Veer Savarkar

Dr. Devendra Kumar Sharma

NISHA PUBLICATIONS
NEW DELHI-110002

Veer Savarkar

First Published : 2018

ISBN : 978-93-85621-37-6

₹ 950/-

Published by

NISHA PUBLICATIONS

G-11 A 4754/23, Akarshan Bhawan,
Ansari Road, Darya Ganj
New Delhi-110002
Mobile: 9811644742, 9899039162
Phone: 011-23258681
e- mail: sales@nishabookdistributors.com
Website: www.nishabookdistributors.com

PRINTED IN INDIA

Contents

Preface

Vinayak Damodar Savarkar ((May 28, 1883-February 26, 1966) was an Indian politician and an Indian Independence Movement activist, who is credited with developing the Hindu nationalist political ideology Hindutva. He is considered to be the central icon of modern Hindu nationalist political parties. Commonly addressed as Veer Savarkar, he is considered to be the central icon of modern Hindu nationalist political parties. His last years were clouded with accusations of involvement in Mahatma Gandhi's assassination.

Savarkar passed away in 1966, after coming under controversy of the assassination of Mahatma Gandhi by Nathuram Godse. The Hindu Mahasabha, an institution Savarkar had helped grow, had opposed creation of Pakistan, and took exception to Gandhi's continued Muslim appeasement stances. Nathuram Godse, a volunteer of the Hindu Mahasabha, assassinated Gandhi in 1948 and upheld his actions till his hanging.

Savarkar is revered in India today as the "Brave Savarkar" (Veer Savarkar), and on the same level as Mahatma Gandhi, Subhash Chandra Bose, and Tilak. The intellectuals as well as commoners in India continue to debate what would have happened if ideas of Savarkar were endorsed by the nation, especially after freedom in 1947. A famous general is said to have quoted Savarkar after the Indians conceded land to the Chinese in a military conflict in 1962.... Savarkar had advocated a militarily strong India. All the matter is just compiled and edited in nature. Taken from the various sources which are in public domain.

The book will prove an informative and most useful asset for students, scholars and teachers in this field.

—*Editor*

1

Introduction

Vinayak Damodar Savarkar ((May 28, 1883-February 26, 1966) was an Indian politician and an Indian Independence Movement activist, who is credited with developing the Hindu nationalist political ideology Hindutva. He is considered to be the central icon of modern Hindu nationalist political parties. Commonly addressed as Veer Savarkar, he is considered to be the central icon of modern Hindu nationalist political parties. His last years were clouded with accusations of involvement in Mahatma Gandhi's assassination.

Savarkar's revolutionary activities began when studying in India and England, where he founded student societies and publications, espousing the cause of complete Indian independence by revolutionary means. Savarkar would publish The Indian War of Independence about the Indian rebellion of 1857 that would be banned by British authorities and was arrested in 1910 for his connections with the revolutionary group India House. Following a failed attempt to escape while being transported from Marseilles, Savarkar was sentenced to 50-years imprisonment and moved to the Cellular Jail in the Andaman and Nicobar Islands.

While in jail, Savarkar would pen the work describing Hindutva, openly espousing Hindu nationalism. He would be released in 1921 under restrictions after signing a controversial plea for clemency in which he renounced revolutionary activities. Travelling widely, Savarkar became a forceful orator and writer, advocating Hindu political and social unity. Serving as the president of the Hindu Mahasabha, Savarkar endorsed the ideal of Hindus as a distinct nation and of India as a Hindu Rashtra and controversially opposed the Quit India struggle in 1942. He became a fierce critic of the Indian National Congress and its acceptance of India's partition, and was one of those accused in the assassination of Indian leader Mahatma Gandhi, though he was acquitted by the Court. He spent the last years of his life writing and expounding on Hindutva.

EARLY LIFE

Vinayak Damodar Savarkar was born in the village of Bhagur, near the city of Nasik, in what is now Maharashtra. He was one of four children-his brothers Ganesh (Babarao) and Narayan, and his sister Mainabai-born to Radhabai and Damodarpant Savarkar. His family was of Hindu and Marathi background, and belonged to the Chitpawan Brahmin community-his ancestral roots and heritage would be an important influence on Savarkar. Descending from a long line of jagirdars (landlords) and scholars of Sanskrit, the Savarkar family was well-respected and both parents encouraged and inculcated a love of learning in all their children. Savarkar's mother died when he was only nine years old, after suffering from an outbreak of cholera. For the next seven years, Savarkar was raised by his father until his father fell victim to plague in 1899.

Savarkar's elder brother Ganesh took the burdens of providing for the family, and would be a strong influence on the teenage Savarkar in this period of hardship. Despite financial difficulties, Babarao supported Savarkar's dreams for higher education. In this period, Savarkar had organised several local young men in a group called the Mitra Mela (Band of Friends), and soon began encouraging revolutionary and nationalist views and passions amongst the band. In 1901, Savarkar was married to Yamunbai, the daughter of Ramchandra Triambak Chiplunkar, who supported Savarkar's university education. After passing his matriculation examination, Savarkar enrolled in the Fergusson College in the provincial capital of Pune (then Poona) in 1902.

As a young man and student, Savarkar was enthralled by the rising Swadeshi (Home-made) campaign, and the political struggle against the partition of Bengal in 1905. His views and passions were guided by a new generation of radical political leaders such as Bal Gangadhar Tilak, Bipin Chandra Pal and Lala Lajpat Rai. Absorbed immediately into nationalist activities, he began organising college students across Pune in the promotion of Swadeshi goods, boycotting foreign-made alternatives and promoting Indian culture in condemnation of European influences. At the occasion of the Hindu festival of Dussehra in 1905, Savarkar and his friends set a large bonfire of foreign goods and clothes. Reorganising his friends and students into a political outfit called Abhinav Bharat, Savarkar committed himself to fighting for India's independence, envisioning a republic united by a common language.

Savarkar was expelled from college for his activities, yet permitted to take examinations to achieve his Bachelor of Arts degree. With the help of nationalist activist Shyam Krishnavarma, Savarkar embarked to study law in England on a scholarship. In the same year, India's main political organisation, the Indian National Congress split, with the followers of Tilak (collectively known as the Garam Dal (Hot Faction) rejecting the moderate Congress leadership, which advocated dialogue and reconciliation with the British Raj. A firebrand nationalist of Marathi background, Tilak advocated Swaraj (Self-Rule) for India and was imprisoned for his support of outright independence and revolutionary activities. His zeal was heightened following Tilak's arrest, and Savarkar took on the Indian leader as his mentor, imbibing the latter's ideas for India's political freedom as well as the revival of the ancient heritage of Indian civilisation. Although generally espousing atheism, Savarkar began studying Indian history, Hindu scripture and observing religious traditions.

Activities at India House

Savarkar enrolled at Gray's Inn, a law college in London and began living with fellow Indian students at the India House. Organised by expatriate social and political activist Pandit

Shyamji, India House was a thriving centre for student political and intellectual activity, and with Savarkar's addition, it soon became a hot-bed of revolutionary thought and activities. Founding the Free India Society, Savarkar sought to organise fellow Indian students for the goal of independence through revolution:

"We must stop complaining about this British officer or that officer, this law or that law. There would be no end to that. Our movement must not be limited to being against any particular law, but it must be for acquiring the authority to make laws itself. In other words, we want absolute independence."

Savarkar envisioned a guerrilla war for independence along the lines of the famous armed Independence Movement of 1857 (incorrectly taught as Sepoy Mutiny by some old fashioned outdated schools). Studying the history of the revolt from English as well as Indian sources, Savarkar wrote a major book, The History of the War of Indian Independence in which he analyzed the revolt and assailed British rule in India as unjust and oppressive. Savarkar became one of the first writers to allude to the revolt as the "First War for Independence." Karl Marx is also said to have written the Sepoy Mutiny of 1857 as the India's First War of Independence.

Banned from publication throughout the British Empire, Savarkar managed to smuggle his work to expatriate Indian revolutionary Madame Bhikaji Cama, who obtained its publication in the Netherlands, France and Germany. Widely smuggled and circulated, the book would attain great popularity and would influence rising young Indians and future revolutionaries, including Subhash Chandra Bose and Bhagat Singh. With a core group of fellow students, Savarkar began studying revolutionary methods and came into contact with a veteran of the Russian Revolution of 1905, who imparted the knowledge of bomb-making to Savarkar and his friends. Savarkar would print and circulate a manual amongst his friends, on bomb-making and other methods of guerrilla warfare.

In 1909, Madan Lal Dhingra, a keen follower and friend of Savarkar, assassinated British MP Sir Curzon Wylie in a public meeting. Dhingra's action provoked controversy across Britain and India, evoking enthusiastic admiration as well as condemnation. Savarkar published an article in which he all but endorsed the murder and worked to organise support, both political and for Dhingra's legal defence. At a meeting of Indians called for a condemnation of Dhingra's deed, Savarkar protested the intention of condemnation and was drawn into a hot debate and angry scuffle with other attendants. A secretive and restricted trial and a sentence awarding the death penalty to Dhingra provoked an outcry and protest across the Indian student and political community. Strongly protesting the verdict, Savarkar struggled with British authorities in laying claim to Dhingra's remains following his execution. Savarkar hailed Dhingra as a hero and martyr, and began encouraging revolution with greater intensity.

Cellular Jail

In India, Ganesh Savarkar had organised an armed revolt against the Morley-Minto reforms of 1909 for which he was arrested and sentenced to transportation for life, moved to the Cellular Jail in the Andaman and Nicobar Islands. The British police implicated Savarkar in the investigation for allegedly plotting the crime. Hoping to evade arrest, Savarkar moved to Madame Cama's home in Paris. He was nevertheless arrested by police on March 13, 1910. In the final days of freedom, Savarkar wrote letters to a close friend planning his escape. Knowing that he would most likely be shipped to India, Savarkar asked his friend to keep track of which ship and route he would be taken through. When the ship S.S. Morea reached the port of Marseilles on July 8, 1910, Savarkar escaped from his cell through a porthole and dived into the water, swimming a long distance to the shore in the hope that his friend would be there to receive him in a car.

But his friend was late in arriving, and the alarm having been raised, Savarkar was re-arrested. Arriving in Mumbai (then Bombay), he was taken to the Yeravda Central Jail (which was a high security prison then reserved for the most illustrious of Indian Freedom Fighters, even Mahatma Gandhi was later housed there). Following a trial, Savarkar was sentenced to 50-years imprisonment and transported on July 4, 1911 to the Cellular Jail in the Andaman and Nicobar Islands.

Infamously known as Kaalapani, his fellow captives included many political prisoners, and were forced to perform hard labour for many years. Reunited with his brother Ganesh, the Savarkars nevertheless struggled in the harsh environment. Forced to arise at 5 a.m., tasks including cutting trees and chopping wood, and working at the oil mill under regimental strictness, with talking amidst prisoners strictly prohibited during mealtime. Prisoners were subject to frequent mistreatment and torture. Contact with the outside world and home was restricted to the writing and mailing of one letter a year. In these years, Savarkar withdrew within himself and performed his routine tasks mechanically. Obtaining permission to start a rudimentary jail library, Savarkar would also teach some fellow convicts to read and write.

Savarkar appealed for clemency in 1911 and again during Sir Reginald Craddock's visit in 1913, citing poor health in the oppressive conditions. In 1920, even as the Indian National Congress and leaders such as Mahatma Gandhi, Vithalbhai Patel and Bal Gangadhar Tilak demanded his unconditional release, Savarkar controversially signed a statement endorsing the trial verdict and British law, and renouncing violence: "I hereby acknowledge that I had a fair trial and just sentence. I heartily abhor methods of violence resorted to in days gone by and I feel myself duty bound to uphold law and constitution to the best of my powers and I am willing to make the [1919 Montague-Chelmsford Reforms] a success in so far as I may be allowed to do so in future." (from facsimile of Savarkar's letter to British authorities, Frontline, April 7, 1995. Pg. 94).

In his appeal and a willingness to sign a statement renouncing revolutionary activities, Savarkar sparked intense criticism and controversy, which has continued till today. Critics allege that he bargained for his freedom at the expense of his ideals, while supporters assert that Savarkar was merely seeking to escape one way or another, and resume his activities.

On May 2, 1921, the Savarkar brothers were moved to a jail in Ratnagiri, and later to the Yeravda Central Jail. He was finally released on January 6, 1924 under stringent restrictions-he was not to leave Ratnagiri District and was to refrain from political activities for the next five years. However, police restrictions on his activities would not be dropped until the Congress came to power in 1937.

It is often alleged by Indian communists that Savarkar was employed by the British government in their 'Divide and rule' strategy to rule India. A more realistic view is that he was a patriot with strong Hindu revivalist feelings, who spent more than a decade in the Cellular Jail, which is something a lot of other 'freedom fighters' escaped.

HINDUTVA

During his incarceration, Savarkar's views began turning increasingly towards Hindu cultural and political nationalism, and the next phase of his life remained dedicated to this cause. In the brief period he spent at the Ratnagiri jail, Savarkar wrote his ideological treatise-Hindutva: Who is a Hindu?. Smuggled out of the prison, it was published by Savarkar's supporters under his alias "Mahratta." In this work, Savarkar promotes a radical new vision of Hindu social and political consciousness. Savarkar began describing a "Hindu" as a patriotic inhabitant of Bharatavarsha, venturing beyond a religious identity. While emphasising the need for patriotic and social unity of all Hindu communities, he described Hinduism, Jainism, Sikhism and Buddhism as one and same. He outlined his vision of a "Hindu Rashtra" (Hindu Nation) as "Akhand Bharat" (United India), purportedly stretching across the entire Indian subcontinent: "the Aryans who settled in India at the dawn of history already formed a nation, now embodied in the Hindus.... Hindus are bound together not only by the tie of the love they bear to a common fatherland and by the common blood that courses through their veins and keeps our hearts throbbing and our affection warm but also by the tie of the common homage we pay to our great civilisation, our Hindu culture."(Page108)"

Scholars, historians and Indian politicians have been divided in their interpretation of Savarkar's ideas. A self-described atheist, Savarkar regards being Hindu as a cultural and political identity. While often stressing social and community unity between Hindus, Sikhs, Buddhists and Jains, Savarkar's notions of loyalty to the fatherland are seen as an implicit criticism of Muslims and Christians, who regard Mecca, Medina and Jerusalem as their holiest places.

Savarkar openly assailed what he saw as Muslim political separatism, arguing that the loyalty of many Muslims was conflicted. After his release, Savarkar founded the Ratnagiri Hindu Sabha on January 23, 1924, aiming to work for the social and cultural preservation of Hindu heritage and civilisation. Becoming a frequent and forceful orator, Sarvakar agitated for the use of Hindi as a common national language and against caste discrimination and untouchability. Focusing his energies on writing, Savarkar authored the Hindu Padpadashashi-a book documenting and extolling the Maratha empire-and My Transportation for Life-an account of his early revolutionary days, arrest, trial and incarcertaion. He also wrote and published a collection of poems, plays and novels.

Leader of the Hindu Mahasabha

Although disavowing revolution and politics, Savarkar grew disenchanted with the Congress's emphasis of nonviolence and criticised Gandhi for suspending Non Cooperation Movement following the killing of 22 policemen in Chauri Chaura in 1922. He soon joined the Hindu Mahasabha, a political party founded in 1911 and avowed to Hindu political rights and empowerment. The party was disengaged from the Indian independence movement, allowing Savarkar to work without British interference.

As his travel restrictions weakened, Savarkar began travelling extensively, delivering speeches exhorting Hindu political unity and criticising the Congress and Muslim politicians. Savarkar and the Mahasabha did not endorse the Salt Satyagraha launched by the Congress in 1930, and neither

Savarkar nor any of his supporters participated in civil disobedience. Savarkar focused on expanding the party's membership, revamping its structure and delivering its message.

In the wake of the rising popularity of the Muslim League led by Muhammad Ali Jinnah, Savarkar and his party began gaining traction in the national political environment. Savarkar moved to Mumbai and was elected president of the Hindu Mahasabha in 1937, and would serve until 1943. The Congress swept the polls in 1937 but conflicts between the Congress and Jinnah would exacerbate Hindu-Muslim political divisions. Jinnah derided Congress rule as a "Hindu Raj," and hailed December 22, 1939 as a "Day of Deliverance" for Muslims when the Congress resigned en masse in protest of India's arbitrary inclusion into World War II.

Savarkar's message of Hindu unity and empowerment gained increasing popularity amidst the worsening communal climate. Even as the League adopted the Lahore Resolution in 1940, calling for a separate Muslim state based on the Two-Nation Theory, Savarkar publicly stated that he did not disagree with Jinnah's contention that Hindus and Muslims were a separate nation. He was firmly opposed, however to the proposed partition of Indian territory, citing the existence of a Muslim homeland in the Middle East.

However, Savarkar and the Mahasabha joined several political parties including the League and the Communist Party of India in endorsing the war effort. Savarkar publicly encouraged Hindus to enlist in the military, which his supporters described as an effort for Hindus to obtain military training and experience potentially useful in a future confrontation with the British. When the Congress launched the Quit India rebellion in 1942, Savarkar criticised the rebellion and asked Hindus to stay active in the war effort and not disobey the government.

Under his leadership, the Mahasabha won several seats in the central and provincial legislatures, but its overall popularity and influence remained small. Towards the end of the war, Savarkar and the Mahasabha became increasingly confrontational with the League and Muslim politicians. Hindu

Mahasabha activists protested Gandhi's initiative to hold talks with Jinnah in 1944, which Savarkar denounced as "appeasement." He assailed the British proposals for transfer of power, attacking both the Congress and the British for making concessions to Muslim separatists. The Mahasabha's popularity was affected when the young and rising politician Syama Prasad Mookerjee left the party, believing it to be too radical and out-of-touch with most Hindus.

IDEOLOGUE OF HINDUTVA

Vinayak Damodar ("Veer") Savarkar can, with some justice, be described as the inspirational force behind the resurgence of militant Hinduism in contemporary India. His fame has been on the ascendancy since the Hindu right captured power in India less than a decade ago, and lately he has been lionized in the film "Veer Savarkar" by the filmmaker Sudhir Phadke, a fellow Maharashtrian.

In May 2002, L. K. Advani spoke glowingly of Savarkar and Hedgewar, the founder of the Rashtriya Swayamsevak Sangh [RSS], as men who had "kindled fierce nationalistic spirit that contributed to India's liberation." Savarkar's advocates view him as a luminous visionary, a supreme patriot who sacrificed much for the defense of Mother India, a great revolutionary and even social reformer; his opponents, who generally do not question his patriotism, nevertheless point to his political conservatism, his support of reactionary movements, and his advocacy of a communal-based politics verging on fascism.

Savarkar was born in Bhagur village in Nasik district of present-day Maharashtra on 28 May 1883 into a Chitpavan Brahmin family. His early exposure to the political activities of the Maharashtrian elite who were opposed to British rule may have come at the hands of his elder brother, Ganesh [Babarao], who is said to have been greatly inspired by the actions of Lokmanya Tilak, the Chapekar Brothers, and other revolutionaries. The Savarkar brothers were active in the Mitra Mela, a secret society formed with the aim of liberating, through the use of armed force, India from British rule. Veer Savarkar attended Fergusson College in Pune: his biographer, Dhananjay Keer, notes that Savarkar gathered around him a group of students who debated European political texts, discussed revolution, and championed swadeshi [self-reliance]. In 1906, Savarkar left for London to get credentialed in law; his passage was paid for by Shyam Krishnavarma, an Indian patriot settled in London who used his journal, The Indian Sociologist, to make a case for Indian independence.

The journal was advocating violent revolution by 1909; but before then, in 1907, Savarkar had published a Marathi translation of Mazzini's autobiography which did very well. By early 1909, according to the senior intelligence officer James Campbell Ker, author of Political Trouble in India 1907-1917 [1917, reprinted 1973 by Oriental Publishers, Delhi], Savarkar had taken charge of India House, the London headquarters of those Indians who claimed revolutionary credentials (p. 177). That year, on July 1, Madan Lal Dhingra assassinated Sir William Curzon-Wyllie at the Imperial Institute.

This assassination, less than a month after Ganesh Savarkar was convicted on the charge of sedition and sentenced to transportation for life, is said to have been instigated by Savarkar's orders; yet Savarkar himself never wielded any arms. His critics, quite rightly, describe this cowardice as typical of Savarkar's conduct; and it is striking, of course, that nearly 40 years later Savarkar was again thought to have encouraged and instigated Nathuram Godse to murder Mahatma Gandhi, without himself having taken up arms. It is more than likely that Savarkar became a master at manipulating those who looked up to him, and sought to conduct his violent activities without explicitly implicating himself in gruesome deeds of murder.

A steady stream of publications emerged from Savarkar's pen over a course of five decades, and his first substantial work, the Indian War of Independence, appeared in 1908, or fifty years after the rebellion of 1857-58 had been crushed. Though in this work Savarkar argued that Hindus and Muslims had stood together in resistance to the British, in later works he showed himself much less enamoured of Hindu-Muslim unity, and for most of his adult life he would, in fact, become known for his advocacy of the rights of Hindus. Hindu Pad-Padashahi [1925], a treatise on Hindu Kingship, or more particularly on the glories of India under Maratha rule, showed as well the impact of political events on Savarkar's thinking: both the Khilafat movement, as well as the Moplah Rebellion, doubtless played a part in turning Savarkar against Muslims.

However, his signature piece, in this respect, was a "treatise" he penned in 1922, "Essentials of Hindutva", a more elaborate version of which appeared in 1928 as Hindutva: Who is a Hindu? (Nagpur, 1928). Savarkar vigorously set forth the idea that Hindus constituted a nation, bound together by common blood, and that Hindus were united "by the tie of a common heritage we pay to our great civilization — our Hindu culture".

Savarkar eschewed the word "Hinduism"; to him, Hindutva represented the essence of the Hindu way of life. As he wrote, "If there be any word of alien growth it is this word Hinduism and so we should not allow our thoughts to get confused by this new fangled term." The Hindus' devotion to their motherland was supreme; indeed, whosoever was devoted to Hindustan, and considered it his or her holy land (punyabhoomi), was a Hindu.

The most elaborate legend, vigorously promoted by Savarkar's friends and admirers, has developed around his supposed bravery. In 1910, as Savarkar was being taken to India after a warrant had been issued for his arrest on charges of sedition and treason, he escaped as his ship docked at Marseilles. Upon being recaptured, Savarkar challenged the legality of his arrest in France, but the international court at Hague, though it took the view that an illegality had been committed when Savarkar was handed over to the British police, nonetheless ruled against Savarkar.

Savarkar was, at his trial in Bombay, sentenced to imprisonment for life, and transported to the Andamans. In 1922, he was sent back to India, but confined to Ratnagiri District until 1937. Yet, to put it mildly, there are serious reasons to doubt whether Savarkar was deserving of the epithet of "Veer" [brave] that was bestowed on him. The indisputable fact remains that throughout his political life, Savarkar showed himself perfectly capable of not merely negotiating with the British, but serving as an active collaborator.

When confined to jail in the Andamans, Savarkar negotiated with the British to have himself set free. Moreover, when Congress refused to form a government in the Central Provinces and Bengal, the Hindu Mahasabha under Savarkar's guidance opted to collaborate with the British. He thought it a God-given opportunity for the Mahasabha to flex its muscles while the Congress was in hibernation.

Similarly, though the Congress declared itself opposed to offering the British any assistance during World War II, Savarkar was keen that Hindus should acquire experience in the use of firearms. Savarkar saw in World War II an opportunity for Hindus, who had been emasculated (in Savarkar's view) by centuries of oppression under Muslim and British rule, and rendered incapable of even elementary knowledge in the discharge of firearms by virtue of legislation that forbid ownership of guns among Indians to become versed in fighting strategies. Not only did the Hindu Mahasabha, whose presidency Savarkar assumed in 1937 upon the rescission of the order which confined him to Ratnagiri District, not oppose the British position in World War II, but the Mahasabha played no role in the Quit India movement and indeed even assisted the British in its suppression.

In the last analysis, Savarkar appears as an extraordinary embodiment of utter mediocrity. In the large corpus of his writings, there is barely anything to suggest a creative mind at work, and one searches in vain for any original idea. Savarkar imbibed the worst of Western political and social traditions, and his warped ideas about race superiority, the survival of the fittest, and the nation as a "blood entity", so to speak, were derived from the most objectionable strands of Western thinking.

In his avid desire to militarize the Hindus, he showed himself hostage to crude notions of realpolitik. He perfected the art of assassination and political intrigue by remote control, and his true disciple in this respect is Bal Thackeray. It is no surprise that he should appeal to the leadership of the present generation of Hindu extremists, who are similarly bereft of intellectual ideas, moral sentiments, and the barest standards of truth in public life, and whose idea of bravery entails murderous onslaught upon religious minorities. If Savarkar is at all to be remembered, let it not be forgotten that as Nathuram Godse plotted to take Mahatma Gandhi's life, Savarkar blessed him and wished him success in his God-given task.

WORKS

Veer Savarkar wrote more than 10,000 pages in the Marathi language. His literary works in Marathi include "Kamala", "Mazi Janmathep" (My Life Sentence), and most famously "1857-The First war of Independence", about what the British referred to as the Sepoy Mutiny. Savarkar popularised the term 'First War of Independence'. Another noted book was "Kala Pani" (similar to Life Sentence, but on the island prison on the Andamans), which reflected the treatment of Indian freedom fighters by the British. In order to counter the then accepted view that India's history was a saga of continuous defeat, he wrote an inspirational historical work, "Saha Soneri Pane" (Six Golden Pages), recounting some of the Golden periods of Indian history.

At the same time, religious divisions in India were beginning to fissure. He described what he saw as the atrocities of British and Muslims on Hindu residents in Kerala, in the book, "Mopalyanche Band" (Muslims' Strike) and also "Gandhi Gondhal" (Gandhi's Confusion), a political critique of Gandhi's politics. Savarkar, by now, had become a committed and persuasive critic of the Gandhian vision of India's future he was great poet & writer he wrote more than 10,000 pages in 'Marathi' & morethan 1,500 pages in 'English' languages.

He is also the author of poems like "Sagara pran talmalala", and "Jayostute" (written in praise of freedom), one of the most moving, inspiring and patriotic works in Marathi literature. When in the Cellular jail, Savarkar was denied pen and paper. He composed and wrote his poems on the prison walls with thorns and pebbles, memorised more than ten thousand lines of his poetry for years till other prisoners returning home brought them to India. Savarkar is credited with several popular neologisms in Hindi, like Digdarshak (leader, one who points in the right direction), Shatkar, Saptahik (Weekly) and Sansad (Parliament).

PARTITION AND GANDHI'S MURDER

Savarkar had become one of the fiercest critics of Mahatma Gandhi, and attacked him and the Congress leadership for acquiescing to the partition of India. During the intense communal violence, Hindu Mahasabha activists were allegedly responsible for carrying out attacks on Muslim civilians. Savarkar blamed Gandhi for weakening Hindu society in face of Muslim separatism, and for agreeing to divide the Hindu homeland.

The anger of some Hindu refugees from Pakistan provoked fears of assassination attempts on Gandhi's life. Gandhi's fast-unto-death in January 1948, demanding immediate communal peace and the payment of outstanding shares of the treasury to Pakistan in spite of the Indo-Pakistani War of 1947 increased the consternation and anger of many Hindu Mahasabha activists, including Savarkar.

Following the murder of Mahatma Gandhi on January 30, 1948, police arrested the assassin Nathuram Godse and rounded up his companions. Police investigation revealed that Godse and his chief conspirator Narayan Apte had been a close political confidantes of Savarkar in the Hindu Mahasabha. Despite having publicly denounced Gandhi's murder, Savarkar was arrested on suspicion of having inspired and planned Gandhi's murder, and accordingly indicted. Witnesses during the trial testified that Savarkar had blessed Nathuram Godse before he shot Gandhi, with the words "Yashasvi howun yaa" (Marathi: Come back with success). Both Godse and Savarkar belonged to the Chitpawan Brahmin community. Even before the trial, However, Sardar Vallabhbhai Patel had, in a letter to Jawaharlal Nehru, clearly stated his doubts over allegations that Savarkar had masterminded the murder. In the court, approvers had testified to the intimate relationship between Savarkar and the Godse brothers, but there was no corroborative evidence to nail down Savarkar's assertion that he had merely formal relationships with them. Godse claimed full responsibility for planning and carrying out the attack, in absence of an independent corroboration of the prosecution witness Digambar Ramchandra Badge's evidence implicating Savarkar directly, the court exonerated him citing insufficient evidence.

Lingering doubts about this version of events led the government of India to appoint the Kapur Commission in the mid-1960s. The Kapur commission was fortunate in having access to testimonies of Savarkar's aides (including his bodyguard and his secretary) and important Hindu Mahasabha functionaries who were not available to the earlier court. The weight of this evidence led Justice Kapur to reverse the conclusions of the court trial and state unambiguously that "all these facts taken together were destructive of any theory other than the conspiracy to murder by Savarkar and his group".

NATHURAM GODSE, THE RSS, AND THE MURDER OF GANDHI

On 30 January 1948, Mohandas Karamchand Gandhi, known around the world as Mahatma Gandhi, and to his countrymen and women as Bapu, the "Father of the Nation", was shot dead by Nathuram Vinayak Godse, a Chitpavan Brahmin from Pune. Much ink has been spilled on determining whether Godse was, at that time, a member of the RSS, or indeed of the Hindu Mahasabha, or perhaps of neither organization. Though Godse single-handedly carried out the execution of Gandhi, others were implicated in the assassination plot, and among those against whom the Indian government filed charges was Veer Savarkar. Godse, as investigations after Gandhi's murder were to reveal, appears to have been close to Savarkar, a prominent leader of the Hindu Mahasabha. Godse was certainly a frequent visitor to Savarkar's residence, and he did not, in the time that intervened between his arrest on January 30 and his execution upon conviction of the charge of murder nearly two years later, ever disown his association with the Mahasabha.

The general consensus appears to be that Nathuram, who saw himself as a passionate and ardent defender of the Hindu motherland against the depredations of Muslims, was at one point active in the RSS but resigned his membership in the early 1930s. This mere fact, if fact it be, has been pounced upon by the RSS in the five decades following Gandhi's assassination to argue that Godse had no association with the RSS, and curiously Nathuram's younger brother, Gopal Godse, who was convicted of partaking in the conspiracy to murder Gandhi and served a fifteen-year jail term and still speaks in the most bitter terms of Gandhi as the betrayer of India, has himself on more than one occasion had to issue a strong rejoinder to the RSS, with whose ideological outlook he is otherwise in complete sympathy, for attempting to disguise his brother's long-term association with the RSS. Thus, shortly after releasing Nathuram's book, Why I Assassinated Mahatma Gandhi, in December 1993, Gopal Godse in an interview with Frontline magazine stated: "All the [Godse] brothers were in the RSS. Nathuram, Dattatreya, myself and Govind. You can say we grew up in the RSS rather than in our home. It was like a family to us. Nathuram had become a baudhik karyavah [intellectual worker] in the RSS. He has said in his statement that he left the RSS. He said it because [Madhav Sadashiv] Golwalkar and the RSS were in a lot of trouble after the murder of Gandhi. But he did not leave the RSS." [See issue of 28 January 1994]

Whether Godse formally remained a member of the RSS is much less important than the fact that though the Hindu Mahasabha and the RSS had some ideological differences, both organizations were united in their extreme hostility to Gandhi as well as to Muslims. Golwalkar and Savarkar shared a platform in Pune in 1952, as Sitaram Yechury's What Is This Hindu Rashtra (Madras: Frontline Publications, 1993) has recently documented, and it is a little-known fact that at one point the RSS, eager to foment the impression that it did not stand by the virulently anti-Muslim sentiments expressed in Golwalkar's influential book, We or Our Nationhood Defined (1938), claimed that the author of the book was Babarao Savarkar, the brother of Veer Savarkar. Sardar Patel, the Deputy Prime Minister and Home

Minister in Nehru's Cabinet, was himself inclined to view the Mahasabha and the RSS as organizations that had together created an atmosphere in which, as he wrote on 18 July 1848 to the Hindu Mahasabha leader, Shyam Prasad Mookerjee, "such a ghastly tragedy [Gandhi's assassination] became possible. There is no doubt in my mind that the extreme section of the Hindu Mahasabha was involved in this conspiracy." Yet, as Patel added, in terms that leave no room to doubt that from his standpoint the RSS also stood implicated in Gandhi's assassination, "The activities of the RSS constituted a clear threat to the existence of Government and the State. Our reports show that those activities, despite the ban, have not died down. Indeed, as time has marched on, the RSS circles are becoming more defiant and are indulging in their subversive activities in an increasing measure."

Two months later, on September 11th, Patel was again unequivocal in his denunciation of the role played by the RSS in Gandhi's assassination: addressing Golwalkar, Patel spoke about the "poison" spread by the RSS. Following Gandhi's murder, "Even an iota of the sympathy of the Government or of the people no more remained for the RSS. In fact opposition grew. Opposition turned more severe, when the RSS men expressed joy and distributed sweets after Gandhiji's death."

It scarcely matters, then, whether Nathuram Godse retained membership in the RSS when he shot Gandhi dead. Godse was involved in Hindu extremist organizations, including the RSS and the Hindu Mahasabha, his entire adult life, and the continuing attempts by RSS to evade responsibility for Gandhi's assassination are characteristic of that extreme pusillanimity and tendency to falsehood which have always been the signal trademarks of an organization that is determined to bring the idea of Hindu Rashtra to fruition.

LATER LIFE

Despite his exoneration, Savarkar's role in the plot remains a source of intense controversy, but at the time the public held him answerable for instigating the murder. Public outrage over Gandhi's murder wrecked the fortunes of the Hindu Mahasabha, whose membership and activity dwindled into insignificance. Hindu nationalist organisations such as the RSS and the Bharatiya Jana Sangh disavowed any links with Savarkar and his ideology. Savarkar's home in Mumbai was stoned by angry mobs, and his political influence and activism sharply curtailed by widespread public anger. His activities remained confined to occasional speeches and publishing his writings.

Although regarded with respect and admiration for his revolutionary activities and work on behalf of Hindus, most political parties refused to be associated with him. Yet Savarkar maintained a standing of a legendary freedom fighter, especially in Maharashtra. He attempted to organise a new political party based on Hindutva, but to no avail. Savarkar exercised Voluntary Euthanasia and passed away on February 27, 1966 and was mourned by large crowds that attended his cremation. His home, possessions and other personal relics have been preserved for public display. Corroboration of Badge's testimony came only after Savarkar's death when his secretary, Gajanan Vishnu Damle and bodyguard Appa Ramachandra Kasar deposed to Justice Kapur that Godse and accomplice Narayan Apte met Savarkar on January 23 or 24 on their return from Delhi well after they had met him on January 17.

SAVARKAR

Savarkar: The crown prince of revolutionaries, has many firsts to his credit, here is the list:

* He was the first Indian political leader to call for Swadeshi, and the first Indian leader who publicly performed a bonfire of foreign clothes (1906). (MANY YEARS BEFORE GANDHIJI)
* He was the first Indian student who was rusticated from a hostel of an institution aided by British Govt. (reason was the bonfire).
* He was the first Indian leader of India to daringly proclaim absolute political independence of India as her goal (EVEN BEFORE LOKMANYA TILAK called Swaraj a birth right)

* Savarkar was the first barrister who was refused the degree on account of his political line of thought by the British Government.
* He was the first graduate to lose the degree from an Indian University (Bombay University) for his love of independence.
* (The same University rescinded its 1911 decision after 49 years in April 1960 and reconferred the degree. Meanwhile Pune and Nagpur had conferred honorary Doctorates on Savarkar).
* Savarkar was again the first Indian leader to invest the problem of Indian independence with international importance.
* Savarkar was the first Indian leader who cleared the myth British historians propagated and showed that 1857 war of independence was not a mutiny of sepoys in few regiments but a revolt of Indian population against the British sustained over for 2 years. He also highlighted the cruelty of British Generals during that period who slaughtered outright ordinary Indians on flimsiest pretexts. He was the first Indian leader to celebrate 50th anniversary of 1857.
* Savarkar was the first Indian leader to organize revolutionary movement in the 'enemy's camp' right in the heart of London.
* He was the first author whose work was proscribed by the governments of two countries (India & UK) even before it was printed or published. (his book 'War of Independence of 1857' which was published clandestinely in US and India Thanks to Dr.Kurien, an Indian Christian)
* Savarkar was the first rebel leader of India who refused to recognize the authority of the British Court of Law.
* He was the first political prisoner in the history of world the issue of whose arrest was fought out in the International Court at the Hague.
* Savarkar was the first political prisoner in the political history who was sentenced to 50 year's transportation.

* Savarkar was the first poet in the world, who deprived of pen and paper, composed and wrote his poems on the prison walls with thorns and pebbles, learnt with Vedic tenacity more than ten thousand lines of his poetry for years till they reached his country thru the mouth of others, and showed how since dawn of humanity sacred Vedas were kept circulating from generation to generation.
* Savarkar also designed the first Indian flag to be unfurled overseas (by Madam Cama, in Stuttgart Germany, on August 22, 1907 at the International Socialist Congress, where British and French socialists moved a resolution to call India an oppressed country).
* He was the first Indian political leader to build a pan-Hindu temple where former 'untouchable' was a priest.
* He was the first president of Marathi Sahitya Parishad (Council of all Marathi writers and poets)
* He was the only Hindu leader honoured by SGPC (Sikh religious body)

Some Interesting Facts about Savarkar

Some interesting facts you should know:

1. Savarkar at the age of 15 took a vow in front of Goddess Durga to drive out British from his Motherland to make her free and great once again.
2. At age 14 he wrote ballads of Tanaji Malusare and Shivaji.
3. At the age 17 he started a Mitra mela which in four years sprouted into Abhinav Bharat Society, the foremost revolutionary group, which later led to a web of revolutionaries in Bengal, Punjab and other states.
4. It was on Lokmanya Tilak's recommendation that got Savarkar a scholarship by India House (by Shri Shyamji Krishna Varma who later became Savarkar's follower)
5. During his stay in London, Savarkar shipped bomb recipes and pistols in books with hollow cavities carved out from the pages.

6. Unlike Gandhi and Nehru who were given Class A prisoner status, Savarkar was given Class C and was made to drive an oil mill He had to make mulch choir and make ropes out of it with bare hands. Even in prison forcible conversions of poor Hindus to Islam were taking place. Savarkar fought for the prison reforms and put a stop to these conversions. He eliminated untouchability among Hindu prisoners in the Andamans.
7. After the arrest of his brother, who also was given a life term in Andamans, and banning of his books in 1909, the British confiscated all his family's personal property. The utensils, clothes were thrown out on the street. His family's belongings were nothing but the clothes they were wearing at the time. All this while he was in Europe. This victimization of his family made him return to London where he was arrested.

   On this sacrifice Savarkar's poetic words are;

   We have not taken this vow to go "Sati", to jump into the burning fire knowing the pain it may cause, blindly. This enlightened sacrifice comes naturally to Hindus. (Many thousands of Hindu women committed Jouhar and many Hindus have donned kesariya before).

   Many youths those days had this poem of Savarkar and the preface his book on Mazzini by heart, and they used to recite it every day. (One such then youth is Rev. Pandurang Shastry Athavale, Leader of Swadhayay movement, a parivar of 6 million plus Hindus).

   Now compare that to Nehru. Indira Gandhi writes in her autobiography that Nehru made her give away a "foreign made" doll Nehru had bought her from London. That's a BIG sacrifice, HAH..
8. Savarkar wrote Mazzini's biography, The history of 1857 war of independence, epic poems Kamla, he wrote news reports from UK, he wrote Hindutva-a unique contribution to Hindu philosophy he wrote novels, he wrote plays, he wrote a grand study of Indian history.

He wrote songs, he wrote 'stotras'. One of his song "praise of Godess Liberty" is in 10th grade texts in Marathi.

9. Unfortunately for us, Savarkar's manuscript on Sikh history was lost and was never found.
10. Savarkar's followers in London also worked with the Gadhar Party in USA mobilising American support for Indian independence movement. Theyorked worked with other European leaders also. The 1912 demands by Wilhem Kaiser's German Govt. from the British included that India be given independence.
11. In 1960 Savarkar exhorted India to make atomic bombs.
12. Savarkar is the only author who tried to put "Kundalini' and sapta chakra experience of a yogi in modern medical terms. Flag Savarkar designed for Hindus has the lotus Kundlini and kripan (a sword) for the defence
13. The book Savarkar worked the longest on is 'Six Gloriuos Epochs of Indian History'- This book has nearly thousand references. This is the true Indian history, not the canned 'British' version of history. If you are a Hindu, you should atleast read this book to know your side of the history.

Judge the man by his words and his actions before you pass an opinion based on British/Nehru inspired rumours passed on by the nitwits and their followers the netwits. Veer Savarkar's 'prophecies' which came remarkably true. Savarkar's political realism and foresight has proved to be correct and unfailing.

In 1925 Savarkar predicted that the separation of Sindh from Bombay province for appeasing Moslems would be disastrous precedent, would destroy Sindh Hindus and would pique the appetite of Panislamists.

We know it snow balled into creation of Pakistan. Plight of Hindus in Sindh keeps getting even worse.

Savarkar foretold (in his speech on Aug. 2, 1942 a week before the start of Quit India movement) that the political leadership of Gandhi and Nehru which according to him lacked historical perspective, would end up dividing India on the basis of religion.

It came true. Savarkar said that if once Pakistan came into being it would raise an army and always disturb the peace, industrialisation and the progress of India. It came true. 3 wars with Pakistan. We have Punjab, Kashmir terrorism supported by Pakistan, Bombings in Bombay at sensitive strategic locations. It is still coming true. He said in January 1954, that Mao hoodwinked Nehru over Tibet and China would pull down the pillars of Panchsheel any moment. (He also commented "In the very six years (after 1947) we criminally wasted, China had equipped her whole nation with most modern and upto date arms and without caring the least for feelings of India, had completely overrun Tibet and destroyed the only buffer state.") (Only other Indian leader to protest vehemantly against China's take over of Tibet was Dr.Ambedkar).

It came true and China invaded India in 1962. He warned in 1941 about Moslem infiltration to Assam from East Bengal. It came true and is coming true even now. We have 15 to 20 million illegal Moslems (100,000 of them in Bombay itself is acknowledged by the Maharashtra Govt.). Thanks to Sayyad Shahbuddin and Ghani Khan Choudhari, Kishan Ganj, Malda districts of Bihar and Bengal are open havens for BD Moslems who are being made into voters of India overnight. Lately Hiteshwar Saikia is after Moslem voters in Assam, ad you know more voters for Congress can be created by importing Moslems from across the border.

In 1910, on the way to Andamans to India Savarkar envisioned a naval base guarding this southeastern gate of India. Guess what Chinese are getting active at a nearby port in Burma. In 1937 Savarkar expressed fear that Congress would one day throttle Vande Mataram. Within a few years Congress did sacrifice Vande Mataram to appease Moslems (prior to Partition). Savarkar sounded a warning about the fate of kashmir in 1938.

We have paid for ignoring his warnings in the 3 wars, 300,000 Kashmiri who are made refugees in their own country are paying for it now. A comparison of Savarkar with other contemporary leaders. Savarkar was a rebel and revolutionary to the last breath (Times of India, Feb. 27, 1966)

Savarkar was the first Indian leader to give the message of absolute political independence and unity to the nation. But the tragedy of Savarkar was that although he was a secularist to the backbone, a great lover of science and a sturdy nationalist, he was cruelly represented as an orthodox leader by those partial to Gandhi and Nehru. (Savarkar said in June 1963 that it was rediculous and irrational to follow astrology when Russians and Americans are striving to land on the Moon and Mars. Earlier Savarkar refused to consider a cow as holy and chose to call it only as a very useful animal). Savarkar was the first Indian leader to give India the message of secularism and modernism before the advent of Nehru and MN Roy. Savarkar was more rational than Gandhi, Cripps or Jayaprakash Narayan and as rational As Nehru and Roy. He was an epic poet and a great rationalist. He was a great author and the Demoshenes of his age in India. His political realism and foresight proved to be correct and unfailing.

Great men are sometimes obsessed with one idea. Likewise Savarkar was obsessed, his critics say, with the idea of Hindu Militarisation. He was not an imperialist or a militarist. It was his sincere desire that having suffered slavery often, India should not fall a prey to any militarist and aggressive country. So many times in the history the holy land of Hindus was devastated and sacked by hoards of barbarians (Huns, Scythians, etc.), so inferior to them in language, religion, culture, philosophy, mercy and all the soft attitudes of man and God; but superior to them in strength alone- the strength that summed up in two words-Fire and Sword! It is in this sense Savarkar wanted Hindus to militarise so never again shall their country be devastated.

Savarkar was the foremost Indian leader to welcome the machine age and he undertood that economic equality is the inevitable outcome of the machine age. As regards the social equality, none of his great contemporaries except Dr.Ambedkar, not even Jawaharlal Nehru fought orthodoxy with such ruthlessness as did Savarkar.

Savarkar was dubbed a communalist because he said that the principle of one man one vote should be followed (then opposed to by Muslim leadership) and because he opposed Muslim Mauliavis and Christian Missionaries trying to convert illiterate, ignorant and poor Hindus.

In every age the nation that had access to superior force defeated the nations that did not have that advantage. Savarkar was the only leader in India who openly said that India should have accession to a superior device, weapon or force. Savarkar held that justice would go down if not backed by a superior force. A nation, however tolerant, just and cooperative would go down if it did not go match (approximate) the power of surrounding nations (Lesson taught to India by China war the hard way). India should believe in noble principles for the progress of humanity but keep her superior weapon ready for her own survival. This was the message of Savarkar to India.

Also beautifully worded by National poet Ramdharisingh "Dinkar" 'Kshamaa shobhati oos Bhujang ko Jis ke paas garal ho' forgiveness befits only that Cobra that still carries the venom.

Savarkar on revolution (Nov.1909)-"Whenever the natural process of national and political evolution is violently suppressed by the forces of wrong, then revolution must step in as a natural reaction and therefore ought to be welcomed as the only effective instrument to reenthrone Truth and Right. You (the British) rule by bayonets and under these circumstances it is a mockery to talk of constitutional agitation when no constitution exists at all. But it would be worse than a mockery, even a crime when there is a constitution that allows the fullest and freest development of a nation. Only because you (British) deny us a gun, we pick up a pistol. Only because you deny us light, we gather in darkness to compass means to knock out the fetters that hold out Mother down."

What others said about Savarkar. Rajagopalachari -Savarkar to him was a national hero, a symbol of courage, bravery and patriotism, an 'abhitirth' in the long battle for freedom. Subhash Chandra Bose wanted Savarkar to join the Congress after Savarkar's release in 1937. M.N.Roy wanted Savarkar to devote his life again to the emancipation of India on Savarkar's own line of thinking.

Dr. Rajendra Prasad, Dr.Radhakrishanan, YB Chavan felicited Savarkar on Dec.1960.

S.M.Joshi (the socialist leader) said he was inspired by Savarkar's call for absolute political independence.

General Cariappa India's first Commander in Chief (C-in-C) in Dec. 1962 after the defeat of Indian Army in the China war said "Had India listened to Savarkar and adopted his policy of militarization and prepared herself she would not have been placed in this predicament.

Gyanpith award winner V.S.Khandekar said that Savarkar was great not only the field of politics but also in the fields of poetry, courage literature. His greatness had the colours of the rainbow. We are all Lilliputians before Savarkar.

On Feb. 3. 1966 Savarkar decided to surrender to death and simply stopped taking any food or drink other than water. He had stopped taking any medicine a month before that.

Congress MPs Violet and Joachim Alva (on Feb. 5, 1966) wrote to Savarkar "We humbly salute your unforgettable daring achievement-Swimming the ocean and regaining freedom- will be long cherished in the pages of freedom struggle"

Among the people who wrote concerned about his health were Jagjivan Ram and then home minister Gulzarilal Nanda.

After 22 days on barely 5 to 6 teaspoonfuls of water a day, on February 26 1966, Savarkar happily surrendered to Death whom he had challenged since his youth. He was conscious to the last hour and did not suffer any serious complications whatsoever.

S.A.Dange (Chairman of the Communist party) said of Savarkar "He was one of the great anti-imperialist revolutionary".

PM Indira Gandhi said "Savarkar was a great figure of contemporary India and his name is byword for daring and patriotism. He was cast in a mould of a classic revolutionary and countless people drew inspiration from him."

Defence minister YB Chavan "Savarkar displayed a unique combination of nationalism, bravery and social unity ".

Haribhau Pataskar ex Govt. of MP and congress leader said "Savarkar was India's bravest son, a great literary genius, an inspiring poet and a great orator."

M.C.Chagla (the then Education minister) said "Savarkar was a great patriot and an illustrious son of India" he added "anyone living in this country who loved and drew inspiration from the great heritage of India and was loyal to India was a Hindu. Revolutionaries like Savarkar created an atmosphere which made it possible for Mahatma Gandhi to succeed. It would be unpatriotic if the people of India failed to give Savarkar a prominent place in the history of India".

(By the way 'Muslim' Chagla's definition of Hindu is close to Savarkar's definition of a Hindu).

Savarkar in his will asked that nobody should observe hartal or close his business to mourn over his death. This to avoid inconvenience to common people.

He was cremated in electric crematorium per his wish because he considered it more clean, efficient (eco-friendly in modern terms).

Chronology of Savarkar's Life

- 28 May 1883-Born in Bhagur, a tiny village in Dist. Nasik, Maharashtra
- 1892-Lost his mother Radhabai
- 1898-Took an oath before the family deity to conduct armed revolt against British Rule
- 09 Sept. 1898-Lost his father Damodarpant
- 01 Jan. 1900-Founded Mitra Mela, a secret revolutionary society
- 01 Mar 1901-Married Yamuna (Mai)
- 19 Dec. 1901-Passed Matriculation examination
- 24 Jan. 1902-Joined Fergusson College, Pune
- May 1904-Founded Abhinav Bharat-A revolutionary organisation
- Nov. 1905-Organised the first public bonfire of foreign clothes in Pune

- Dec. 1905-Passed B.A. examination
- June 1906-Left for London
- 10 May 1907-Celebrated Golden Jubilee of Indian War of Independence 1857 in London
- June 1907-Wrote the book "Joseph Mazzini" which was later published by Babarao Savarkar
- 1908-Wrote 'Indian War of Independence 1857'. It was secretly published in Holland
- May 1909-Passed Bar-at-Law examination, but granting of permission to practice was denied
- 01 July 1909-Madanlal Dhingra shot dead Curzon Wyllie in London
- 24 Oct. 1909-Vijayadashmi celebrated under the Chairmanship of Gandhi at India House, London
- 13 Mar 1910-Arrested on arrival in London from Paris
- 08 Jul. 1910-Epic escape through the port hole of SS Morea while being taken to India
- 24 Dec. 1910-Awarded Transportation for Life
- 31 Jan. 1911-Awarded Transportation for Life for the second time, the only person in the history of the British Empire to have received it twice
- 04 Jul. 1911-Entered the Cellular Jail, Andamans
- April 1919-Yesuvahini, the wife of his elder brother passed away
- 21 May 1921-Both brothers brought back to the Indian mainland
- 1921-1923-Lodged at Alipore and Ratnagiri Jails
- 06 Jan. 1924-Released from Yerawada Prison and interned in Ratnagiri on condition that he would not participate in politics
- 07 Jan. 1925-Daughter Prabhat was born
- 10 Jan. 1925-A new weekly "Shraddhanand" launched in memory of Swami Shraddhanandji of Arya Samaj
- Mar 1925-Dr. Hedgewar, who was to found the RSS later, met Savarkar

- 01 Mar 1927-Gandhi called on Savarkar at Ratnagiri
- 17 Mar 1928-Son Vishwas was born
- 16 Nov. 1930-First interdining organized as a part of social reform campaign
- Feb. 1931-Instrumental in establishment of Patitpavan Mandir open to all Hindus
- 25 Feb. 1931-Presided over Bombay Presidency Untouchability Eradication Conference
- 26 Apr 1931-Chairman of the Somvanshi Mahar Parishad in the premises of Patitpavan Mandir
- 17 Sept. 1931-Arranged programmes such as keertan by a person belonging to the bhangi caste, interdining of 75 ladies as a part of social reform campaign
- 22 Sept. 1931-Prince of Nepal, Hem Bahadur Samsher Singh called on Savarkar
- 10 May 1937-Unconditional release from internment at Ratnagiri
- 10 Dec. 1937-Elected as President of Akhil Bharat Hindu Mahasabha at its 19th Session at Karnavati (Ahmedabad) and continued to be re-elected President for the next seven years
- 15 Apr 1938-Elected as President of Marathi Sahitya Sammelan
- 01 Feb. 1939-Started unarmed resistance against the Nizam of Bhaganagar (Hyderabad)
- 22 Jun 1941-Netaji Subhas Chandra Bose called on Savarkar
- 25 Dec. 1941-Bhagalpur struggle
- May 1943-Public felicitations on the occasion of 61st birth anniversary
- 14 Aug. 1943-University of Nagpur conferred Honorary D.Litt. on Savarkar
- 05 Nov. 1943-Elected president of Marathi Natya Sammelan at Sangli
- 16 Mar 1945-Elder brother Babarao passed away

- 19 Apr 1945-Presided over All India Princely States Hindu Sabha Conference at Baroda (Gujarat)
- 08 May 1945-Daughter Prabhat married at Pune
- Apr 1946-Bombay Government lifted ban on Savarkar's literature
- 15 Aug. 1947-Hoisted both Bhagwa and Tricolour Flags on Savarkar Sadanto celebrate India's independence
- 05 Feb. 1948-Arrested under the Preventive Detention Act after Gandhi's murder
- 10 Feb. 1949-Acquitted in Gandhi Murder Trial
- 19 Oct. 1949-Youngest brother Dr. Narayanrao Savarkar passed away
- Dec. 1949-Inaugurated Calcutta session of the Akhil Bharat Hindu Mahasabha
- 04 Apr 1950-Was arrested and dctaincd in Belgaum jail on the eve of arrival of Pakistani Prime Minister Liaquat Ali in Delhi
- May 1952-Public function held at Pune to announce the dissolution of Abhinav Bharat, the revolutionary society having achieved its aim of freeing India
- Feb. 1955-Presided over Silver Jubilee celebrations of Patitpavan Mandir at Ratnagiri
- 23 Jul. 1955-Was the Chief Speaker at Lokmanya Tilak Centenary Celebrations in Pune
- 10 Nov. 1957-Main speaker at the Centenary Celebrations of the Indian War of Independence 1857 held in New Delhi
- 28 May 1958-Accorded a civic reception by Greater Bombay Municipal Corporation on the occasion of his Diamond Jubilee
- 08 Oct. 1959-University of Pune conferred honorary D. Litt. at his residence
- 24 Dec. 1960-Mrityunjay Divas celebration-a day set down for the release of Savarkar after completing the sentences of two Transportation for Life

- 15 Apr 1962-Sri Prakash, Governor of Bombay called upon Savarkar at his residence to pay his respects
- 29 May 1963-Hospitalized for a fracture in the leg
- 08 Nov. 1963-Savarkar's wife Yamuna passed away
- Sept. 1965-Taken seriously ill
- 01 Feb. 1966-Takes a decision to fast unto death
- 26 Feb. 1966-10.30 a.m., at the age of 83, Savarkar left his mortal coil
- 27 Feb. 1966-Cremation at the electric crematorium, the final salute given by 2500 uniformed swayamsevaks of the RSS and millions of admirers across the country

REMEMBERING VEER SAVARKAR

In the history of struggle for Indian independence, V.D. Savarkar's place is unique. He had a firm belief that only a strong, armed revolt by Indians would liberate India from British. An extraordinary Hindu scholar (he is one who coined Indian words for telephone, photography, the parliament, among others), a recklessly brave revolutionary (tried to swim a sea and escape when captured by the enemy) and fiercely patriotic leader, he uncovered the truth about Sepoy Mutiny. His disagreements with Gandhi's nonviolent methods and Pakistan pleasing efforts appealed to a large number of Hindus who were wronged by Pakistanis and led to the assassination of Mahatma Gandhi by Nathuram Godse.

Born Leader

Savarkar could be called a born rebel. He organized a gang of kids ,Vanarsena (Monkey Brigade) when he was just eleven. A fearless individual, he wanted everybody around him to become physically strong and able to face any disasters— natural or man-made. He conducted long tours, hiking, swimming and mountaineering around Nasik, his birthplace in Maharashtra.

During his high school days, he used to organize Shivaji Utsav and Ganesh Utsav, started by Tilak (whom Savarkar considered as his Guru) and used these occasions to put up plays on nationalistic themes. He started writing poems, essays, plays, etc. to inspire people, which he had developed as a passion. Later he went to Pune for college education and founded the "Abhinav Bharat Society". As a serious student of nationalism he found bigger venue now; with growing youngsters, he bloomed as a leader as well. All political activities were banned by the ruling British then and he had to undertake all transactions, communications in secret and was expelled from hostel and at one point from the college as well. But since he managed to get the prestigious Shivaji scholarship (named after Shivaji) to study law at London, the college authorities had to make way for his scholastic journey!

Magnum Opus

Savarkar greatly nurtured the idea of bringing out an authentic informative researched work on The Great Indian Revolt, which the British termed as "Sepoy Mutiny" of 1857. Since India Office Library was the only place which contained all records and documents, he was determined to undertake a detailed study, but was cautious enough not to make his intentions known. Hence after landing in London, he wrote a biography of Gieuseppe Mazzini, the great revolutionary and leader of modern Italy who inspired his countrymen to overthrow the Austrian Empire's yoke (Holy Roman Empire). Written in Marathi language, the manuscript was smuggled out with great care which was published by his brother Baba. The book created a wave. 2000 copies sold out secretly, read and reread. By British estimate, each copy was read by at least 30 people. Some could reproduce page after page in their voice! His brother however was imprisoned for printing the book.

At London, Savarkar undertook the task, his mission in life, to create awareness regarding the first Armed National Revolt in India in 1857. Through friends, he could get access to all much-needed first hand information regarding men, this earlier countrywide effort, was a sincere one on the part of the leaders, princes, soldiers and commoners to drive away the British, (though grossly misrepresented by British historians.) It was the first national effort towards getting political independence and rightly called his book "The Indian War of Independence 1857"

He wrote in Marathi and could not get it printed in Europe. Though the manuscript found its way to India, due to British vigilance, all printing presses were raided and in the nick of time, the manuscript had to be taken out due to a friendly police officer's information before seizure. It went back to Europe and got unfortunately got lost.

But the English version became a necessity. Savarkar was helped in this venture by the other revolutionaries who had come to study Law and Civil Service. But printing it in Britain was out of question, so also in France, as British and French spies were working together to face the imperial Germany which was becoming a great threat. Ultimately the book was published in Holland by Madam Cama without a cover or name. The cover pages of popular classics like "Don Quixote", "Oliver Twist", etc. were used for the book and successfully smuggled to India. One box with false bottom was used to take books at great risk by a Muslim friend who later became Chief Minister of Punjab! The book reached the right people through secret sympathizers in Ireland, France, Russia, U.S.A., Egypt, Germany and Brazil as well.

Fierce Nationalist

While in London, Savarkar organized festivals like Rakshabandhan and Guru Gobind Singh Jayanti and tried to create awareness among Indian students that it was banned. The slogan Savarkar coined for Indian festivals became a unifying factor.

"One Country. One God
One Caste, One Mind
Brothers all of us
Without Difference
Without Doubt"

It was during this period that Savarkar helped design the first Indian National Flag, which Madam Bhikaji Cama unfurled at the World Socialist Conference at Stuttgart, Germany.

The Scotland Yard Police noose was tightening on Savarkar. Revolutionary activities in London, Mumbai, Pune, Nasik were traced to his guidance! His speeches, articles, smelt sedition, his friends were traced as those learning the preparation of bombs and transporting arms (pistols) illegally. Finally he was arrested and ordered to be sent back to India. In India, punishments were very harsh, tortuous and the greatest crime of the land was that of sedition which could easily send one to the gallows. He was sent on a ship "Morena" which was to halt briefly at Marseilles. (1910)

Swimming the Ocean

Savarkar and his friends then attempted a brave escape which has since become legendary. Savarkar was to jump from a sailing ship, swim the sea waters and his friends were supposed to pick him there and lead to freedom. Savarkar was under a strict watch. There was no way out. With constable waiting outside, he entered the toilet, broke the window, wriggled out somehow, and jumped into the ocean to swim his way to Marseilles port. Alas! The rescue party was late by a few minutes and the French Police on guard returned the prisoner to British cops, now chained and stricter watch.

After a formal trial, Savarkar was charged with serious offences of illegal transportation of weapons, provocative speeches and sedition and was sentenced to 50 years' of jail and deported to the Blackwaters (kalapani) at Andaman cellular jail.

Conditions in jail were inhuman: backbreaking job of stone breaking, rope making, and milling. For the last prisoners had to grind the copra in the mill, tied like oxen. Each had to take out 30 pounds of oil everyday. Some died of sheer exhaustion and inhuman treatment of beating and whipping. Bad food, unsanitary conditions, stone bed and cold weather in winter used to take their toll.

Talented Mr. Savarkar

Since political prisoners were treated like hardened criminals, they had no access to "luxury" like pen and paper. The poet in

Savarkar was restless and uneasy. Finally he found a nail and wrote (itched) his epic "Kamala" consisting thousands of lines on the plastered mud wall of his cell in the darkness. A Hindi journalist friend who was taught Marathi by Savarkar came to his cell when Savarkar was removed all of a sudden to another remote cell. The friend learnt the entire poem by heart and later when he was released, put it on paper and sent it to Savarkar's relatives.

After spending 16 years in Andamans, Savarkar was transferred to the Ratnagiri jail and then kept under a house arrest. He was reunited with his wife. (He had married before leaving for England and it was a long separation). A daughter and later a son were born.

Books, poems, and articles came out. But now he was known for his book on 1857 (War of Independence) throughout the world. Two generations of Indians were influenced by his magnum opus. The second edition was printed in the U.S.A. by Savarkar's revolutionary friends. Third edition was brought out by Bhagat Singh and its Punjabi and Urdu translations followed and were widely read in India and far east. Even in the Indian National Army of Subhash Chandra Bose, Tamil translation of this work was read out like a Bible by the South Indian soldiers in Singapore, though nobody knows till the day, who translated it in Tamil.

Savarkar stood by what he wrote till the last and never compromised with "adjustments," "reforms" and peaceful solution which according to him meant nothing! As a great scholar full of originality and independent standing, he coined several new technical terms of parliamentary usage and of Indian parlance such as chhayachitra (photography), Sansad (Senate), Vyangyachitra (Cartoons) etc.

He earnestly believed that Indian Independence was a reality not because of a few individuals, leaders or sections of society. It was possible because of the participation of a commoner who prayed to his family deity everyday. But the youngsters who went to gallows to see their motherland free, were the greatest ("Veeradhiveers") he said.

LEGACY

Savarkar passed away in 1966, after coming under controversy of the assassination of Mahatma Gandhi by Nathuram Godse. The Hindu Mahasabha, an institution Savarkar had helped grow, had opposed creation of Pakistan, and took exception to Gandhi's continued Muslim appeasement stances. Nathuram Godse, a volunteer of the Hindu Mahasabha, assassinated Gandhi in 1948 and upheld his actions till his hanging. Savarkar is revered in India today as the "Brave Savarkar" (Veer Savarkar), and on the same level as Mahatma Gandhi, Subhash Chandra Bose, and Tilak. The intellectuals as well as commoners in India continue to debate what would have happened if ideas of Savarkar were endorsed by the nation, especially after freedom in 1947. A famous general is said to have quoted Savarkar after the Indians conceded land to the Chinese in a military conflict in 1962.... Savarkar had advocated a militarily strong India.

2

His Struggle for Freedom

After matriculation in 1901, he took admission in Fergusson College of Poona. He was however more interested in India's freedom from British rule. The young college students in Poona were charged by the speeches by the patriots and political leaders like Bal Gangadhar Tilak, Bhopatkar etc. The news papers in Poona were also actively participating in creating anti-British atmosphere in the society and appealing society's feelings of Nationalism. Savarkar was the uncrowned leader of the youth in this movement. In 1905 he burnt the imported clothes as a token of India's protest to imported clothes. In May 1904, he established an International Revolution Institute named "Abhinav Bharat". His instigating patriotic speeches and activities irritated the British Government. As a result his B.A. degree was withdrawn by the Government. In June 1906 he left for London to become Barrister. However, once in London, he united and inflamed the Indian students in England against British. He believed in use of arms against the foreign rulers and created a network of Indians in England, equipped with weapons. Although he passed Barrister Examination in England, because of his anti-government activities, he was denied the Degree.

He was the prime inspiration for the Indian students to rise against British rule. The British Government Officers were waiting for some opportunity to arrest him. He was arrested in London on 13 March 1910 on some fabricated offenses. The case against him was to be heard by the court in India. So he was to be sent to India. During his travel in a ship, as the ship neared

Marseilles in France, he jumped through a porthole and swam to the port. This was on 8 July 1910. As per the plan, his colleagues were to reach there beforehand. However, they reached late and he was caught by French Police. The French Government denied him asylum.

After the case was decided in India, he was sentenced to 50 years rigorous life imprisonment in Andaman on 24 December 1910. Since 4 July 1911, he was in Andaman Jail in solitude. On 2nd May 921 he was brought to India from Andaman. Since 1921 to 1922, he was in Alipur (Bengal) and Ratnagiri (Maharashtra) Jails. On 6th January 1924, he was released from the jail on two conditions viz. (a) He will not actively participate in politics and (b) he will stay in Ratnagiri District. He was in house arrest at Ratnagiri. Thereafter he spent his life in different fields of social work. He breathed his last at the age of 83, on Saturday, February 26, 1966. "Prayopveshana", meaning fast till death, was what he observed and refused any intake of food. His death was like a true warrior. Death did not grab him, he approached death with erect head.

SAVARKAR AND THE PRESENTATION OF HINDUTVA

Hindutva is based on a certain definition of the Hindu identity and is developed through certain premises of historical events. The question of identity is raised in this critique of Savarkar's thesis.

Savarkar's Hindutva has become the foundation of a certain form of religious nationalism in India. Dominant forces within the Bharatiya Janata Party and the Rashtriya Swayamsevak Sangh would like to mould India by such an ideology. They would like to see policies and laws promulgated and institutions set up that reflect this ideology. For that reason, it is important to read and analyze the basis of this framework and its implications to India in specific and South Asia in general.

The central thesis of his argument is around the question of Hindu and Hindutva. A Hindu, he claims is an individual defined by the land described by Sindhu-Sindhu, the old name for the river Indus and Sindhu, the oceans. But it is not enough to be related to this land. Savarkar argues that you were a Hindu if your forefathers came from this land, if you find yourself connected to this land AND your religious commitment evolved from this land. Hindutva, he argues, is not about the religion of Hinduism but the cultural essence of the Hindu. There is a sleight of hand in that the culture itself is defined by religion.

Thus, he argues, a Sikh is a Hindu as is a Jain or a Buddhist. Their religion evolved from within the subcontinent and they are as much part of the Hindutva consciousness. On the other hand, Muslims and Christians are not part of this Hindu tradition. Their religions evolved in Western Asia.

Savarkar argues that even though most Muslims and Christians in India were converts-converted through various processes from Hindu families as he defines them-and even though their forefathers were Hindus, by committing their loyalties to Islam or Christianity, they have lost their connectivity to the Hindu traditions-traditions which describe Hindutva. Having lost their commitment to these traditions, or at the very least, having split commitments to the tradition of Islam or Christianity on one hand and the land they live in, on the other, they embody an intrinsic conflict of loyalties.

Significant implications follow-if a certain community is defined to have an intrinsic conflict of loyalties based on the geography of the source of its belief, it is easily argued that the community cannot be trusted and every action of that community must be questioned. The community becomes defined as a community of second class citizens. While individuals of that community may become first class citizens owing to something special that they contribute-such as sporting superstars, military heroes, etc.-they do have an unenviable position. Every individual within that community is intrinsically untrustworthy unless proven otherwise.

Such an understanding destroys the fabric of a society. On one hand it affects policies. Most democracies have a variety of policies designed to empower minority groups to help them access opportunities more equally; now one can question the rights to such opportunities of minorities that are intrinsically semi-loyal. And having questioned these rights, one can begin to promulgate policies that limit the rights of these minorities. This however is a rather obvious problem that can be stymied by watchful citizens groups. The problem that is more heinous relates to the changing perception of this group of minorities in the eyes of the Hindu (as defined above by Savarkar) majority. The larger majority within the Indian society begins to form a worldview that their neighbours, friends and members of their communities who believe in another religion are less loyal to their nation, or their community and cannot always be trusted. This sentiment leads to suspicion against members of another religion. It affects the stability of society. Housing societies in numerous cities have been known to refuse ownership or tenancy to Muslims. Social relationships have become more tenuous. Usual social conflicts that exist in any community-fights between kids, arguments between neighbours-suddenly takes on a different hue, a malicious intent is seen. A people cannot exist this way, a society cannot live at peace.

Annihilating an entire community is neither possible nor desirable. The Nazis, with their immense access to resources and power, could not do it. The Americans with their power have not been able to destroy another less powerful community of Native Americans nor were they able to keep subdued another seemingly powerless community of African Americans. The anger, and hatred that breeds in even envisaging such a process makes a society numb; it arrests all development and growth. We are seeing the effects of such ideas in central Europe, in Kurdistan, among numerous other places. For generations afterwards, fear and revenge guide the ethos of the society and all its energies are caught up this quagmire. Even a powerful nation like the USA recognized this and its domestic policies attempt to reflect this recognition.

Clearly, then, Savarkar's understanding of Hindutva cannot be the worldview that the Indian people can accept without hurting their own people, their own nation. Hindutva cannot become the basis on which a stable, prosperous Indian nation can be built and any nationalist ideology must come to recognize this especially in times when economic development is the basis of progress and it demands peace. These are implications that some of the nationalists recognized clearly.

While the implications of such a worldview were disastrous, the basis of the worldview also had to be critiqued. Mainly, two kinds of critiques persist. One is based on questioning the correctness of the history that Savarkar cites. Groups have questioned his reading of the events during the wars between the Mughals, other Muslim kingdoms and the Rajputs and Marathas. Yet others have questioned the role of the Marathas themselves, arguing that they were largely interested in their own power and influence-like any other ambitious ruling class-citing various treaties signed and alliances struck up between Muslim rulers and Marathas, sometimes at the expense of other Hindu kingdoms, and the oppression and plunder that they inflicted on various groups in what is now Chattisgarh, and Orissa.

While the historical basis of some of these events is questionable, given the paradigm of modern history, it is not clear that the bravery or patriotic leanings of one ruler can be questioned in any unbiased fashion. Thus, the protagonists of such a critique often get trapped in the similar biases and propaganda that they accuse Savarkar and his followers of disseminating.

Another critique is based on the premise that the central question of Savarkar's thesis-who is a Hindu-is not really relevant to the modern nation state. We are a secular society where religion is a private matter, and identities derived from religion are irrelevant. Given that we have equal rights with respect to the state and this is a democratic state, this question is of little consequence. In fact, this critique stands on rather shaky grounds. For one, arguments of minority pandering (that in fact has been strategically used by political parties) have been use to shake up the premise of this critique. In addition, the state finds it difficult to resolve injustices within the communities-such as marriage laws or inheritance laws, for example-without engaging with the question of identities that are derived from religion. It becomes even more difficult for it to resolve problems between communities that are perceived to be tied to such identities-the slaughter of cows is one example and the Babri Masjid demolition is another. Most significantly, for most people in India, religious identity and other social identities derived from religious beliefs are important. Thus, any critique based on the irrelevancy of the religious identity is acceptable only to a certain elite; it certainly is not accepted by the larger Indian populace.

Thus, the two dominant critiques of the premises that are the foundation of Savarkar's Hindutva, fail. Even though the implications of this worldview are frightening, its appeal to a certain kind of tradition, and its easy apportionment of the blame for the problems of the Indian nation also appeal to many. The one critique that had found success in presenting the misinterpretations which form the basis of Hindutva-one that perhaps found much success in the pre-independence era thanks to Gandhi and one that has not found favour with the secular intelligentsia since independence is based on questioning Savarkar's answers to "Who is a Hindu?".

It is a critique that shows that Savarkar's attempt to construct the Hindu identity was based on misrepresentations and might even have been politically motivated like the white supremacist identities in various parts of the world. In addition, by providing a different worldview derived from a religious framework, such a definition of a Hindu in fact provides an identity that is relevant and meaningful to a large population and helps create a stable society that can provide an environment of economic, intellectual and spiritual growth for its citizens. This quandary is not unique to the Indian society. Various societies around the world-in the Islamic world, in the USA, in Europe-are confronted with this question. In this modern world, with homogenization and mass production of identities that seem irrelevant to people, religious worldviews seem to provide that relevant identity. The secularist claim, that the religious worldview is irrelevant, is unfounded. It has provided a language that is widely understood and used for communities to find their own identities, and understand their relationship to the rest of the world. While there is justifiable focus on the problems with religion, there really is no framework that is not problematic-including the framework of modern science, and that of humanities. The framework of modern science tied by assumptions of objectivity and reductionism do not provide a meaningful identity-and when they do provide an identity it is that of a consumerist or manufacturer, etc., which are in fact even more frightening and as violent. The framework of humanities is for most part inaccessible to the common people, shrouded as it is by jargon and fortified as it is within the ivory towers of academe. Even so, humanities itself had a rather oppressive birth and a violent history.

It is this quandary that various groups around the world are beginning to face today-those working for religious harmony in India, those working on issues of religious identity in Europe, those looking at the religious right and religious supremacist groups in USA as well as those working to counter religious extremism in the North Africa and Middle East. For most part, these groups have attempted to solve religious extremism by arguing that the religious framework is irrelevant-and this method has been of limited effect. As we see people make choices that are driven by this sense of identity and often counter to their own economic or other personal needs, it is clear that this identity is certainly not irrelevant. And that is not necessarily a bad thing.

Any feasible alternative then has to recognize this question of identity and make it central to the evolution of the alternative. In addition, it must be able to express the worldview and the identity in a language that people understand, can talk about and mould for themselves. What such an alternative might be is another issue.

Founded the Abhinav Bharat Society and Free India Society; brought out an authentic informative researched work on The Great Indian Revolt of 1857 called "The Indian War of Independence 1857"; founded Hindu Mahasabha.

Veer Savarkar occupies a unique place in the history of Indian freedom struggle. His name evokes controversy. While some consider him as one of the greatest revolutionaries in the Indian freedom struggle, others consider him a communalist and Machiavellian manipulator. Vir Savarkar was also a great orator, prolific writer, historian, poet, philosopher and social worker. He was an extraordinary Hindu scholar. He coined Indian words for telephone, photography, the parliament, among others.

Veer Savarkar's original name was Vinayak Damodar Savarkar. He was born on May 28, 1883 in the village of Bhagur near Nasik. He was one among four children born to Damodarpant Savarkar and Radhabai. Veer Savarkar had his initial education at the Shivaji School, Nasik. He lost his mother when he was only nine. Savarkar was a born rebel. He organized a gang of kids ,Vanarsena when he was just eleven.

During his high school days, Veer Savarkar used to organize Shivaji Utsav and Ganesh Utsav, started by Bal Gangadhar Tilak (whom Savarkar considered as his Guru) and used these occasions to put up plays on nationalistic themes. Savarkar lost his father during the plague of 1899. In March 1901, he married Yamunabai. Post marriage, in 1902, Veer Savarkar joined Fergusson College in Pune.

In Pune, Savarkar founded the "Abhinav Bharat Society". He was also involved in the Swadeshi movement and later joined Tilak's Swaraj Party. His instigating patriotic speeches and activities incensed the British Government. As a result the British Government withdrew his B.A. degree.

In June 1906, Veer Savarkar, left for London to become Barrister. However, once in London, he united and inflamed the Indian students in England against British rule in India. He founded the Free India Society. The Society celebrated important dates on the Indian calendar including festivals, freedom movement landmarks, and was dedicated to furthering discussion about Indian freedom. He believed and advocated the use of arms to free India from the British and created a network of Indians in England, equipped with weapons.

In 1908, brought out an authentic informative researched work on The Great Indian Revolt, which the British termed as "Sepoy Mutiny" of 1857. The book was called "The Indian War of Independence 1857". The British government immediately enforced a ban on the publication in both Britain and India. Later, it was published by Madame Bhikaji Cama in Holland, and was smuggled into India to reach revolutionaries working across the country against British rule.

In 1909, Madanlal Dhingra, a keen follower of Savarkar shot Sir Wyllie after a failed assassination attempt on the then Viceroy, Lord Curzon. Savarkar conspicuously did not condemn the act. When the then British Collector of Nasik, A.M.T. Jackson was shot by a youth, Veer Savarkar finally fell under the net of the British authorities. He was implicated in the murder citing his connections with India House. Savarkar was arrested in London on March 13, 1910 and sent to India. After a formal trial, Savarkar was charged with serious offences of illegal transportation of weapons, provocative speeches and sedition and was sentenced to 50 years' of jail and deported to the Kalapani (Blackwaters) at Andaman cellular jail.

In 1920, many prominent freedom fighters including Vithalbhai Patel, Mahatma Gandhi and Bal Gangadhar Tilak demanded the release of Savarkar. On May 2, 1921, Savarkar was moved to Ratnagiri jail, and from there to the Yeravada jail. In Ratnagiri jail Savarkar wrote the book 'Hindutva'. On January 6, 1924 he was h freed under the condition that he would not leave Ratnagiri district and abstain from political activity for the next five years. On his release, Veer Savarkar founded the Ratnagiri Hindu Sabha on January 23, 1924 that aimed to preserve India's ancient culture and work for social welfare.

Later Savarkar joined Tilak's Swaraj Party and founded the Hindu Mahasabha as a separate political party. He was elected President of the Mahasabha and toiled for building Hindu Nationalism and later joined the Quit India movement.

The Hindu Mahasabha opposed creation of Pakistan, and took exception to Gandhi's continued Muslim appeasement stances. Nathuram Godse, a volunteer of the Hindu Mahasabha, assassinated Gandhi in 1948 and upheld his actions till his hanging. Veer Savarkar was arrested and indicted by the Government of India in the Mahatma Gandhi assassination case.

VEER SAVARKAR'S FAMILY MEMBERS DR. NARAYAN DAMODAR SAVARKAR

Younger brother of Veer Savarkar. Born on 25 May 1888. Dentist by profession. Made great efforts to get his two elder brothers released. Participated in revolutionary activities in Nashik.

Participated in Tilakite political activities. He published the Shraddhananda weekly for three years in memory of Swami Shraddhananda who was murdered by a Muslim called Abdul Rashid. Was a senior worker of the Mumbai Hindu Sabha and president of the Mumbai Hindu Sabha for some years. The first shakha (branch) of the Rashtriya Swayamsevak Sangh (RSS) in Mumbai started in his clinic. Was physically assaulted in the aftermath of the Gandhi murder. Never fully recovered and died on 19 October 1949.

Yamunabai Vinayak or Mai Savarkar

Savarkar's wife. Born on 04 December 1888 or Margashirsh shukla 1, Vikram samvat 1945. Her father Bhaurao Chiplunkar rose to become dewan (minister) of Jawhar principality near Thane. Married Savarkar in February 1901 or Magh Vikram samvat 1957.

It was Mai's father Bhaurao Chiplunkar who bore Savarkar's expenses in London. Supported Savarkar silently throughout her life. Organized haldi-kumkum programmes in Ratnagiri as part of Savarkar's campaign of social reform. Bore Savarkar four children in all. The eldest Prabhakar died while Savarkar was in London. Their daughter Prabhat was born in Satara in January 1925. Their second daughter Shalini was a sickly child and expired in childhood when the Savarkars were in Ratnagiri. Their son Vishwas was born in Mumbai in March 1928. Mai Savarkar died on 08 November 1962 or Kartik 8 Vikram samvat 2020 in Mumbai.

The Oath of Abhinav Bharat

BANDE MATARAM

In the name of God,

In the name of Bharat Mata,

In the name of all the Martyrs that have shed their blood for Bharat Mata,

By the Love, innate in all men and women, that I bear to the land of my birth, wherein the sacred ashes of my forefathers, and which is the cradle of my children, By the tears of Hindi Mothers for their children whom the Foreigner has enslaved, imprisoned, tortured, and killed, I, ... Convinced that without Absolute Political Independence or Swarajya my country can never rise to the exalted position among the nations of the earth which is Her due,

And Convinced also that Swarajya can never be attained except by the waging of a bloody and relentless war against the Foreigner,

Solemnly and sincerely Swear that I shall from this moment do everything in my power to fight for Independence and place the Lotus Crown of Swaraj on the head of my Mother;

And with this object, I join the Abhinav Bharat, the revolutionary Society of all Hindusthan, and swear that I shall ever be true and faithful to this my solemn Oath, and that I shall obey the orders of this body;

If I betray the whole or any part of this solemn Oath, or if I betray this body or any other body working with a similar object, May I be doomed to the fate of a perjurer!

Savarkar in London

Savarkar played a significant role in putting forth the case for India's independence on the international scene. He fearlessly went to the enemy camp and carried out his revolutionary activities in the heart of the British Empire. Barrister Sardarsingh Rana (born 12 April 1870, in Katharia in Saurashtra) had announced three travelling fellowships of Rs. 2000 each. These fellowships were named after Maharana Pratap, Chhatrapati

Shivaji and Akbar. Savarkar received the Shivaji fellowship on the recommendation of Lokmanya Tilak and Kaal editor Shivrampant Paranjpe. As had been decided, Tilak paid the first instalment of Rs. 400. Savarkar was to initially leave India on 26 May 1907. However, this plan changed. Finally, on 09 June 1909, Savarkar embarked on S.S. Persia and reached London on 24 June 1906.

Savarkar came to London with the following aims in mind:

1. To observe at first hand, the strengths of the British people which enabled them to rule over India and also to note their weaknesses and to think of ways of using them to achieve India's freedom.
2. To meet students from all parts of India. Such meetings were much more easier in London than in India. People back home looked to these men with admiration and expected direction and leadership from them. According to report 'Indian Students in U.K.' compiled by Secretary of State for India in 1907 there were some 700 of them in U.K at that time.
3. To kindle the spirit of fighting among these youth for Indian independence.
4. To meet professionals, Rajahs, merchants and rich people, who came to London and possibly, also visited Europe. Savarkar sought their assistance in the freedom struggle too.
5. To establish contacts with revolutionaries of other countries like Russia, China, Ireland, Turkey, Egypt and Iran. He wanted to learn the art of making bombs from them, and put that knowledge and friendship into use for concerted attempts to overthrow the British rule. He also wanted to smuggle pistols and ammunition into India.

Savarkar carried out the following activities in London:

1. He started regular Sunday meetings to discuss various topics related to India's future. These soon became popular among Indian students. Revolutionaries from other countries such as Egypt, Ireland, Russia, China

and Turkey used to attend. Lenin was one of them. One of the topics of discussion was "Future constitution of India."

These meetings were intended to increase one's knowledge of all current affairs. Savarkar was able to maintain this tradition even in the Cellular Jail in the Andaman Islands.

2. Savarkar organized the days of the remembrance of national heroes such as Shivjayanti (birthday of Chhatrapati Shivaji) and celebrations of festivals like Diwali and Dassara. He also celebrated the golden jubilee of the 1857 War of Independence against the British in India House.
3. Savarkar had started his secret revolutionary society called the Abhinav Bharat (similar to Young Italy of Mazzini) in India in 1905. Savarkar carried on the activities of the Abhinav Bharat while in London. Copies of bomb manual were printed in India House in London. One copy reached Lokmanya Tilak in Pune.
4. Savarkar completed his biography of Mazzini in Marathi in September 1906. His elder brother Babarao published it in India in June 1907. A year later, the British proscribed the book. He wrote his famous book Indian War of Independence 1857 in Marathi. His friends in India House translated it into English. It was published secretly in Holland in 1909 and immediately banned in India. Savarkar's book served as a source of inspiration to Indian revolutionaries for next 40 years.

Sikhs are an important part of the Hindu society. In the Indian Army their percentage was quite high. Savarkar therefore learned Gurumukhi and studied the holy books, Adigranth, Panthprakash and Vichitra Natak.

While in England, Savarkar prepared notes for his book 'History of the Sikhs' which he completed while in Paris. Savarkar sent 43 newsletters from India House during the period from 17 August 1906 to 26 November 1909.

These were related to politics and current affairs and were published in the Marathi newspaper, Vihari. Three leaflets were printed in India House.

1. Gurumukhi leaflet-This appealed to the Sikhs to revolt against the British.
2. 'Oh Martyrs!'. This was addressed to the fighters of the 1857 war. Savarkar assured them 'your blood oh martyrs, shall be avenged. We will continue your fight and drive the British out of India.
3. 'Choose, oh Indian Princes'

This was sent out to Indian Princes, Rajas and Maharajas after Dhingra's martyrdom in August 1909. Savarkar appealed to them to join in the freedom struggle.

Chronology

1906

- April
- On the 14th, a protest meeting against the partition of Bengal was held at Barisal (now in Bangladesh). Police used brute force to disperse the gathering. Surendranath Banerjee was heavily fined.
- May
- 5th-A meeting to condemn the police action was held at Shyamji's home by the Indian Home Rule Society. At this meeting, Vitthalbhai Patel (elder brother of Sardar Patel) and Bhai Paramanand were present. Dadabhai Naoroji and Gokhale were invited but did not attend.
- 6th-Similar meeting was held in Paris by Mr Banker, Mr Godrej, Barrister Rana and others.
- Vande Mataram became our national anthem because it was banned in Dacca by Sir Banfield Fuller, Lt Governor of East Bengal
- June
- 9th-Savarkar left Bombay for London by S.S. Persia
- 14th-Report on Savarkar by Special Branch, Pune was dispatched to London

- 24th-Savarkar probably reached London.
- 26th-Savarkar enrols with Grays Inn for his studies.
- July
- 18th-Savarkar called on Sir Curzon Wyllie, by appointment for obtaining an order for the House of Commons to hear the debate on the Indian Budget on 20th July
- 20th-Debate in House of Commons on Indian Budget.
- 22nd-Public meeting in Chandos Hall. Lecture by Barrister Parekh

  Subject-The Recent Persecution in Bengal. Social Democratic Federation arranged series of lectures. Parekh's was one of them
- October
- Letter of R C Dutt

  Daily News/ Daily Chronicle/ Mirror / Telegrap
- 20th-Gandhi reached London. He headed a delegation to protest against injustices suffered by Indians in South Africa. He met Savarkar in India House.
- November
- 23rd Dadabhai going to India to accept office of President of Congress Party.. Public celebrations in London
- P M (Senapati) Bapat wrote a book India demands Home Rule. As a result Bombay university withdrew Mangaldas Nathubhai scholarship

1907

- January
- Suffragette movement-Daily News, Tribune,
- February
- Irish Home Rule movement
- March
- 14th-Morley sets up a committee for condition of Indian students in U.K.
- May
- Shyamji left London for Paris

- 10th-Savarkar celebrated anniversary of 1857 War at 78 Goldsmith Avenue, Acton, London W3 (riots in Rawalpindi, Daily Graphic, Daily Telegraph, Evening News, Tribune)
- Lala Lajpat Rai and Sardar Ajit Singh were deported to Mandalay (Burma). So strict was the security that the two leaders did not know that they were kept in prison in the same place, Mandalay.
- August
- Madame Cama unfurled Indian National flag in front of 1,000 delegates from all over the world at the International Socialist Conference in Stuttgart, Germany. Ramsey MacDonald was one of the delegates. He later became British Prime Minister. Others included Lenin and Rosa Luxemburg who was hanged during Communist uprising in the days of Weimar Republic.
- November
- 30th-Indian students in U.K.-report was published.

City	*Number of students*
London	380 (320 studied Law)
Edinburgh	150
Cambridge	085
Oxford	032
Manchester	016
Birmingham	011
Others	016
Total	700

1908

- February
- Turmoil in Portugal. King and Prince killed, younger prince on throne.
- May
- Shivaji's birthday celebrated in London. Programme arranged by Free India Society

- 10th-50th anniversary of the 1857 War was celebrated in India House, Dramas in English theatres
- September
- 21 Meeting in Caxton Hall to protest against the sentence of Transportation for 6 years given to Tilak
- October
- Board of Trade figures-effect of Swadeshi, Mill-owners want to reduce wages by 5%- labour unrest
- Bipin Chandra Pal in London-news in papers
- December
- 20th-Annual session of Indian National Congress held in Caxton Hall-It was to be held in Nagpur, but Govt. banned it there
- 29th-Savarkar organised celebration of birthday of Guru Govind Singh, in Caxton Hall (Times, Daily Telegraph, Mirror, Daily Express)

1909

- February
- 28 Babarao Savarkar arrested in Mumbai
- April
- 3rd Savarkar left India House
  - o Standard-representative meets Savarkar
  - o Sunday Chronicle-representative meets Savarkar
  - o Also Daily Mail, Manchester Guardian, Dispatch also sent representatives to meet Savarkar.
- May
- On the 1st, Shyamji Krishnavarma was struck off the register of Barristers by benchers of the Inner Temple.
- June
- 8th Babarao sent to Transportation for Life and forfeiture of all his property.
- Three days later, Viceroy Lord Minto sent a telegram to the Secretary of State for India, "Ganesh Damodar Savarkar convicted under section 121 and 124A of the

India Penal Code and sentenced to transportation for life and forfeiture of property."

- July
- 1st Madanlal Dhingra shot dead Sir Curzon Wyllie
- 5th Meeting in Caxton Hall to condemn Dhingra. Savarkar protests
- 6th Savarkar's letter of explanation published in Times (London) Daily Dispatch-news
- In 1903, Shyamji had endowed a sum of 1,000 pounds to the Oxford University in memory of philosopher Herbert Spencer who died in that year. This was returned to him in July 1909. The once venerated Sanskrit scholar had suddenly become a persona non grata because now he was seeking independence for India.
- 14th-At the end of all the farce the benchers of Grays Inn ruled, "None of the charges was proven. Savarkar is a permanent member of this society (Grays Inn) and would continue to enjoy the privileges of membership. There was still suspicion about him and, as such he would not be called to the Bar as yet. (What happened to the principle that an accused person is innocent unless proved guilty? It was conveniently set aside by those who practised and taught law!!) He may be called later, if his behaviour is satisfactory."
- 23rd-Savarkar wrote in his newsletter, "When it became obvious that the evidence was collected by the Government of India, it was clear who was behind this episode."
- August
- On 3rd August Viceroy Lord Minto sent a telegram from Simla to India Office, "It is understood that Madanlal Dhingra is to be executed on the 17th August. If body cremated, undesirable that ashes should be sent to India."
- The Times reported on 11 August 1909, "The mail from India brings the following notification issued at Simla on July 23-' In exercise of the power conferred by section 19

of the Sea Customs Act 1878 (viii of 1878) the Governor-General is pleased to prohibit the bringing by sea or land into British India of any copy of the book or pamphlet in Marathi on the subject of the Indian Mutiny by Vinayak Damodar Savarkar or any English translation or version of the same.' Savarkar's book served as a source of inspiration to Indian revolutionaries for next 40 years]

- 16th Dhingra's statement published as handbill in London.
    - o Newspapers-Daily Mirror-"we challenge the police"
    - o Times/Standard etc. Check-American and Irish Newspapers for news.
- 17th Dhingra was sent to the gallows at Pentonville Prison at 09:00 hrs
- November
- 5th-Queens Road Hall-meeting of Vijayadashmi. Gandhi praises Savarkar. This was the last newsletter sent by Savarkar
- December
- 21st Mr Jackson, Collector of Nashik was shot dead in Nashik by Kanhere.

1910

- March
- 13th-Savarkar was arrested at London (Victoria) station.
- 14th-Savarkar was brought in front of Bow Street Magistrate.
- July
- 8th-Savarkar's dramatic attempt to escape from S.S. Moria at Marseilles

HIS READING HABITS

Right from his childhood he used to like reading. Invariably found in Library, he used to read the news papers like Kesari, Kal, Dnyanprakash etc. He read "Short History of the World" in childhood. He studied History of India from Vedic time. History was his favourite subject. He had good command over Sanskrit and thoroughly read Sanskrit as well as English literature. Amongst other books, he was impressed by the biographies of Mazini, Garibaldi, Napoleon etc. He read Bible, and Holy Koran, philosophers like Spencer, Mill, Darwin, Huxlay, Emerson etc. He also studied Economics, Geology etc. He could by heart half of Ravindranath Tagore's literature. He had also carefully studied Lenin and Trotsky.

Pioneer

He is proved to be pioneer in many fields such as:

- He studied the original records available in London about India's history and proposed that the "mutiny" of 1957 in India, as stamped by British, was not a mutiny but a freedom fight.
- While in Andaman Jail, he took lead in uniting the prisoners and made representation to the British Government against the subhuman conditions of the jail and worst treatment given to the prisoners. This persuaded the Government to improve the jail conditions and some facilities were sanctioned to the prisoners.
- He made history in Marathi Poetry by writing an epoch making poetry "Kamala", in Andaman Jail. He was a gifted poet who wrote poems, which can be compared to those of Kalidas in Sanskrit.
- He was the pioneer to get back the converted Indians to Hindu Religion.
- To follow the guiding principle of "Swadeshi movement" by Lok Manya Tilak, he was the first to set ablaze imported clothes.

Purification of Mother Tongue

He was against the influence of Urdu, English or any other languages on Marathi-his mother tongue Hence he professed for use of pure Marathi Language. To replace many conversant words adopted from languages like Urdu, Persian or English, he coined many words and brought them in use. Since Marathi originates from Sanskrit, which is a proliferate language, why should invasion of words from other languages be tolerated, he used to emphasis. The following Marathi words, which we use in day to day language are brought in by Savarkar-Prashala (High school), Aacharya (Principal), Dhani (Malak-Owner), Dinank (Tarikh-date), Upasthita (hajar-present), Nabhowani (radio), Mahapour (mayor), Vishwasta (Trustee) etc.

Realizing the importance and influence of print media, he made appropriate changes in the Devnagari script, so as to ease printing. "Savarkar script" reduced print type faces from 200 to 80.

He was the President of Hindu Mahasabha and toiled for building Hindu Nationalism.

He campaigned for incorporation of Hindus in Indian Military from 30% to 65% during British Raj apparently this was misunderstood as helping British for fighting the Second World War. However military training was very essential for the revolution, which could be used against British Rule on opportune time. That was the purpose of this campaign. This was appreciated by Netaji Subhash Chandra Bose saying that this movement facilitated supply of trained soldiers to his "Swatantra Sena".

At his instance, Madam Cama represented India in the International Socialists Conference with India's flag. The participants in the conference not only saluted Indian Flag, but also agreed that they should support the freedom movement in India. After India's independence, while deciding the flag of the country, Savarkar's suggestion to adopt Dharmachakra on the Sarnath Pillar (Ashok Stambh) was accepted and implemented.

HIS LITERATURE

Savarkar was a prolific writer and poet. His literature from the age of 11 till 70 can be divided in five parts.

The first part consists of poems and ballads, mainly related to freedom movement.

The second part consists of his writings while being in England. Amongst them "Joseph Mazini"- a biography of the famous Italian freedom fighter-is world famous. Another one is "Sattavanche watryantsamar"-"The freedom fight of 1857", which is a deep study of the 1857 "Mutiny" (as called by British) in India. He also wrote "Shikhancha Itihas" (History of Shikhs). He used to write in the Indian news papers called "Kal" and "Vihari" on various politics related topics.

The third part is during his imprisonment in Andaman. While enduring the rigorous imprisonment, he did not get even pen and paper to write. In such adverse conditions he wrote "Kamala"-an epic on the prison walls with the help of shart thorns.

The fourth part is after he was shifted to Ratnagiri under house arrest. The immortal book "Mazi Janmathep" (My life imprisonment) was written during this period. It describes the dreadful life in prison. This part also includes his "Vidnyannishtha Nibandh" (scientific essays), three dramas named "Ushshap", "Sanyasta Khadga" and "Uttarkriya" regarding imancipation of untouchables, conversion of religion and the adverse effects of extremity of "Ahinsa" on the nation, "Kale Pani" (Black water)-a novel based on his experiences in Andaman Jail and "Mala kay tyache" (What do I care?), on the background of the mutiny of Mopla- Muslims in Malbar. He wrote two books in English named "Hindutwa" and "Hindupadapadshahi" on the history of Marathas.

After he was released from house arrest he became the President of Hindu Mahasabha. His presidential addresses have been compiled in "IIindurashtra-Darshan" which throws light on his political thinking. In the fifth and the last part, after he retired from day to day political work, he wrote "Hindurashtrachya itihasateel saha soneri pane" (Six golden pages in the History of Hindu Nation) about the critical study of History of Hindus. So far the impression was that Hindus have always been losing the battle, which is not true. He has quoted the heroism of Hindus, which gives Hindus stimulus and pride of their glorious legacy.

His contribution of Marathi literature is invaluable. Therefore he was selected as the President of Maharashtra Sahitya Sammelan in 1938. Nagpur University and Poona University conferred on him the Honorary D.Lit. degree on 14th August 1943 and on 8th October 1959 respectively.

After India's independence, he had to face the judicial inquiry for assassination of Gandhiji, since Nathuram Godse, Gandhiji's assassinator was the disciple of Savarkar. No charges were proved against him. His two very famous poems are Sagara Pran Talamalala and Jayostute.

He was a living "Sthitapradnya" as described in "Bhatwat Geeta" and used to live as per the philosophy of "Bhatwat Geeta".

His house in Bhagur, 9 kilometres away from Nashik, is being preserved as National Monument by the Government of India

Martyrs and Revolutionaries of India's Freedom-XI

Veer Savarkar has been rightly hailed as a Prince among Indian revolutionaries. An incomparable freedom fighter, a historian, a gifted playwright, an ethic poet and a fiery orator, he was indeed a Carlylean hero cast in a truly magnificent mould. He led a consecrated life. He was an inspiration alike to the young and the old.

Chakravarthi Rajagopalachari (1878-1972) paid this tribute to him: 'Veer Savarkar was my first Revolutionary Idol. 'When he gave up his Law studies in London and declared rebellion against the British Rule, he caught the imagination of us all.'

Vinayak Damodar Savarkar was born on 28 May, 1883 into a family of jagirdars (landlords) in the village of Bhagpur near Nasik. Vinayak was one of four children others being, Ganesh (Babarao), Mainabai and Narayan, born to Damodarpant Savarkar and Radhabai. Being descendents of a line of Sanskrit scholars, the Savarkars inculcated the love of learning into their children. Vinayak and Babarao were sent to the Shivaji School in Nasik. When Vinayak was nine years old, his mother died of cholera. Damodarpant himself looked after his children thereafter.

There was an outbreak of plague epidemic in Nasik in 1899 and Savarkar's father died of plague in 1899. The burden of the family fell on Babarao's shoulders. Savarkar's patriotic spirit found an outlet through an organisation called the Mitra Mela that he formed. Savarkar inducted young patriotic men like himself into the Mela. He encouraged the members of the Mela to strive for 'absolute political independence for India' by whatever means necessary. In the event of an armed revolt the young crusaders toughened themselves through physical training. The Mitra Mela served the city of Nasik in many ways, especially during the plague when the group carried victims for cremation.

In March 1901, Savarkar was married to Yamunabai, daughter of Ramchandra Triambak Chiplunkar, who agreed to help in the matter of Savarkar's university education. After his matriculation examination, Savarkar enrolled in the Fergusson College in Poona in 1902. Savarkar very soon dominated the Fergusson College campus life. He, along with a group of students began dressing alike like Nationalists and started using Swadeshi goods only. He renamed the 'Mitra Mela' as 'ABHINAV BHARAT' in 1904 and declared that 'India must be independent; India must be united; India must be a republic; India must have a common language and common script.' This secret organisation started growing in leaps and bounds and turned into a Revolutionary Party.

In 1905, a huge Dussehra bonfire of foreign goods was lit in Poona by Savarkar and his friends to express their violent resentment toward the partition of Bengal. Savarkar organised in Pune a mammoth procession at the close of which he made a big bonfire of foreign clothes. Lokmanya Tilak (1856-1920) also participated in the rally. For organising the nation's first bonfire of foreign clothes, Savarkar was fined Rs 10 and expelled from the College Hostel by his principal. Savarkar left for London to study Law in June 1906 on receiving a scholarship.

Savarkar stayed at the India House in London, which was established by Pandit Shyamaji Krishnavarma (1857-1930), a patriot, scholar and social reformer. Shyamaji Krishnavarma started a journal Indian Sociologist, for the propagation of the ideals of freedom and revolution. He was the man who had announced liberal scholarships for Indian students desiring to study in Europe. Savarkar was able to go to England only with the help of Shyamaji's scholarship. Interestingly it was Lokmanya Tilak who had recommended his scholarship to Shyamaji. In London, Savarkar founded the Free India Society which held weekly meetings and celebrated Indian festivals and anniversaries of important figures and days in the Indian struggle for freedom. On 10 May, 1907, scuffles broke out between Indians and Britishers at the celebration of the Golden Jubilee of the 1857 martyrs of the First War of Indian Independence (described by British Historians as the Indian Mutiny) organised by the Free India Society. In 1908, Savarkar completed his historic and immortal work 'THE HISTORY OF THE WAR OF INDIAN INDEPENDENCE.' This book was originally written in Marathi and later translated into English by the well-known revolutionary of Tamilnadu, V V S Iyer (1881-1925) who was also staying along with Savarkar in India House at that time. This book was proscribed by the British government for being 'revolutionary, explosive and seditious' even before it was published. This book was later published in France and Germany and it played a very significant role in inspiring great revolutionaries like Bhagat Singh (1907-1931) and Subhash Chandra Bose (1897-1945).

In 1909, Madanlal Dhingra, follower of Savarkar, shot Sir Wyllie of the India Office after failing in his attempt on the life of the then Indian Viceroy, Lord Curzon, for the atrocities committed on Nationalist Indians in India. Madanlal Dhingra was imprisoned and a meeting of Indians in London took place at which it was proposed to unanimously condemn Madanlal Dhingra's action. At that meeting Savarkar angrily shouted, 'No, not unanimously!' The meeting became unruly, Savarkar's spectacles broke and blood ran down his face. The meeting was broken up with the prominent Indian Nationalist leader Surendranath Banerjea (1848-1925) leaving in protest of the physical attack on Savarkar. That very night Savarkar wrote to the London Times to clarify the reasons for his action. Savarkar wrote: 'The meeting had no right to condemn Madanlal Dhingra like a Law Court.'

What is interesting to note is that at that time simultaneously in India, Savarkar's elder brother Babarao led an armed movement against the Minto-Morley reforms. Babarao was sentenced to transportation for life to the Andamans jail. In protest, a youth called Kanhere shot dead the British Collector of Nasik, A M T Jackson. Savarkar was implicated in the murder of Jackson because of his contacts with the India House. Savarkar soon moved to Madame Cama's residence in Paris. A warrant was issued and Savarkar was arrested on 13 March, 1910. In one of his last letters to a close friend before his arrest, Savarkar conveyed the plan of his intended attempt to escape from the custody at Marseilles. His friend was expected to be waiting there with a car. The escape attempt at Marseilles failed since the car arrived too late. When he was being taken to India as a prisoner in the P & O Liner SS Morea, Veer Savarkar made a daring attempt to escape by jumping into the sea at Marseilles Port. Though he swan across to the pier, he was arrested by the French Police and handed over to the Scotland Yard Officer. Savarkar was tried and found guilty on the counts of 'waging war by instigation using printed matter, and providing arms... (and) for abetting the murder of Mr. Jackson. Savarkar was awarded 25 years imprisonment on the former charge and 25 years for the latter. A sum total of 50 years imprisonment which he was to serve at the Andamans prison. Veer Savarkar was only 27 years old at the time of his sentencing!

Savarkar arrived at the Andamans prison on 4 July, 1911. Life for the prisoners was very harsh. Savarkar's day began at 5 a.m. chopping trees with a heavy wooden mallet and then he would be yoked to the oil mill. If prisoners talked or broke the queue at mealtime, their 'once a year letter writing privilege' was revoked. Savarkar withdrew within himself, quietly and mechanically doing the tasks presented to him. He was successful in getting permission to start a jail library. With great effort and patience he taught the illiterate convicts to read and write. On 2 May, 1921, the Savarkar brothers were brought back to India on the SS Maharaja.

Savarkar remained imprisoned in Ratnagiri Jail and then in Yeravada Jail until 6 January, 1924 when he was freed under the condition that he would not leave Ratnagiri district and abstain from political activity for the next five years. While in Ratnagiri Jail, Savarkar wrote 'Hindutva' which was smuggled out and published under the pen-name 'Maharatta.' On his release, Savarkar founded the Ratnagiri Hindu Sabha on 23 January, 1924 which aimed to preserve India's ancient culture and work for social welfare. He appealed for a wider use of Hindi as the mother tongue and suggested reforms to the Devanagiri script to facilitate printing.

While in Ratnagiri, he wrote the 'Hindu Padpadashashi' and 'My Transportation for Life' and a collection of poems, plays and novels. At the end of his five- year confinement in Ratnagiri, Savarkar joined Tilak's Swaraj Party and founded the Hindu Mahasabha as a separate political party. He warned of the Muslim League's designs of partitioning the nation. In 1937, Savarkar was elected President of the Hindu Mahasabha. He toured the nation widely and delivered the simple message to the effect that followers of Vedism, Jainism, Buddhism and Sikhism were all Hindus.

Savarkar agreed to join hands with the Congress in support of Gandhiji's Quit India Movement in 1942 as long as the Congress did not compromise the unity of the nation to the Muslim League. 'The Quit India Movement must not end in a Split India Movement!' he thundered on a BBC broadcast of his speech. On 15 August, 1947, Savarkar proudly unfurled the national flag along with the saffron flag of the Hindu Mahasabha.

The government of India deliberately implicated him in the case relating to the assassination of Mahatma Gandhi in 1948. He was honourably acquitted by the Court on 10 February, 1949. He passed away on 27 February, 1966.

M C Chagla, the then Union Education Minister paid this tribute to him: 'Savarkar was a great patriot and an illustrious son of India. He was always of the view that anyone living in this country who loved and drew inspiration from the great heritage of India and was loyal to India was a Hindu.

Revolutionaries like Savarkar created an atmosphere which made it possible for Mahatma Gandhi to succeed. It would be unpatriotic if the people of India fail to give Savarkar a prominent place in the history of India.'

The life of Vinayak Damodar Savarkar is a story of resistance, strife, struggle, suffering and sacrifice for the cause of political, social and economic emancipation of India. V.D. Savarkar was born on 28th May, 1883 at Bhagur a village near Nasik, in a family of Chitpavan Brahmins, a community which has produced noted revolutionaries like Nana Saheb (of 1857 fame) and Lokmanya Tilak. Savarkar matriculated from Nasik and went to Poona where he joined the Fergusson College. There, he found group of students, who vowed themselves to a spartan way of life in the cause of country's freedom.

In 1904, Savarkar, still an undergraduate, convened a meeting of nearly 200 of his trusted comrades and founded the "Abhinav Bharat"- an organisation dedicated to wresting freedom from the British rulers, if necessary with the help of arms. After graduation in 1905, he studied law in Bombay. The following year Savarkar went to London to study law on a scholarship on the recommendation, among others of Lokmanya Tilak and in due course, was admitted in Gray's Inn. Soon, the young revolutionary started the "Free India Society" in London as a recruiting ground for his secret organisation, the "Abhinav Bharat" and enfolled a number of Indians including Madame Cama. Repression in India continued to agited the minds of the members of the "Abhinav Bharat", and on July 1,1909, one of the members, Madan Lal Dhingra shot and killed Cuzon Wyllie in the hall of Imperial Institute.

This incident shook London and Savarkar came under suspicion. As a result, when he passed the final examination of the Gray's Inn, the benchers of the Inn declined to confer the degree upon Savarkar, unless Savarkar give a written understanding that he would not participate in politics. Savarkar rejected the offer.

In London, Savarkar, wrote a book entitled the "First war of Independence" about the 1857 revolution. This book was promptly confiscated by the Government even before its publication. Later, Veer Savarkar was arrested in London in 1910 in connection with the Nasik Conspitacy case. When he was being taken by ship to India for trial, off Marseilles, Savarkar jumped into the sea and swamto the French coast braving the flringfrom the ship. He was arrested at Marseilles by the British Police. The French Government protested against this arrest on French soil to the Hague International Court. This brought Veer Savarkar and other Indian freedom fighters to prominence throughout the world. Savarkar was tried for sedition in 1910 at Bombay and was sentenced to double transportation for life totalling about 50 years rigorous imprisonment. He was lodged in the Cellular Jail in the Andamans where he spent 12 long years of hard labour.

This did not, in any way, dampen his spirit or quench his thirst for freedom. Veer Savarkar was brought to Tantnagiri in 1924 and was interned there till 1937, he joined the Hindu Mahasabha for about seven years. Veer Savarkar worked relentlessly for the removal of untouchability through the Hindu Mahasabha. He build a temple called "Patit-Pawan Mandir" and appointed a 'harijan' as the priest in attendance. When British Government was holding talks with the Indian political leaders, Veer Savarkar had participated on behalf of the Hindu Mahasabha in the discussions connected with the Cripps Mission and Wavell Plan and Sressed the need for keeping.

India united. Veer Savarkar was the happiest man when India achieved freedom in 1947. In 1951, he dissolved the revolutionary organisation "Abhinav Bharat" and devoted his time and energy for the ideals of the Hindu Mahasabha. On February 26,1966, Veer Savarkar passed away at the ripe old age of 83. His memory will always remain green in the hearts of his countrymen, and he will always be counted among the great men of his generation. The P.& T. Department is proud to celebrate the memory of this great son of India by issuing a special commemorative stamp in his honour.

3

Associates in Hindutva and Savarkar

WHO IS A HINDU?

The words Hindutva and Hinduism both of them being derived from the word Hindu, must necessarily be understood to refer to the whole of the Hindu people. Any definition of Hinduism that leaves out any important section of our people and forces them either to play false to their convictions or to go outside the pale of Hindutva stands self-condemned.

Hinduism means the system of religious beliefs found common amongst the Hindu people. And the only way to find out what those religious beliefs of the Hindus are, i.e., what constitutes Hinduism, you must first define a Hindu.

But forgetting this chief implication of the word, Hinduism which clearly presupposes an independent conception of a Hindu many people go about to determine the essentials of Hinduism and finding none so satisfactory as to include, without overlapping all our Hindu communities, come to the desperate conclusion-which does not satisfy them either -that therefore those communities are not Hindus at all; not because the definition they had framed is open to the fault of exclusion but because those communities do not subject themselves to the required tenets which these gentlemen have thought it fit to lable as 'Hinduism'. This way of answering the question 'who is a Hindu' is really preposterous and has given rise to so much of bitterness amongst some of our brethren of Avaidik school of thought, the Sikh, the Jain, the Devsamaji and even our patriotic and progressive Aryasamajis.

'Who is a Hindu ?' -he who is subject to the tenets of Hinduism. Very well. What is Hinduism ?- those tenets to which the Hindus are subjected. This is very nearly arguing in a circle and can never lead to a satisfactory solution. Many of our friends who have been on this wrong track have come back to tell us 'there are no such people as Hindus at all!' If some Indian, as gifted as that Englishman who first coined the word Hinduism, coins a parallel word 'Englishism' and proceeds to find out the underlying unity of beliefs amongst the English people, gets disgusted with thousands of sects and societies from Jews to the Jacobins, from Trinity to Utility, and comes out to announce that 'there are no such people as the English at all,' he would not make himself more ridiculous than those who declare in cold print' there is nothing as a Hindu people.' Any one who wants to see what a confusion of thought prevails on the point and how the failure to analyse separately the two terms Hindutva and Hinduism renders that confusion worst confounded may do well to go through the booklet 'Essentials of Hinduism ' published by the enterprising ' Natesan and Co.'

Hinduism means the ' ism ' of the Hindu; and as the word Hindu has been derived from the word Sindhu, the Indus, meaning primarily all the people who reside in the land that extends from Sindhu to Sindhu, Hinduism must necessarily mean the religion or the religions that are peculiar and native to this land and these people. If we are unable to reduce the different tenets and beliefs to a single system of religion then the only way would be to cease to maintain that Hinduism is a system and to say that it is a set of systems consistent with, or if you like, contradictory or even conflicting with, each other. But in no case can you advance this your failure to determine the meaning of Hinduism as a ground to doubt the existence of the Hindu nation itself, or worse still to commit a sacrilege in hurting the feelings of our Avaidik brethren and Vaidik Hindu brethren alike, by relegating any of them to the Non-Hindu pale.

The limits of this essay do not permit us to determine the nature or the essentials of Hinduism or to try to discuss it at any great length. As we have shown above the enquiry into what is Hinduism can only begin after the question ' who is a Hindu'? is rightly answered determining the essentials of Hindutva ; and as it is only with these essentials of Hindutva, which enable us to know who is a Hindu, that this our present enquiry is concerned, the discussion of Hinduism falls necessarily outside of our scope. We have to take cognizance of it only so far as it trespasses on the field of our special charge. Hinduism is a word that properly speaking should be applied to all the religious beliefs that the different communities of the Hindu people hold. But it is generally applied to that system of religion which the majority of the Hindu people follow. It is natural that a religion or a country or community should derive its name from the characteristic feature which is common to an overwhelming majority that constitutes or contributes to it. It is also convenient for easy reference or parlance. But a convenient term that is not only delusive but harmful and positively misleading should not any longer be allowed to blind our judgement. The majority of the Hindus subscribes to that system of religion which could fitly be described by the attribute that constitutes its special feature, as told by Shruti. Smriti and Puranas or Sanatan Dharma.

They would not object if it even be called Vaidik Dharma. But besides these there are other Hindus who reject either partly or wholly, the authority-some of the Puranas, some of the Smritis and some of the Shrutis themselves. But if you identify the religion of the Hindus with the religion of the majority only and call it orthodox Hinduism, then the different heterodox communities being Hindus themselves rightly resent this usurpation of Hindutva by the majority as well as their unjustifiable exclusion. The religion of the minorities also requires a name. But if you call the so-called orthodox religion alone as Hinduism then naturally it follows that the religion of the so-called heterodox is not Hinduism. The next most fatal step being that, therefore, those sections are not Hindus at all!! But this inference seems as staggering even to those who had unwillingly given wholehearted support to the premises which have made it logically inevitable that while hating to own it they hardly know to avoid arriving at it.

And thus we find that while millions of our Sikhs, Jains, Lingayats, several Samajis and others would deeply resent to be told that they-whose fathers' fathers up to the tenth generation had the blood of Hindus in their veins-had suddenly ceased to be Hindu!-yet a section amongst them takes it most emphatically for granted that they had been faced with a choice that either they should consent to be a party to those customs and beliefs which they had in their puritanic or progressive zeal rejected as superstitions, or they should cease to belong to that race to which their forefathers belonged.

All this bitterness is mostly due to the wrong use of the word, Hinduism, to denote the religion of the majority only. Either the word should be restored to its proper significance to denote the religions of all Hindus or if you fail to do that it should be dropped altogether. The religion of the majority of the Hindus could be best denoted by the ancient accepted appellation, the Sanatan dharma or the Shruti-smriti-puranokta Dharma or the Vaidik Dharma; while the religion of the remaining Hindus would continue to be denoted by their respective and accepted names Sikha Dharma or Arya Dharma or Jain Dharma or Buddha Dharma. Whenever the necessity of denoting these Dharmas as a whole arises then alone we may be justified in denoting them by the generic term Hindu Dharma or Hinduism. Thus there would be no loss either in clearness, or in conciseness but on the other hand a gain both in precision and unambiguity which by removing the cause of suspicion in our minor communities and resentment in the major one would once more unite us all Hindus under our ancient banner representing a common race and a common civilization.

The earliest records that we have got of the religious beliefs of any Indian community-not to speak of mankind itself-are the Vedas. The Vedic nation of the Saptasindhus was sub-divided into many a tribe and class. But although the majority then held a faith that we for simplicity call Vedic religion, yet it was not contributed to by an important minority of the Sindhus themselves. The Panees, the Dasas, the Vratyas and many others from time to time seem to have either seceded from or never belonged to the orthodox church and yet racially and nationally they were conscious of being a people by themselves. There was such a thing as Vedic religion, but it could not even be idenitfied with Sindhu Dharma; for the latter term, had it been coined, would have naturally meant the set of religions prevailing in Saptasindhu, othodox as well as heterodox. By a process of elimination and assimilation the race of the Sindhus at last grew into the race of Hindus, and the land of the Sindhus *i.e.* Sindhustan, into the land of the Hindus i.e.- Hindusthan. While their orthodox and the heterodox schools of religions have,-having tested much, dared much and known much,-having subjected to the most searching examination possible till then, all that lay between the grandest and the tiniest, from the atom to the Atman-from the Paramanu to the Parabrahma,-having sounded the deepest secrets of thoughts and having soared to the highest altitudes of ecstasy,- given birth to a synthesis that sympathises with all aspirants towards truth from the monist to the atheist. Truth was its goal, realization its method. It is neither Vedic nor non-Vedic, it is both. It is the veritable science of religion applied. This is Hindudharma-the conclusion of the conclusions arrived at by harmonising the detailed experience of all the schools of religious thought-Vaidik, Sanatani, Jain, Baudda, Sikha or Devasamaji. Each one and every one of those systems or sects which are the direct descendants and developments of the religious beliefs Vaidik and non-Vaidik that obtained in the land of the Saptasindhus or in the other unrecorded communities in other parts of India in the Vedic period, belongs to and is an integral part of Hindudharma.

Therefore the Vaidik or the Sanatan Dharma itself is merely a sect of Hinduism or Hindu Dharma, however overwhelming be the majority that contributes to its tenets. It was a definition of this Sanatan Dharma which the late Lokamanya Tilak framed in the famous verse. Belief in the Vedas, many means, no strict rule for worship-these are the features of the Hindu religion.

In a learned article that he had contributed to the Chitramayajagat which bears the mark of his deep erudition and insight Lokmanya in an attempt to develop this more or less negative definition into a positive one, had clearly suggested that he had an eye not on Hindutva as such but only on what was popularly called Hindudharma, and had also admitted that it could hardly include in its sweep the Aryasamajis and other sects which nevertheless are racially and nationally Hindus of Hindus. That definition, excellent so far as it goes, is in fact not a definition of Hindudharma, much less of Hindutva but of Sanatan Dharma-the Shruti-Smriti-puranokta sect, which being the most popular of all sects of Hindu Dharma was naturally but loosely mistaken for Hindu Dharma itself.

Thus Hindu Dharma being etymologically as well as actually and in its religious aspects only, (for Dharma is not merely religion) the religion of the Hindus, it necessarily partakes of all the essentials that characterise a Hindu. We have found that the first important essential qualification of a Hindu is that to him the land that extends from Sindhu to Sindhu is the Fatherland, (Pitribhu) the Motherland (Matribhu) the land of his patriarchs and forefathers. The system or set of religions which we call Hindu Dharma-Vaidik and Non-Vaidik-is as truly the offspring of this soil as the men whose thoughts they are or who 'saw' the Truth revealed in them. To Hindu Dharma with all its sects and systems this land, Sindhusthan, is the land of its revelation, the land of its birth on this human plane. As the Ganges, though flowing from the lotus feet of Vishnu himself, is even to the most orthodox devotee and mystic so far as human plane is concerned the daughter of the Himalayas, even so, this land is the birth-place-the Matribhu (motherland) and the Pitribhu (fatherland)-of that Tatvajnana (philosophy) which in its religious aspect is signified as Hindu Dharma.

The second most important essential of Hindutva is that a Hindu is a descendant of Hindu parents, claims to have the blood of the ancient Sindhu and the race that sprang from them in his veins. This also is true of the different schools of religion of the Hindus; for they too being either founded by or revealed to the Hindu sages, and seers are the moral and cultural and spiritual descendants and development of the Thought of Saptasindhus through the process of assimilation and elimination, as we are of their seed. Not only is Hindu Dharma the growth of the natural environments and of the thought of the Indus, but also of the Sanskriti or culture of the Hindus. The environmental frames in which its scenes, whether of the Vaidik period or of Bauddha, Jain or any extremely modern ones of Chaitanya, Chakradhar, Basava, Nanak, Dayananda or Raja Rammohan, are set, the technical terms and the language that furnished expression to its highest revelation and ecstasies, its mythology and its philosophy, the conceptions it controverted and the conceptions it adopted, have the indelible stamp of Hindu culture, of Hindu Sanskriti, impressed upon them. Hindu Dharma of all shades and schools, lives and grows and has its being in the atmosphere of Hindu culture, and the Dharma of a Hindu being so completely identified with the land of the Hindus, this land to him is not only a Pitribhu but a Punyabhu, not only a fatherland but a holyland.

Yes, this Bharatbhumi this Sindusthan, this land of ours that stretches from Sindhu to Sindhu is our Punyabhumi, for it was in this land that the Founders of our faith and the Seers to whom 'Veda' the Knowledge was revealed, from Vaidik seers to Dayananda, from Jina to Mahavir, from Buddha to Nagasen, from Nanak to Govind, from Banda to Basava, from Chakradhar to Chaitanya, from Ramdas to Rammohan, our Gurus and Godmen were born and bred. The very dust of its paths echoes the footfalls of our Prophets and Gurus. Sacred are its rivers, hallowed its groves, for it was either on their moonlit ghats or under their eventide long shadows, that the deepest problems of life, of man, soul and God, of Brahma and Maya, were debated and discussed by a Buddha or a Shankar. Ah! every hill and dell is instinct with memories of a Kapil or a Vyas. Shankar or Ramdas.

Here Bhagirath rules, there Kurukshetra lies. Here Ramchandra made his first halt of an exile, there Janaki saw the golden deer and fondly pressed her lover to kill it. Here the divine Cowherd played on his flute that made every heart in Gokul dance in harmony as if in a hypnotized sleep. Here is Bodhi Vriksha, here the deer-park, here Mahaveer entered Nirvana. Here stood crowds of worshippers amongst whom Nanak sat and sang the Arati 'the sun & the moon are the lights in the plate of the sky!' Here Gopichand the king look on vows of Gopichand the Jogi and with a bowl in his hand knocked at his sister's door for a handful of alms! Here the son of Bandabahadur was hacked to pieces before the eyes of his father and the young bleeding heart of the son thrust in the father's mouth for the fault of dying as a Hindu! Every stone here has a story of martyrdom to tell! Every inch of thy soil, O Mother! has been a sacrificial ground! Not only 'where the Krishnasar is found' but from Kasmir to Sinhar it is ' Land of sacrifice,' sanctified with a Jnana Yajna or an Atmaajna (self-sacrifice). So to every Hindu, from the Santal to the Sadhu this Bharata bhumi this Sindhusthan is at once a Pitribhu and a Punyabhu-fatherland and a holy land.

That is why in the case of some of our Mohammedan or Christian countrymen who had originally been forcibly converted to a non-Hindu religion and who consequently have inherited along with Hindus, a common Fatherland and a greater part of the wealth of a common culture-language, law, customs, folklore and history-are not and cannot be recognized as Hindus. For though Hindusthan to them is Fatherland as to any other Hindu yet it is not to them a Holyland too. Their holyland is far off in Arabia or Palestine. Their mythology and Godmen, ideas and heroes are not the children of this soil. Consequently their names and their outlook smack of a foreign origin. Their love is divided. Nay, if some of them be really believing what they profess to do, then there can be no choice-they must, to a man, set their Holy-land above their Fatherland in their love and allegiance. That is but natural. We are not condemning nor are we lamenting. We are simply telling facts as they stand. We have tried to determine the essentials of Hindutva and in doing so we have discovered that the Bohras and such other

Mohammedan or Christian communities possess all the essential qualifications of Hindutva but one and that is that they do not look upon India as their Holyland.

It is not a question of embracing any doctrine propounding any new theory of the interpretation of God, Soul and Man, for we honestly believe that the Hindu Thought-we are not speaking of any religion which is dogma-has exhausted the very possibilities of human speculation as to the nature of the Unknown-if not the Unknowable, or the nature of the relation between that and thou. Are you a monist-a monotheist-a pantheist -an atheist-an agnostic? Here is ample room, O soul! whatever thou art, to love and grow to thy fullest height and satisfaction in this Temple of temples, that stands on no personal foundation but on the broad and deep and strong foundation of Truth. Why goest then to fill thy little pitcher to wells far off, when thou standest on the banks of the crystal-streamed Ganges herself? Does not the blood in your veins, O brother, of our common forefathers cry aloud with the recollections of the dear old scenes and ties from which they were so cruelly snatched away at the point of the sword? Then come ye back to the fold of your brothers and sisters who with arms extended are standing at the open gate to welcome you-their long lost kith and kin. Where can you find more freedom of worship than in this land where a Charvak could preach atheism from the steps of the temple of Mahakal -more freedom of social organisation than in the Hindu society where from the Patnas of Orissa to the Pandits of Benares, from the Santalas to the Sadhus, each can develop a distinct social type of polity or organize a new one? Verily whatever, could be found in the world is found here too. And if anything is not found here it could be found nowhere.

Ye, who by race, by blood, by culture, by nationality possess almost all the essentials of Hindutva and had been forcibly snatched out of our ancestral home by the hand of violence-ye, have only to render wholehearted love to our common Mother and recognize her not only as Fatherland (Pitribhu) but even as a Holyland (punyabhu); and ye would be most welcome to the Hindu fold.

This is a choice which our countrymen and our old kith and kin, the Bohras, Khojas, Memons and other Mohammedan and Christian communities are free to make -a choice again which must be a choice of love. But as long as they are not minded thus, so long they cannot be recognized as Hindus. We are, it must be remembered, trying to analyse and determine the essentials of Hindutva as that word is actually understood to signify and would not be justified in straining it in its application to suit any pre-conceived notions or party convenience. A Hindu, therefore, to sum up the conclusions arrived at, is he who looks upon the land that extends from Sindu to Sindu-from the Indus to the Seas,-as the land of his forefathers -his Fatherland (Pitribhu), who inherits the blood of that race whose first discernible source could be traced to the Vedic Saptasindhus and which on its onward march, assimilating much that was incorporated and ennobling much that was assimilated, has come to be known as the Hindu people, who has inherited and claims as his own the culture of that race as expressed chiefly in their common classical language Sanskrit and represented by a common history, a common literature, art and architecture, law and jurisprudence, rites and rituals, ceremonies and sacraments, fairs and festivals; and who above all, addresses this land, this Sindhusthan as his Holyland (Punyabhu), as the land of his prophets and seers, of his godmen and gurus, the land of piety and pilgrimage. These are the essentials of Hindutva-a common nation (Rashtra) a common race (Jati) and a common civilization (Sanskriti). All these essentials could best be summed up by stating in brief that he is a Hindu to whom Sindhusthan is not only a Pitribhu but also a Punyabhu. For the first two essentials of Hindutva-nation and Jati-are clearly denoted and connoted by the word Pitrubhu while the third essential of Sanskriti is. pre-eminently implied by the word Punyabhu, as it is precisely Sanskriti including sanskaras i.e. rites and rituals, ceremonies and sacraments, that makes a land a Holyland. To make the definition more handy, we may be allowed to compress it in a couplet:

A Sindu Sindhu paryanta, Yasya Bharatbhumika
Pitribhuh Punyabhushchaiva sa vai Hinduriti smritah

HINDUS IN SINDH

The rough analysis to which the conception of Hindutva was subjected in the foregoing pages has enabled us to frame a working definition embodying or rather indicating the salient essentials of it. It now remains to see how far this general definition can stand a detailed examination that could be best conducted by testing a few typical and some of the most different cases which have in fact made the necessity of a definition so badly felt. While developing it we have tried at each step to free it, so far as it is possible to do so in the case of so comprehensive and elusive a generalization as that, from the defect of being too wide. If we find in testing a few typical cases in the light of this definition that they all fit in well then we may be sure that it is free from the opposite defect of being too narrow. We have seen that it is not open to Ativyapti, it remains to be seen whether it is not open to Avyapti also.

The geographical divisions that obtain amongst the Hindus would, at a glance, be seen to harmonize well with the spirit of our definition. The fundamental basis of it is the land from Sindhu to Sindhu, and although many of our brethren, and especially those who had been the most undoubted descendants of the ancient Sindhus and who besides are the very people that to this day have never changed the ancient name either of their land or of their race, and are called to day as five thousand years ago, Sindhi, the children of Sindhudesha, inhabit the other bank of the Indus; yet, as in the mention of a river the mention of both its banks is implied as a matter of course so that part of Sindh which constitutes the western bank of the Indus is a natural part of Sindhusthan and is covered by our definition. Secondly, accessories to the mainland are always known by the name of the latter. And thirdly, our Hindu people on that side of the Sindhu had throughout history looked upon this land of Bharatvarsha as their real Pitribhu as well as Punyabhu. They had never been guilty of matricide in attempting to set up the patch they inhabit as their only Pitribhu or only Punyabhu. On the other hand their Baharas and Kailas and Gangotri are our Banaras and Kailas and Gangotri. From the Vedic time they are a part integral of Bharatvarsha, Sindhushivisauveers are mentioned in Ramayan and Mahabharat as the rightful constituents of the great Hindu confederacy and commonwealth. They belong to our Rashtra, to our Jati and to our Sanskriti. Therefore they are Hindus and their case is well-covered by our definition.

But even if one rejects the contention that the ownership of a river does employ, unless otherwise stated, the ownership of both its banks yet the definition remains as sound as ever and applies to our Sindhi brethren on other grounds. For apart from the special case of our Sindhi brethren that inhabit the other side of the Indus, there are hundreds of thousands of Hindus who have settled in all parts of the world. A time may come when these our Hindu colonists, who even today are the dominating factor in trade, numbers, capacity and intellect in their respective lands, may come to own a whold country and form a separate state. But will this simple fact of residence in lands other than Hindusthan render one a non-Hindu? Certainly not; for the first essential of Hindutva is not that a man must not reside in lands outside India, but that wherever he or his descendants may happen to be he must recognize Sindhusthan as the land of his forefathers. Nay more; it is not a question of recognition either.

If his ancestors came from India as Hindus he cannot help recognizing India as his Pitribhu. So this definition of Hindutva is compatibls with any conceivable expansion of our Hindu people. Let our colonists continue unabated their labours of founding a Greater India, a Mahabharat to the best of their capacities and contribute all that is best in our civilization to the upbuilding of humanity. Let them enrich the people that inhabit the earth from Pole to Pole with their virtues and let them in return enrich their own country and race by imbibing all that is healthy and true wherever found. Hindutva does not clip the wings of the Himalayan eagles but only adds to their urge. So long as ye, O Hindus! look upon Hindusthan as the land of your forefathers and as the land of your prophets, and cherish the priceless heritage of their culture and their blood, so long nothing can stand in the way of your desire to expand. The only geographical limits of Hindutva are the limits of our earth!

So far as the racial aspect of our definition is concerned we cannot think of any exception that can seriously challenge its validity. Just as in England we find Iberians, Kelts, Angles, Saxons, Danes, Normans now fused, in spite of the racial restrictions on intermarriages into one nation, so the ancient racial distinctions of Aryans, Kolarians, Dravidians and others even if they had ever been keen, can no longer be recognized. We have dealt with the point as exhaustively as necessary in the foregoing pages and pointed out that the Anulom and Pratilom systems recognized in our law-books bear indisputable testimony to the fact that a fusion sufficient to keep the flow of common blood through our body politic vigorous and fresh was even then an accomplished fact. Nature again broke the barriers where custom refused to pull them down in time. Bheemsen was neither the first nor the last of Aryans to make love to a Hidimba, nor the Brahmin lady the mother of Vyadhakarma, to whom we have referred already, wave the only Aryan girl that took a fancy to a Vyadha youth. Out of a dozen Bhils or Kolis or even Santals, a youth or a girl may at times be picked up and dropped in a city school without any fear of being recognized as such either by a physical or by a moral test. The race that is born of the fusion, which on the whole is a healthy one, because gradual, of the Aryans, Kolarians, Dravidians and all those of our ancestors, whose blood we as a race inherit, is rightly called neither an Aryan, nor Kolarian, nor Dravidian-but the Hindu race; that is, that People who live as children of a common motherland, adoring a common holyland-the land that lies between the Sindhus. Therefore the Santals, Kolis, Bhils Panchamas, Namashudras and all other such tribes and classes are Hindus. This Sindhusthan is as emphatically, if not more emphatically, the land of their forefathers as of those of the so-called Aryans; they inherit the Hindu blood and the Hindu culture; and even those of them who have not as yet come fully under the influence of any orthodox Hindu sect, do still worship deities and saints and follow a religion however primitive, are still purely attached to this land, which therefore to them is not only a Fatherland but a Holyland.

There would have been no serious objection raised against the cultural aspect of Hindutva too, but for the unfortunate misunderstanding that owes its origin to the confusing similarity between the two terms Hindutva and Hinduism. We have tried already to draw a clear line of demarcation between the two conceptions and protested against the wrong use of the word Hinduism to denote the Sanatan Dharma alone. Hindutva is not indentical with Hindu Dharma; nor is Hindu Dharma indentical with Hinduism. This twofold mistake that indentifies Hindutva with Hindu Dharma and both with Sanatani sect is justly resented by our non-Sanatani sects or religious systems and goads a small section of people amongst them-not to explode this mistaken notion, but unfortunately to commit another grave and suicidal mistake in the opposite direction and disown their Hindutva itself. We hope that our definition will leave no ground for any such bitterness of feelings on either side and based on truth as it is, would be acknowledged by all the fair-minded people throughout our Hindu society. But as in the general treatment of this question we could not take any notice of any special case we shall do so now. Let us first take the case of our Sikh brotherhood.

No one could be so silly as to contest the statement that Sindusthan, Asindhu Sindhu Paryanta yasya Bharatbhumika', is their Fatherland-the land that ever since the first extant records of the Vedic Period has been the land where their forefathers lived and loved and worshipped and prayed. Secondly, they most undoubtedly inherit the Hindu blood in their veins as much as any one in Madras or Bengal does Nay more, while we Hindus in Maharashtra or Bengal inherit the blood of the Aryans as well as of those other ancient people who inhabited this land, the Sikhs are the almost direct descendants of those ancient Sindhus and can claim to have drunk their being at the very fountain of this Ganges of our Hindu life before she had descended down to the plains. Thirdly, they have contributed and to therefore are the rightful copartners in our Hindu culture,

For Saraswati was a river in the Punjab before she became the Deified Image of Learning and Art. To this day, do millions of Hindus throughout Hindusthan join in the enchanted chorus ' with which the Sindhus, your forefathers, oh Sikhs, paid the tribute of a grateful people to, and extolled the glories of the River on whose banks the first seeds of our culture and civilization were sown and catching their Rigvedic accents sing 'Ambitame, Naditame, Devitame Saraswati; the Vedas are theirs as they are ours, if not as a revelation yet as revered work that sings of the first giant struggles of man to tap the sources of nature.

The first giant struggle of Light against the forces of darkness and ignorance, that had stolen and kept imprisoned the spirited waters and refused to allow the rays of Illumination touch man and rouse the soul in him. The story of the Sikhs, like any one of us must begin with the Vedas, pass on through the palaces of Ayodhya, witness the battlefield of Lanka, help Lahu to lay the foundation of Lahore and watch prince Sidhartha leave the confines of Kapilavastu and enter the caves to find some way out to lighten the sorrows of man. The Sikhs along with us bewail the fall of Prithviraj, share the fate of a conquered people and suffer together as Hindus. Millions of Sikh udasis, Nirmalas, the Gahangambhirs and the Sindhi. Sikhs adore the Sanskrit language not only as the language of their ancestors but as the sacred language of their land. While the rest cannot but own it as the tongue of their forefathers and as the Mother of Gurumukhi and Punjabi, which yet in its infancy is still sucking the milk of life at its breast. Lastly the land Asindhu Sindhuparyanta is not only the Pitribhu also the Punyabhu to the Sikhs. The land spread from the river, Sindhu, to the seas is not only the fatherland but also the holyland to the Sikhs. Guru Nanak and Guru Govind, Shri Banda and Ramsing were born and bred in Hindusthan; the lakes of Hindusthan are the lakes of nectar (Amritsar) and of freedom-(Muktasar); the land of Hindusthan is the land of prophets and prayer- Gurudvar and Gurughar. Really if any community in India is Hindu beyond cavil or criticism it is our Sikh brotherhood in the Punjab, being almost the autochthonous dwellers of the Saptsindhu land and the direct descendants of the Sindhu or Hindu people. The Sikh of today is the Hindu of yesterday and the Hindu of today may be the Sikh of tomorrow. The change of a dress, or a custom, or a detail of daily life cannot change the blood or the seed, nor can efface and blot out history itself.

To the millions of our Sikh brethren their Hindutva is self-evident. The Sahajdhari, udasi, Nirmal, Gahangambhir and the Sindhi Sikhs are proud of being Hindus by race and by nationality. As their Gurus themselves had been the children of Hindus they would fail to understand if not resent any such attempt to class them as Non-Hindus. The Gurugrantha is read by the Sanatanis as well as by the Sikhs as a sacred work; both of them have fairs and festivals in common. The Sikhs of the Tatkhalsa sect also so far as the bulk of their population is concerned, are equally attached to their racial appellation and live amongst Hindus as Hindus. It cannot be but shocking to them to be told that they had suddenly ceased to be Hindus. Our racial Unity is so unchallenged and complete that inter-marriages are quite common amongst the Sikhs and Sanatanis.

The fact is that the protest that is at times raised by some leaders of our Sikh brotherhood against their being classed as Hindus would never have been heard if the term Hinduism was not allowed to get identical with Sanatanism. This confusion of ideas and the vagueness of expression resulting therefrom, are at the root of this fatal tendency that mars at time the cordial relations existing between our sister Hindu communities. We have tried to make it clear that Hindutva is not to be determined by any theological tests. Yet we must repeat it once more that the Sikhs are free to reject any or all things they dislike as superstitions in Sanatandharma, even the binding authority of the Vedas as a revelation.

They thereby may cease to be Sanatanis, but cannot cease to be Hindus. Sikhs are Hindus in the sense of our definition of Hindutva and not in any religious sense whatever. Religiously they are Sikhs as Jains are Jains, Lingayats are Lingayats, Vaishnavas are Vaishnavas ; but all of us racially and nationally and culturally are a polity and a people, one and indivisible, most fitly and from times immemorial called Hindus. No other word can express our racial oneness-not even Bharatiya can do that for reasons dealt with in the forgoing pages. Bharatiya indicates an Indian and expresses a larger generalization but cannot express racial unity of us Hindus. We are Sikhs, and Hindus and Bharatiyas. We are all three put together and none exclusively.

Another reason besides this fear of being indentified with the followers of Sanatanpanth which added to the zeal of some of our Sikh brothers and made them insist on getting classed separately as non-Hindus, was a political one. This is not the place of entering into merits or demerits of special representation. The Sikhs were naturally anxious to guard the special interests of their community and if the Mohammedans could enjoy the privilege of a special and communal .representation, we do not understand why any other important minority in India should not claim similar concession. But we feel that, that claim should not have been backed up by our Sikh brothers by an untenable and suicidal plea of being non-Hindus. Sikhs, to guard their own interests could have pressed for and succeeded in securing special and communal representation on the ground of being an important minority as our non-Brahmins and other communities have done without renouncing their birthright of Hindutva. Our Sikh brotherhood is certainly not a less important community than the Mohammedans -in fact to us Hindus they are more important than any non-Hindu community in India.

The harm that a special and communal representation does is never so great as the har done by the attitude of racial aloofness. Let the Sikhs, the Jains, the Lingayats, the non-Brahmins and even, for the matter of that. Brahmins press and fight for the right of special and communal representation, if they honestly look upon it as indispensable for their communal growth. For their growth is the growth of the whole Hindu-society. Even in ancient times our four main castes enjoyed a kind of special representation on communal basis in our councils of State as well as in local bodies. They could do that without refusing to get fused into the larger whole and incorporated into the wider generalization of Hindutva, Let the Sikhs be classed as Sikhs religiously, but as Hindus racially and culturally.

The brave people placed their heads by hundreds under the executioner's axe rather than disown their Guru. Will they disown their seed, forswear their fathers and sell their birthright for a mess of pottage? God forbid! Let our minorities remember that if strength lies in union, then in Hindutva lies the firmest and yet the dearest bond that can effect a real, lasting and powerful union of our people. You may fancy that it pays you to remain aloof for the passing hour, but it would do incalculable harm to this our ancient race and civilization as a whole -and especially to yourselves. Your interests are indissolubly bound with the interests of your other Hindu brethren.

Whenever in the future as in the past a foreigner raises a sword against the Hindu civilization it is sure to strike you as deadly as any other Hindu community. Whenever in future as in the past the Hindus as a people come to their own and under a Shivaji or a Ranjit, a Ramchandra or a Dharma, an Ashoka or an Amoghwarsha feeling the quickening touch of life and activity mount the pinnacles of glory and greatness-that day would shed its lustre on you as well as on any other members of our Hindu commonwealth.

So, brothers, be not lured by the immediate gains, partly or otherwise, nor be duped by misreadings and misinterpretations of history. I was once told by one who posing as a Granthi was nevertheless convicted for committing a dacoity in the house of a Brahmin to whom he owed money and whom he consequently murdered, that the Sikhs were not Hindus and that they could incur no guilt by killing a Brahmin as the sons of Govindsing were betrayed by a Brahmin cook. Fortunately there was another Sikh gentleman and a real Granthi and was recognized as such by all learned Sikhs who immediately contradicted and cornered him by several examples of Matidas and others, who had sheltered the Guru and proved true to the Sikhs even unto martyrdom. Was not Shivaji betrayed by his kith and kin and his grandson again by a Pisal who too was a Hindu?

But did Shivaji or his nation disown their race and cease to be Hindus? Many of the Sikhs have acted treacherously first at the time of desertion of the heroic Banda, then again at the time of the last war of the Khalsa forces with the English. Guru Govindsing himself was deserted by a number of Sikhs in the very thick of the fight and it was this act of treacherous cowardice of these Sikhs which by forcing our lion-hearted Guru to try a desperate sortie gave occasion to that cursed Brahmin wretch to betray his two sons. If, therefore, for the crime of the latter we cease to be Hindus, then for the crime of the former we ought to cease to be Sikhs too!

This minority of the Hindus as well as the major communities of them did not fall from the skies as separate creations. They are an organic growth that has its roots embedded deep in a common land and in a common culture. You cannot pick up a lamb and by tying a Kachchha and Kripan on it, make a lion of it! If the Guru succeeded in forming a band of martyrs and warriors he could do so because the race that produced him as well as that band was capable of being moulded thus. The lion's seed alone can breed lions. The flower cannot say 'I bloom and smell: surely I came out of the stalk alone-I have nothing to do with the roots!' No more can we deny our seed or our blood. As soon as you point at a Sikh who was true to his Guru you have automatically pointed at a Hindu who was true to the Guru for before being a Sikh he was, and yet continues to be a Hindu. So long as our Sikh brethren are true to Sikhism they must of necessity continue to be Hindus for so long must this land, this Bharatbhumika from Sindhu to the seas, remain their Fatherland and their Holyland. It is by ceasing to be Sikhs alone that they may, perhaps, cease to be Hindus.

We have dealt at some length with this special case of our Sikh brotherhood as all those arguments and remarks would automatically test all similar cases of our other non-Vaidik sects and religions in the light of our definition. The Devsamajis for example are agnostics but Hindutva has little to do with agnosticism, or for the matter of that, atheism. The Devsamajis look on this land as the land of their forefathers, their fatherland as well as their Holyland and are therefore Hindus. Of course, it is superfluous, after all this to refer to our Aryasamaj. All the essentials of Hindutva hold good in their case so eminently that they are Hindus. We, in fact, are unable to hit upon any case that can lay our definition open to the charge of exclusiveness.

In one case alone it seems to offer some real difficulty. Is, for example. Sister Nivedita a Hindu? If ever an exception proves the rule it does so here. Our patriotic and noble-minded sister had adopted our land from Sindu to the seas as her Fatherland. She truly loved it as such, and had our nation been free, we would have been the first to bestow the right of citizenship on such loving souls. So the first essential may, to some extent, be said to hold good in her case. The second essential of common blood of Hindu parentage must, nevertheless and necessarily, be absent in such cases as these.

The sacrament of marriage with a Hindu which really fuses and is universally admitted to do so, two beings into one may be said to remove this disqualification. But although this second essential failed, either way to hold good in her case, the third important qualification of Hindutva did entitle her to be recognized as a Hindu. For she had adopted our culture and come to adore our land as her Holyland. She felt, she was a Hindu and that is, apart from all technicalities, the real and the most important test. But we must not forget that we have to determine the essentials of Hindutva in the sense in which the word is actually used by an overwhelming majority of people. And therefore we must say that any convert of non-Hindu parentage to Hindutva can be a Hindu, if bona fide, he or she adopts our land as his or her country and marries a Hindu, thus coming to love our land as a real Fatherland, and adopts our culture and thus adores our land as the Punyabhu. The children of such a union as that would, other things being equal, be most emphatically Hindus. We are not authorized to go further.

But by coming to believe into the tenets of any sects of the Hindus a foreign convert may be recognized as a Sanatani, or a Sikh, or a Jain; and as these religions being founded by or revealed to Hindus, go by he name of Hindudharma the convert too, may be religiously called a Hindu. But it must be understood that a religious or cultural convert possesses only one of the three essentials of Hindutva and it is owing to this disqualification that people generally do not recognise as a Hindu any one and every one who subscribes to the religious beliefs of our race. So deep our feeling of gratitude is towards a Sister Nivedita or an Annie Besant for the services they rendered to the cause of our Motherland and our culture, so soft-hearted and sensitive to the touch of love as a race we Hindus are, that Sister Nivedita or a person like her who so completely identifies his or her being with the Being of our people, is almost unconsciously received in the Hindu fold. But it should be done as an exception to the rule. The rule itself must neither be too rigid nor too elastic The several tests to which we have subjected our definition of Hindutva have, we believe, proved that it satisfies both these requirements and involves neither Avyapti nor Ativyapti; neither contraction nor expansion of the exact connotation.

UNIQUE NATURAL BLESSINGS TO HINDUSTHAN

So far we have not allowed any considerations of utility to prejudice our inquiry. But having come to its end it will not be out of place to see how far the attributes, which we found to be the essentials of Hindutva, contribute towards the strength, cohesion, and progress of our people. Do these essentials constitute a foundation so broad, so deep, so strong that basing upon it the Hindu people can build a future which can face and repel the attacks of all the adverse winds that blow ; or does the Hindu race stand on feet of clay ?

Some of the ancient nations raised huge walls so as to convert a whole country into a fortified castle. Today their walls are trodden to dust or are but scarcely discernible by a few scattered mounds here and there; while the people they were meant to protect are not discernible at all. Our ancient neighbours, the Chinese, laboured from generation to generation and raised a rampart, embracing the limits of an empire, so wide, so high, so strong, a wonder of the human world. That too, as all human wonders must, sank under its own weight. But behold the ramparts of Nature! Have they not, these Himalayas, been standing there as one whose desires are satisfied-so they seemed to the Vedic bard -so they seem to us today. These are our ramparts that have converted this vast continent into a cosy castle.

You take up buckets and fill your trenches with water and call it a moat. Behold, Varuna himself, with his one hand pushing continents aside, fills the gap by pouring seas on seas with the other! This Indian ocean with its bays and gulfs, is our moat. These are our frontier lines bringing within our reach the advantages of an island as well as an insular country.

She is the richly endowed, daughter of God-this our Motherland. Her rivers are deep and perennial. Her land is yielding to plough and her fields loaded with golden harvests. Her necessaries of life are few and a genial nature yields them all almost for the asking. Rich in her fauna, rich in her flora, she knows she owes it all to the immediate source of light and heat-the sun. She covets not the icy lands; blessed be they and their frozen latitudes. If heat is at times ' enervating' here, cold is at times benumbing there. If cold induces manual labour, heat removes much of its very necessity. She takes more delight in quenched thirst than in the parched throat. Those who have not, let them delight in exerting to have. But those who have-may be allowed to derive pleasure from the very fact of having. Father Thames is free to work at feverish speed, wrapped in his icy sheets. She loves to visit her ghats and watch her boats gliding down the Ganges on her moonlit waters. With the plough, the peacocks, and lotus, the elephant and the Gita, she is willing to forego, if that must be, whatever advantage the colder latitudes enjoy. She knows she cannot have all her own way. Her gardens are green and shady, her granaries well-stocked, her waters crystal, her flowers scented, her fruits juicy and her herbs healing. Her brush is dipped in the colours of Dawn and her flute resonant with the music of Gokul. Verily Hind is the richly endowed daughter of God.

Neither the English nor the French with the exception of the Chinese and perhaps the Americans, no people are gifted with a land that can equal in natural strength and richness the land of Sindusthan. A country, a common home is the first important essential of a stable strong nationality; and as of all countries in the world our country can hardly be surpassed by any in its capacity to afford a soil so specially fitted for the growth of a great nation; we Hindus whose very first article of faith is the love we bear to the common Fatherland, have in that love the strongest talismanic tie that can bind close and keep a nation firm and enthuse and enable it to accomplish things greater than ever.

The second essential of Hindutva puts the estimate of our latent powers of national cohesion and greatness yet higher. No country in the world with the exception of China again, is peopled by a race so homogeneous, yet so ancient and yet so strong both numerically and vitally. The Americans too, whom we found equally fortunate with us so far as excellent geographical basis of nationality is concerned, are decidedly left behind. Mohammedans are no race nor are the Christians. They are a religious unit, yet neither a racial nor a national one. But we Hindus, if possible, are all the three put together, and live under our ancient and common roof. The numerical strength of our race is an asset that cannot be too highly prized.

And culture? The English and the Americans feel they are kith and kin because they possess a Shakespeare in common. But not only Kalidas or a Bhasa but, Oh Hindus! ye possess a Ramayan and Mahabharat in common-and the Vedas! One of the national songs the American children are taught to sing attempts to rouse their sense of eternal self-importance by pointing out to the hundred years twice told that stand behind their history. The Hindu counts his years not by centuries but by cycles-the Yuga and the Kalpa and amazed asks. The Uttra Kosala of Raghupathi is nowhere to be seen, nor is Shri Krishna's city of Mathura.

He does not attempt to rouse the sense of self-importance so much as the sense of proportion which is Truth. And that has perhaps made him last longer than Ramses and Nebuchadnezzar. If a people that had no past has no future, then a people that had produced an unending galaxy of heroes and hero-worshippers and who are conscious of having fought with and vaquished the forces whose might struck Greece and Rome, the Pharaohs and the Incas, dead, have in their history a guarantee of their future greatness more assuring than any other people on earth yet possess.

But besides culture the tie of common holyland has at times proved stronger than the chains of a Motherland. Look at the Mohammedans. Mecca to them is a sterner reality than Delhi or Agra. Some of I them do not make any secret of being bound to sacrifice all India if that be to the glory of Islam or could save the city of their prophet. Look at the Jews; neither centuries of prosperity nor sense of gratitude for the shelter they found, can make them more attached or even equally attached to the several countries they inhabit. Their love is, and must necessarily be divided between the land of their birth and the land of their Prophets. If the Zionists' dreams are ever realized-if Palestine becomes a Jewish State and it will gladden us almost as much as our Jewish friends-they, like the Mohammedans would naturally set the interests of their Holyland above those of their Motherland in America and Europe and in case of war between their adopted country and the Jewish State, would naturally sympathise with the latter, if indeed they do not bodily go over to it. History is too full of examples of such desertions to cite particulars. The crusades again, attest to the wonderful influence that a common holyland exercises over peoples widely separated in race, nationality and language, to bind and hold them together.

The ideal conditions, therefore, under which a nation can attain perfect solidarity and cohesion would, other things being equal, be found in the case of those people who inhabit the land they adore, the land of whose forefathers is also the land of their Gods and Angels, of Seers and Prophets; the scenes of whose history are also the scenes of their mythology. The Hindus are about the only people who are blessed with these ideal conditions that are at the same time incentive to national solidarity, cohesion and greatness. Not even the Chinese are blessed thus. Only Arabia and Palestine, if ever the Jews can succeed in founding their state there, can be said to possess this unique advantage. But Arabia is incomparably poorer in the natural, cultural, historical, and numerical essentials of a great people; and even if the dreams of the Zionists are ever realized into a Palestine State still they too must be equally lacking in these.

England, France, Germany, Italy, Turkey proper, Persia, Japan, Afghanistan, Egypt of today (for the old descendants of 'Punto' and their Egypt is dead long since), and other African states, Mexico, Peru, Chile (not to mention states and nations lesser than all these), though racially more or less hemogeneous are yet less advantageously situated than we are in geographical, cultural, historical and numerical essentials, besides lacking the unique gift of a sanctified Motherland.

Of the remaining nations, Russia in Europe, and United states in America, though geographically equally well-gifted with us, are yet poorer, in almost every other requisite of nationality. China alone of the present comity of nations is almost as richly gifted with the geographical, racial, cultural essentials as the Hindus are. Only in the possession of a common, a sacred and a perfect language, the Sanskrit, and a sanctified Motherland, we are so far as the essentials that contribute to national solidarity are concerned more fortunate.

Thus the actual essentials of Hindutva are, as this running sketch reveals, also the ideal essentials of nationality. If we would, we could build on this foundation of Hindutva a future greater than what any other people on earth can dream of, greater even than our own past; provided we are able to utilize our opportunities. For let our people remember that great combinations are the order of the day. The league of Nations, the alliances of powers Pan-Islamism, Pan-Slavism, Pan-Ethiopism, all little beings are seeking to get themselves incorporated into greater wholes, so as to be better-fitted for the struggle for existence and power. Those who are not naturally and historically blessed with numerical or geographical or racial advantages are seeking to share them with others. Woe to those who have them already as their birthright and know them not; or worse, despise them!

The nations of the world are desperately trying to find a place in this or that combination for aggression-can any one of you, Oh Hindus! whether Jain or Samaji or Sanatani or Sikh or any other subsection afford to cut yourselves off or fall out and destroy the ancient, the natural and the organic combination that already exists?-a combination that is bound not by any scraps of paper nor by the ties of exigencies alone, but by the ties of blood, birth and culture? Strengthen them if you can: pull down the barriers that have survived their utility, of castes and customs, of sects and sections: What of interdining?-but intermarriages between provinces and provinces, castes and castes, be encouraged where they do not exist.

But where they already exist as between the Sikhs and Sanatanies, Jains and Vaishnayas, Lingayats and Non-Lingayats-suicideal be the hand that tries to cut the nuptial tie. Let the minorities remember they would be cutting the very branch on which they stand. Strenghten every tie that binds you to the main organism, whether of blood or language or common Motherland. Let this ancient and noble stream of Hindu blood flow from vein to vien, from Attock to Cuttack till at last the Hindu people get fused and welded into an indivisible whole, till our race gets consolidated and strong sharp as steel.

Just cast a glance at the past, then at the present: Pan-Islamism in Asia, the political Leagues in Europe, the Pan-Ethiopic movement in Africa and America- and then see, O Hindus, if your future is not entirely bound up with the future of India and the future of India is bound up in the last resort, with Hindu strength. We are trying our best, as we ought to do, to develop the consciousness of and a sense of attachment to the greater whole, whereby Hindus, Mohammedans, Parsis Christians, and Jews would feel as Indians first and every other thing afterwards.

But whatever progress India may have made to that goal one thing remains almost axiomatically true- not only in India but everywhere in the world-that a nation requires a foundation to stand upon and the essence of the life of a nation is the life of that portion of its citizens whose interests and history and aspirations are most closely bound up with the land and who thus provide the real foundation to the structure of their national state.

Take the case of Turkey. The young Turks after the revolution had to open their Parliament and military institutions to Armenians and Christians on a non-religious and secular basis. But when the war with Servia came the Christians and Armenians first wavered and then many a regiment consisting of them went bodily over to the Servians, who politically and racially and religiously were more closely bound up with them. Take the case of America: when the German war broke out she suddenly had to face danger of desertions of her German citizens; while the Negro citizens there sympathise more with their brethren in Africa than with their white countrymen. American State, in the last resort, must stand or fall with the fortunes of its Anglo-Saxon constituents. So with the Hindus, they being the people, whose past,present and future are most closely bound with the soil of Hindusthan as Pitribhu, as Punyabhu, they constitute the foundation, the bedrock, the reserved forces of the Indian state.

Therefore even from the point of Indian nationality, must ye, O Hindus, consolidate and strengthen Hindu nationality ; not to give wanton offence to any of our non-Hindu compatriots, in fact to any one in the world but in just and urgent defence of our race and land ; to render it impossible for others to betray her or to subject her to unprovoked attack by any of those 'Pan-isms' that are struggling forth from continent to continent. As long as other communities in India or in the world are not respectively planning India first or mankind first, but all are busy in organizing offensive and defensive alliances and combinations on entirely narrow racial or religious or national basis, so long, at least, so long O Hindus, strengthen if you can those subtle bonds that like nerve threads bind you in one organic social being.

Those of you who in a fit suicidal try to cut off the most vital of those ties and dare to disown the name Hindu will find to their cost that in doing so they have cut themselves off from the very source of our racial life and strength.

The presence of only a few of these essentials of nationality which we have found to constitute Hindutva enabled little nations like Spain or Portugal to get themselves lionized in the world. But when all of those ideal conditions obtain here what is there in the human world that the Hindus cannot accomplish ? Thirty crores of people, with India for their basis of operation, for their Fatherland and for their Holyland with such a history behind them, bound together by ties of a common blood and common culture can dictate their terms to the whole world. A day will come when mankind will have to face the force.

Equally certain it is that whenever the Hindus come to hold such a position whence they could dictate terms to the whole world-those terms cannot be very different from the terms which Gita dictates or the Buddha lays down. A Hindu is most intensely so, when he ceases to be Hindu; and with a Shankar claims the whole earth for a Benares ' Waranasi Medini !' or with a Tukaram exclaims: 'my country! Oh brothers, 'the limits of the Universe-there the frontiers of my country lie ?'

GAJANAN VISHWANATH KETKAR

Grandson of Lokmanya Tilak. BA, LLB. Editor of Kesari and Mahratta. Senior worker of Hindu Mahasabha. Managed the office work during the Bhaganagar (Hyderabad) unarmed resistance in 1938. Participated in the 1941 Bhagalpur Hindu Mahasabha session that was banned by the Government. Was treasurer of Maharashtra Hindu Sabha for several years. Raised funds for the defence of Savarkar when the latter was implicated by the Nehru Government in the Gandhi murder. Mediated in the talks between the Nehru Government and the then banned Rashtriya Swayamsevak Sangh (RSS) in 1948. Was imprisoned again for four months in 1950 and again in 1964.

Vasudeo Balwant Gogate

Studied LLB and BA in Miraj and Pune. Settled in Pune. While he was studying in Fergusson College, Pune in 1931, the Government hanged to death sixteen innocent people for violating the martial law. As revenge, Gogate attempted to assassinate

Hotson the then Governor by firing shots at him. Was sentenced to seven years imprisonment for this.

Released in 1937. Thereafter did LLB and started practicing law. Was imprisoned in the aftermath of the Gandhi murder in 1948. Was member of Hindu Mahasabha. Was member and later Mayor of the Pune Municipal Corporation. Was elected from the Graduates' constituency to the Maharashtra Vidhan Parishad (Upper House). Was Leader of Opposition in the Maharashtra Vidhan Parishad. Played leading role in erecting memorial to revolutionary Vasudeo Balwant Phadke. Died on 24 November 1974.

Gajanan Vishnu Damle

Son of Vishnupant Damle of Shirgaon. Savarkar had stayed from 24 November 1924 to 20 June 1925 at Vishnupant Damle's house when there was plague in Ratnagiri. It was there that Savarkar wrote his English book Hindu padpaadshahi. Became Savarkar's personal secretary when Savarkar came to Mumbai in 1937. Accompanied Savarkar on his whirlwind tours. Participated and imprisoned in the Bhaganagar (Hyderabad) unarmed resistance in 1938. Arrested in the Mumbai riots in 1946. Was imprisoned for a long time in the aftermath of the Gandhi murder in 1948. Selfless worker of the Hindu Mahasabha.

APPA KASAR

Hailed from Miraj. Participated and imprisoned in the Bhaganagar (Hyderabad) unarmed resistance in 1938. Worked as Savarkar's personal bodyguard during his tours. Selfless worker of the Hindu Mahasabha. Was imprisoned and tortured severely (his nails were plucked out) after the Gandhi murder in 1948 so that he might implicate Savarkar. Bravely withstood police brutality but refused to unjustly implicate Savarkar. Participated and imprisoned during the agitation against the Eucharist Congress held in Mumbai in 1963.

Narsimha Chintaman or Tatyasaheb Kelkar

Born 24 August 1872; BA, LLB, started as a lawyer in Satara (Maharashtra); was called by Lokmanya Tilak to Pune in 1896.

Was editor of Kesari-Mahratta newspapers for 41 years; was trustee of Kesari trust. In 1916, took the lead in organizing the 60th birthday celebrations of Tilak and collected Rs. one lac for that purpose. After the death of Tilak in 1920, he became one of the foremost leaders of the Tilakites in the Congress. Was a member of the Viceroy's Council from 1924-1929. Was president of Akhil Bharat Hindu Mahasabha twice (Jabalpur, 1928 and Delhi 1932). Noted literature, popularly called Sahityasamrat. Died on 14 October 1947.

Mahamahopadhyaya Siddheshwarshastri Chitrao

Sanskrit scholar; adorned with the titles of Mahamahopadhyaya and Vidyanidhi. Wrote extensively on dharmic issues. For some years, did editorial work in Shridhar Vyankatesh Ketakar's 'Dnyankosh' (Encyclopedia). In 1926-1927, he produced the first ever Marathi translation of the Rgveda samhita. He prepared the rites for shuddhi and wrote an insightful Marathi preface to this work. Gave great impetus to shuddhi movement in Maharashtra. From 1924 to 1933, he was president of the Pune city Hindu Sabha. Later, he formed the Bharatiya charitrakosh mandal (Indian biographical encyclopedia circle) and prepared biographies on ancient and modern personalities. Survived the Panshet floods that submerged Pune by sitting on the roof of the Amruteshwar temple.

Shankar Ramchandra or Mamarao Date

Born 28 September 1898. Educated in Pune; secured BA degree in 1920. Worked in editorial department of 'Loksangraha' newspaper from 1920-1923. After 1923, did research in typing and printing of Devnagari alphabet. In 1931-1932, made the printing of Devnagari alphabet possible on 'mono type'. Was secretary of Pune Hindu Sabha from 1924-1930; organized shuddhi programmes. Surveyed riot-hit Mahad in 1928. In 1938, surveyed and reported condition of Hindus under Nizam rule. Imprisoned during the Bhaganagar (Hyderabad) unarmed resistance in 1939. Was secretary of Maharashtra Hindu Sabha from 1940-1945. Imprisoned in 1948 and 1950. Became secretary of Akhil Bharat Hindu Mahasabha in 1950. Organized session of the Akhil Bharat Hindu Mahasabha in Pune in 1950. Became vice-president of Akhil Bharat Hindu Mahasabha in 1975. Published Chitraoshastri's Marathi translation of the Rgveda, Mate's book on the plight of untouchables, Balshastri Hardas' lectures in Pune and Savarkar's collected works. Edited Kaal newspaper from 1940-1955. Started Kaal weekly in 1967.

Ganpat Mahadev Nalawade

Born in Pune on 10 February 1898. Studied till matriculation. Initially worked with his father who was a tobacconist. Later did farming. Started printing press in 1922. Published 'Sangram' weekly from 1925-1932. Member of Pune Corporation from 1928-1954. Became chairman and later member and Mayor of the Pune Municipal Corporation in 1942. Elected to the Mumbai legislative Council in 1964. Was chairman of Merchants' Cooperative Bank for 44 years and its president for six terms. President of Maharashtra provincial Hindu Sabha from 1954-1962. His printing press was burnt down in the riots following the Gandhi murder in 1948. Was imprisoned for four months each in 1948 and 1950. Was president of reception committee during the Hindu Mahasabha session held in Pune in 1975.

Literature

Savarkar was a poet, novelist, writer of short stories, playwright, historian and a champion of purification of language.

Savarkar composed his first poem 'Swadeshicha phatka' at the tender age of eleven years. He composed his poems as a school and college student, in London, in the horrible Cellular Jail in Andamans and while interned in Ratnagiri. He is the first and probably the only poet in the world to have written his poems on the prison walls with thorns.

These poems were committed to memory by fellow prisoners and transmitted to the outside world. Besides composing poetry in conventional meters, he introduced a new meters called vainayak. He also composed blank verse. Savarkar's two novels 'Kaalepani' and 'Malaa kaay tyache' are descriptive and instructive respectively. Savarkar's three plays 'Usshaap', 'Sanyastakhadga' and 'Uttarkriya' are notable for their dialogues and dramatic content. Savarkar's collection of short stories, public statements and reports are readable.

Savarkar wrote three books on history viz. 'The Indian War of Independence 1857', 'Hindupadpaadshaahi' and 'Six Glorious Epochs '. His 'History of the Sikhs' is not available. These books reveal his deep study of and insight into history, penchant for detail and inspirational but well-researched content.

Savarkar has many 'firsts' to his credit, as far as the Marathi literature goes. He was the first to compose powadas (ballads) in modern times and was the first to use modern imagery in the powadas. He was the first Marathi journalist to contribute newsletters to Marathi periodicals -'Londonchi baatmipatre' (Newsletters from London)- from foreign countries. His 'taarakaas pahun' (gazing at the stars) is the first Marathi poem composed outside Indian shores. His 'Joseph Mazzini' is the first Marathi book written outside India. As an offshoot of his movement of purification of Marathi language, he has introduced so many new words in Marathi, that one can verily identify two ages of Marathi literature viz. pre- and post- Savarkar.

SAANTVAN (CONSOLATION)

In 1909, Savarkar wrote a poetic letter of consolation from London to his dear sister-in-law Yesuvahini. She had earlier written to him expressing anguish at the arrest of Savarkar's youngest brother Narayanrao. Days earlier on 21 November 1909, the higher court had confirmed the prison sentence to Yesuvahini's own husband Babarao. Savarkar himself was in London. It was Yesuvahini who was single-handedly bearing the brunt of the Government's onslaught. This remarkable letter entitled Saantvan (Consolation) is a landmark in Marathi literature.

Savarkar wrote:

Saantvan: One

My loving salutations to thee, O my sister

Whose love hath so tenderly nursed me as to make me forget

The early loss of my mother.

Received your letter of blessing, have taken to heart what you hath written

Thy letter gladdened my heart and made me feel truly blessed,

Blessed indeed is this family of ours in as much as it is

Thus privileged to serve the Lord Ram and administer to his Will!

Two

Many a flower blooms and withers away

Who has kept their count or note

But behold, the lotus flower that was plucked by Gajendra's trunk

And offered at the feet of Srihari and thus withered away there

Became immortal and holy effecting moksha (deliverance)

Thus is our Mother Bharat like the pious Gajendra seeking deliverance

Let her come to our garden and offer our dark blue black lotus flower

And pluck it from the bough to offer it at the feet of Sri Rama.

Blessed indeed is our family tree, definitely touched by the divine

In as much as it is privileged to serve Sri Rama

Three

Let then the rest of our flowers too be plucked thus

And offered at the feet of Sri Rama

Let this mortal body be put to good use

Immortal is the family tree that has extinguished itself for the nation

Its fragrance of human welfare spreads all around
O Mother, weave a garland of all in bloom for the
Festival of the Nine Nights
Once the momentous Ninth Night passes
And the ninth garland is woven and offered
Kali the Terrible will reveal Herself
And grant Victory to her votaries

Four

Sister! Thou hast ever been the symbol of courage, the source of my inspiration.

Thou too art a consecrated and avowed votary to Ram's noble mission

Thy consecration to this great and noble cause
Calls upon thee to be great and noble thyself.

Behold! On one side stand watching the past souls of sages and saints

Of our race gone before and on the other side the
Future generations yet unborn!
May we be able to acquit ourselves today in a manner
As to evoke universal approval from these godly spectators

NECESSITY OF REVENGE

A piece from Veer Savarkar's Play "Usshap"

Kamalini (She displays the blood-stained dagger)

Have you seen this! This is the thorn of the beautiful flower of young Hindu maidens!

Oh Hindu Virgins, take look at this blood stained dagger! When our men and Gods cannot protect chastity and religion, then they are protected, either by the sacred fire of Chittor or this dagger of revenge! There is big difference between them. The sacred fire of Chittor makes victim of Godly for the satanics. It hangs an innocent in place of thief. It destroys the weak to deny opportunity to aggressors. It sets fire to one's own house so that the incendiary could not set fire to one's own house. The sacred fire of Chittor disappoints the evil doer, but is unable to destroy him. But this dagger of revenge, this dagger of anger accomplishes both the tasks. One who violates our bodies or religion to him, if not today, tomorrow, if not at night at day, now or later, during daylight or in darkness, during seizure or embrace, awake or asleep, wherever the opportunity occurs, this indignant dagger of righteous anger seeks out and punishes for his misdeed. Hence aggressor is more afraid of this dagger of revenge than of the sacred fire of Chittor.

This dagger may not probably help to save the chastity of a young girl! But it surely will revenge the violated chastity. The prowess of this revenge will also save the chastity of other hundreds of virgins. The evil violator will be afraid to keep in his harem such women who are carrying such secret daggers, just like a man who is afraid of carrying fire in his sleeve. That rascal wanted to hunt me as a deer! You fool, the eyes of Hindu girls are like those of a deer.

But see their nail! (shows dagger)! It is more pointed, hard and cruel, than the nail of a lioness! My revenge, the revenge of my religion! I have taken revenge for those virgins who have been violated by this evil man. No other officer will dare to wander with free and shameless arrogance in the Hindu garden plucking the beautiful flowers of Hindu beauties! Because like a serpent this dagger moves in the garden and bites him. This they have experienced. If not, taste this poison again!!! (Samagra Savarkar Vangmay Vol. 7 page 531)

Arms will Rule the World

A piece from Veer Savarkar's Play 'Sanyast Khadg'

Vikram : Let it happen as God desires! Mankind's greatest enemy is man, the destroyer of human beings. Let this stain on mankind be wiped out and let the honour of establishing peace on earth fall to our Lord Buddha! But gentlemen, with deep anguish I declare my fear that twenty-five years hence this world will, because of its bad luck, be ruled by arms only. Might is right! Blood- stained empires' victory horse will be trampling on the earth and under its hoops those will be first trodden who thinking the dreams of peace as coming times will renounce the arms-and who becoming enfeebled will have to depend on others' mercy. They will shallow the hook of violence by the bait of non-violence.

Bharat will be forced to endure the dreadful consequences of this terrible mistake-for the next 25 generations mistake of permitting anyone to become a monk and thus make lacks of people enfeebled by vow of renouncing arms! But I am following the wishes of our Lord Buddha because future generations should not feel that this experiment failed because Buddha, the greatest man, did not receive co-operation in his noble task, and I enter the monastery from today. (He ungirdles the sword) This sword dedicated to the service of the race of Shakya and my son Vallabha I entrust to the hands of my Shakya race and I enter the monastery as a monk. (Samagra Savarkar Vangmay Vol. 7 Page 570)

BASIS OF HINDU MUSLIM UNITY

A piece from Veer Savarkar's Play Uttarkriya

Madhavrao: Convey our message to the Emperor not to indulge in hate of the Marathas in future. May be through such relations a common Indian Empire could evolve where Hindus and Muslims would be able to function as brothers on the basis of equality! One who becomes an emperor with the consent and prowess of the Hindus, it does not matter if he is Muslim or not by religion!

Hence forward if the Muslims treat Bharatmata as mother and Hindus as brothers then we Hindus will treat them as brothers. If they want unity, it will occur on this basis. If not, then we are not afraid of disunity! Phadanis, when my brave Sardars return to Poona, take them round in a victorious procession. And shower Commander-in-Chief Biniwale with flowers made of Gold! I give you leave to depart, I want some private moments. (Phadanis goes). At last, we have discharged the duty that had fallen to our generation. We have avenged the defeat of Panipat! There is nothing permanent in the world. It is the duty of the future generations to foster or to end this

Kingdom of Swadharma. But today, at least, there is no Muslim power in Hindustan worth taking notice. My Hindu Kingdoms now blossoming. Now you, tuberculosis, if you today take away my tired body, it is not a matter of worry.

INFORMATION OF BRITISH SECRET POLICE

Indian War of Independence 1857

Most historians, British as well as Indian, have described and dismissed the rising of 1857 as a 'Sepoy Mutiny' or at best 'The Indian Mutiny'. Indian revolution is on the other hand, and national minded leaders thinkers have regarded it as a planned and organised political and military rising aimed at destroying the British power in India.

Savarkar attempted to look at the incidents of 1857 from the Indian point of view. A leading revolutionary himself, he was attracted and inspired by the burning zeal, the heroism, bravery, suffering and tragic fate of the leaders of 1857, and he decided to re-interpret the story and to relate it in full with the help of all the material available to him at the time. He spent days and months at the India Office Library studying the period. Savarkar wrote this book originally in Marathi and completed writing it in 1908. As it was impossible to get this book published in India, the manuscript was returned back to Savarkar. Attempts to get this book published in Germany also failed. Some Indian students staying in India House translated this book into English. Finally, this work was published in Holland in 1909, under the title "The Indian War of Independence -1857".

The second edition of this book was published by Lala Hardayal on behalf of the Gadar Party in America, the third edition was published by Sardar Bhagat Singh, while the fourth edition was published by Netaji Subhas Chandra Bose in the Far East. This book was translated into Urdu, Hindi, Punjabi and Tamil. Further, one edition was published secretly in India after the end of World War II.

The original Marathi manuscript was kept in the safe custody of Madame Cama in Paris. This manuscript was handed over to Dr. Coutinho of the Abhinav Bharat when Paris was in turmoil during World War I. Dr. Coutinho preserved it like a holy scripture for nearly 40 years. After India became independent, he returned it to Ramlal Vajpeyee and Dr. Moonje who in turn gave it back to Savarkar. The ban on this book was finally lifted by the Congress Government of Bombay in May 1946.

Oh Martyrs: This is a dedication to the Martyrs of 1857 which was written by Savarkar on the occasion of the fiftieth anniversary of the Indian War of Independence 1857. It was then published under the title 'Oh Martyrs' and circulated on the 10 May 1908 at the time of the Golden Jubilee ceremony which was celebrated in England on a grand scale.

Oh Martyrs
The battle of freedom once begun
And handed down from sire to son
Though often lost is ever won!!

Today is the tenth of May! It was on this day, that in the ever memorable year of 1857, the first campaign of the War of Independence was opened by you, Oh Martyrs, on the battlefield of India. The Motherland, awakened to the sense of her degrading slavery, unsheathed her sword, burst forth from the shackles and struck the first blow for her liberty and for her honour. It was on this day that the war-cry 'Maro Feringhee Ko' was raised by the throats of thousands. It was on this day that the sepoys of Meerut, having risen in a terrible uprising, marched down to Delhi, saw the waters of the Jamuna, glittering in the sunshine, caught one of those historical moments which close past epoch to introduce a new one, and 'had found, in a moment, a leader, a flag and a clause, and converted the mutiny into a national and a religious war.'

All honour be to you, oh Martyrs. For it was for the preservation of the honour of the race that you performed the fiery ordeal of a revolution when the religions of the land were threatened with a forcible and sinister conversion, when the hypocrete threw off his friendly garb and stood up into the naked heinousness of a perfidious foe breaking treaties, smashing crowns, forging chains and mocking all the while our merciful mother for the very honesty with which she believed the pretensions of the white liar, then you, oh Martyrs of 1857, awoke the mother, inspired the mother, and for the honour of the mother, rushed to the battlefield terrible and tremendous with the war-cry 'Maro Feringhee Ko' on your lips, and with the sacred mantra God and Hindusthan on your banner! Well did you do in rising. For otherwise, although your blood might have been spared, yet the stigma of servility would have been the deeper, one more link would have been added to the cursed chain of demoralizing patience, and the world would have again contemptuously pointed to our nation saying, 'She deserves slavery, she is happy in slavery.' For even in 1857, she did not raise even a finger to protect her interest and her honour!'

This day, therefore, we dedicate, oh Martyrs, to your inspiring memory! It was on this day that you raised a new flag to be upheld, you uttered a mission to be fulfilled, you saw a vision to be realized, you proclaimed a nation to be born!

We take up your cry, we revere your flag, we are determined to continue that fiery mission of 'away with the foreigner', which you uttered, amidst the prophetic thunderings of the Revolutionary war. Revolutionary, yes, it was a Revolutionary war. For the War of 1857 shall not cease till the revolution arrives, striking slavery into dust, elevating liberty to the throne. Whenever a people arises for its freedom, whenever that seed of liberty gets germinated in the blood of its fathers, whenever that seed of liberty gets germinated in the blood of its Martyrs, and whenever there remains at least one true son to avenge that blood of his fathers, there never can be an end to such a war as this. No, a revolutionary war knows no truce, save liberty or death. We, inspired by your memory, determine to continue the struggle you began in 1857, we refuse to acknowledge the armistice as a truce; we look upon the battles you fought as the battles of the first campaign-the defeat of which cannot be the defeat of the war. What? Shall the world say that India has accepted the defeat as the final one? That the blood of 1857 was shed in vain? That the sons of Ind betray their fathers' vows?

No, by Hindusthan, no! The historical continuity of the Indian nation is not cut off. The war began on the 10th of May 1857 is not over on the 10th of May 1908, nor shall it ever cease till a 10th of May to come sees the destiny accomplished, sees the beautiful Ind crowned, either with the lustre of victory or with the halo of martyrdom.

But, O glorious Martyrs, in this pious struggle of your sons help. O help us by your inspiring presence! Torn in innumerable petty selves, we cannot realise the grand unity of the Mother. Whisper, then, unto us by what magic you caught the secret of Union. How the feringhee rule was shattered to pieces and the Swadeshi thrones were set up by the common consent of Hindus and Mahomedans.

How in the higher love of the mother, united the difference of castes and creeds, how the venerated and venerable Bahadur Shah prohibited the killing of cows throughout India, Hew Shreemant Nanasahib after the first salute of the thundering cannon to the emperor of Delhi, reserved for himself the second one! How you staggered the whole world by uniting under the banner of mother and forced your enemies to say 'Among the many lessons the Indian Mutiny conveys to the historian and administrator, none is of greater importance than the warning that it is possible to have a revolution in which Brahmins and Shudras, Mahomedans and Hindus were united against us and that it is not safe to suppose that the peace and stability of our dominion in any great measure depends on the continent being inhabited by different races with different religious systems, for they mutually understand each other and respect and take part in each other's modes and ways and doings.

The mutiny reminds us that our dominions rest on a thin crust ever likely to be rent by titanic fires of social changes and revolutions.' Whisper unto us the nobility of such an alliance of Religion and Patriotism, the true religion whichever is on the side of patriotism, the true patriotism which secures the freedom of religion.

And give us the marvellous energy daring and secrecy with which you organized the mighty volcano; show us the volcanic magma that underlie the green thin crust on which the foe is to be kept lulled into a false security; tell us how the chapatti, that fiery Cross of India flew from village to village and from valley to valley, setting the whole intellect of the nation on fire by the very vagueness of its message and then let us hear the roaring thunder with which the volcano at last burst forth with an all shuttering force, rushing, smashing, burning and consuming into one continuous fiery flow of red-hot lava-flood! With in a month, regiment after regiment, prince after prince, city after city, sepoys, police, zemindars, Pundits, Moulvis, the multiple-headed Revolution sounded its tocsin and temples and mosques resounded with the cry 'Maro feringhee Ko' Away with the foreigners! MEERUT ROSE, Delhi rose, rose Benares, Agra, Patna, Lucknow, Allahabad, Jadagalpoor, Jhansi, Banda, Indore- from Peshwar to Calcutta and from the Narmada to the Himalayas, the volcano burst forth into a sudden, simultaneous and all consuming conflagration! !

And then, oh Martyrs, tell us the little as well as the great defects which you found out in our people in that great experiment of yours. But above all, point out that most ruinous, nay, the only material draw-back in the body of the nation which rendered all your efforts futile- the mean selfish blindness which refuses to see its way to join the nation's cause. Say that the only cause of the defeat of Hindusthan was Hindusthan herself, that shaking away the slumber of centuries, the mother rose to hit the foe, but while her right hand was striking the Feringhee dead, her left hand struck, alas, not the enemy, but her forehead! So she staggered and fell back into the inevitable swoon of 50 years.

Fifty years are past, but, oh restless spirits of 1857, we promise you with our hearts' blood that your Diamond Jubilee shall not pass without seeing your wishes fulfilled!! We have heard your voice and we gather courage from it. With limited means you sustained a war, not against tyranny alone, but against tyranny and treachery together. The Daub and Ayodhya making a united stand, waged a war, not only against the whole of the British power but against the rest of the India too; and yet you fought for three years and yet you had well-nigh snatched away the crown of Hindusthan and smashed the hollow existence of the alien rule. What an encouragement this! What the Duab and Ayodhya could do in a month, the simultaneous, sudden and determined rising of the whole of Hindusthan can do in a day. This hope illumines our hearts and assures us of success. And so we allow that your Diamond Jubilee year 1917 shall not pass without seeing the resurging Ind making a triumphant entry into the world.

For, the bones of Bahadur Shah are crying vengeance from their grave! For, the blood of dauntless Laxmi is boiling with indignation! For, the shahid Peer Ali of Patna, when he was going to the gallows for having refused to divulge the secrets of the conspiracy whispered defiance to the Feringhee said in prophetic words 'You may hang me today, you may hang such as me everyday, but thousands will still rise in my place- your object will never be gained.'

Indians, these words must be fulfilled! Your blood, oh Martyrs, shall be avenged.

HINDUTVA IS DIFFERENT FROM HINDUISM

To this category of names which have been to mankind a subtle source of life and inspiration belongs the word Hindutva, the essential nature and significance of which we have to investigate into. The ideas and ideals, the systems and societies, the thoughts and sentiments which have centered round this name are so varied and rich, so powerful and so subtle, so elusive and yet so vived that the term Hindutva defies all attempts at analysis. Forty centuries, if not more, had been at work to mould it as it is. Prophets and poets, lawyers and lawgivers, heroes and historians, have thought, lived, fought and died just to have it spelled thus. For indeed, is it not the resultant of countless actions- now conflicting, now commingling, now cooperating- of our whole race? Hindutva is not a word but a history.

Not only the spiritual or religious history of our people as at times it is mistaken to be by being confounded with the other cognate term Hinduism, but a history in full. Hinduism is only a derivative, a fraction, a part of Hindutva. Unless it is made clear what is meant by the latter the first remains unintelligible and vague. Failure to distinguish between these two terms has given rise to much misunderstanding and mutual suspicion between some of those sister communities that have inherited this inestimable and common treasure of our Hindu civilization. What is the fundamental difference in the meaning of these two words would be clear as our argument proceeds. Here it is enough to point out that Hindutva is not identical with what is vaguely indicated by the term Hinduism. By an 'ism' it is generally meant a theory or a code more or less based on spiritual or religious dogma or creed.

Had not linguistic usage stood in our way then 'Hinduness' would have certainly been a better word than Hinduism as a near parallel to Hindutva. Hindutva embrases all the departments of thought and activity of the whole Being of our Hindu race. Therefore, to understand the significance of this term Hindutva, we must first understand the essential meaning of the word Hindu itself and realize how it came to exercise such imperial sway over the hearts of millions of mankind and won a loving allegiance from the bravest and best of them. But before we can do that, it is imperative to point out that we are by no means attemption a definition or even a description of the more limited, less satisfactory and essentially sectarian term Hinduism. How far we can succeed or are justified in doing that would appear as we proceed.

What is a Hindu?

Although it would be hazardous at the present state of oriental research to state definitely the period when the foremost band of the intrepid Aryans made it their home and lighted their first sacrificial fire on the banks of the Sindhu, the Indus, yet certain it is that long before the ancient Egyptians, and Babylonians had built their magnificent civilization, the holy waters of the Indus were daily witnessing the lucid and curling columns of the scented sacrificial smokes and the valleys resounding with the chants of Vedic hymns- the spiritual fervour that animated their souls. The adventurous valour that propelled their intrepid enterprizes, the sublime heights to which their thoughts rose-all these had marked them out as a people destined to lay the foundation of a great and enduring civilization.

By the time they had definitely cut themselves aloof from their cognate and neighbouring people especially the Persians, the Aryans, had spread out to the farthest of the seven rivers, Sapta Sindhus, and not only had they developed a sense of nationality but had already succeeded in giving it 'a local habitation and a name!' Out of their gratitude to the genial and perennial network of waterways that run through the land like a system of nerve-threads and wove them into a Being, they very naturally took to themselves the name of Sapta Sindhus an epithet that was applied to the whole of Vedic India in the oldest records of the world, the Rigveda itself. Aryans or the cultivators as they essentially were, we can well understand the divine love and homage they bore to these seven rivers presided over by the River, 'the Sindhu' which to them were but a visible symbol of the common nationality and culture.

The Indians in their forward march had to meet many a river as genial and as fertilizing as these but never could they forget the attachment they felt and the homage they paid to the Sapta Sindhus which had welded them into a nation and furnished the name which enabled their forefathers to voice forth their sense of national and cultural unity. Down to this day a Sindhu- a Hindu-wherever he may happen to be, will gratefully remember and symbolically invoke the presence of these rivers that they may refresh and purify his soul.

Not only had these people been known to themselves as 'Sindhus' but we have definite records to show that they were known to their surrounding nations- at any rate to one of them- by that very name, 'Sapta Sindhu'. The letter 's' in Sanskrit is at times changed into h in some of the Prakrit languages, both Indian and non-Indian. For example, the word Sapta has become Hapta not only in Indian Prakrits but also in the European languages too: we have Hapta *i.e.*, week, in India and 'Heptarchy' in Europe, Kesari in Sanskrit becomes Harhvati in Persian and Asuri becomes Ahur. And then we actually find that the Vedic name of our nation Sapta Sindhu had been mentioned as Hapta Hindu in the Avesta by the ancient Persian people. Thus in the very dawn of history we find ourselves belonging to the nation of the Sindhus or Hindus and this fact was well known to our learned men even in the Puranic period. In expounding the doctrine that many of the Mlechha tongues had been but the mere offshoots of the Sanskrit language the Bhavishya Puran clearly cites this fact and says:

> *Thus knowing for certain that the Persians used to designate the Vedic Aryans as Hindus and knowing also the fact that we generally call a foreign and unknown people by the term by which they are known to those through whom we come to know them, we can safely conclude that most of the remoter nations that flourished then must have applied the same epithet 'Hindu' to our land and people as the ancient Persians did. Not only that but even in the very region of the Sapta Sindhus the thinly scattered native tribes too, must have been knowing the Aryans as Hindus in the local dialects in accordance with the same linguistic law. Further on, as the Vedic Sanskrit began to give birth to the Indian Prakrits which became the spoken tongues of the majority of the decendants of these very Sindhus as well as the assimilated and the crossborn castes, these too might have called themselves as Hindus without any influence for the foreign people. For the Sanskrit S changes into H as often in Indian Prakrits as in the non-Indian ones. Therefore, so far as definite records are concerned, it is indisputably clear that the first and almost the cradle name chosen by the patriarchs of our race to designate our nation and our people, is Sapta Sindhu or Hapta Hindu and that almost all nations of the then known world seemed to have known us by this very epithet, Sindhus or Hindus.*

Name Older Still

So far we have been treading on solid ground of recorded facts, but now we cannot refrain ourselves from making an occasional excursion into the borderland of conjecture. So far we have not pinned our faith to any theory about the original home of the Aryans. But if the most widely accepted theory of their entrance into India be relied on, then a natural curiousity arises as to the origin of the names by which they called the new scenes of their adopted home. Did they coin all those name from their own tongue? Could they have done so? Is it not generally true that when we meet a new scene or enter a new country we call them by the very names- may be in a slightly changed form so as to suit our vocal ability or taste- by which they are known to the native people there? Of course, at times we love to call new scenes by names redolent with the memory of the clear old ones- especially when new colonies are being established in a virgin and but thinly populated continent. But this explanation could only be satisfactory when it is proved that the name given to the new place already existed in the old country and even then it could not be denied that the other process of calling new scenes by the names which they already bear is more universally followed. Now we know it for certain that the region of the Sapta Sindhus was, though very thinly, populated by scattered tribes. Some of them seem to have been friendly towards the newcomers and it is almost certain that many an individual had served the Aryans as guides and introduced them to the names and nature of the new scenes to which the Aryans could not be but local strangers.

The Vidyadharas, Apsaras, Yakshas, Rakshas, Gandharvas and Kinnaras were not all or altogether inimical to the Aryans as at times they are mentioned as being benevolent and good-natured folks. Thus it is probable that many names given to these great rivers by the original inhabitants of the soil may have been sansritised and adopted by the Aryans. We have numerous proofs of this nature in the assimilative expansion of those people and their tongues; witness the words Shalakantakata, Malaya, Milind, Alasada, (Alexandria) Suluva (Selucus) etc. If this be true then it is quite probable that the great Indus was known as Hindu to the original inhabitants of our land and owing to vocal peculiarity of the Aryans it got changed into Sindhu when they adopted it by the operation of the same rule that S is the Sanskritised equivalent of H. Thus Hindu would be the name that this land and the people that inhabited it bore from time so immemorial that even the Vedic name Sindhu is but a later and secondary form of it. If the epithet Sindhu dates its antiquity in the glimmering twilight of history then the word Hindu dates its antiquity from a period so remoter than the first that even mythology fails to penetrate- to trace it to its source.

Hindus, a Nation

The activities of so intrepid a people as the Sindhus or Hindus could no longer be kept cooped or cabined within the narrow compass of the Panchanad or the Punjab. The vast and fertile plains farther off stood out inviting the efforts of some strong and vigorous race. Tribe after tribe of the Hindus issued forth form the land of their nursery and led by the consciousness of a great mission and their Sacrificial Fire that was the symbol thereof, they soon reclaimed the vast, waste and but very thinly populated lands. Forests were felled, agriculture flourished, cities rose, kingdoms thrived,- the touch of the human hand changed the whole face of the wild and unkemp nature. But while these great deeds were being achieved the Aryans had developed to suit their individualistic tendencies and the demands of their new environments a policy that was but loosely centralised. As time passed on, the distances of their new colonies increased, and different settlements began to lead life politically very much centred in themselves.

The new attachments thus formed, though they could not efface the old ones, grew more and more pronounced and powerful until the ancient generalizations and names gave way to the new. Some called themselves Kurus, others Kashis or Videhas or Magadhas while the old generic name of the Sindhus or Hindus was first overshadowed and then almost forgotten. Not that the conception of a national and cultural unity vanished, but it assumed other names and other forms, the politically most important of them being the institution of a Chakarvartin. At last the great mission which the Sindhus had undertaken of founding a nation and a country, found and reached its geographical limit when the valorous Prince of Ayodhya made a triumphant entry in Ceylon and actually brought the whole land from the Himalayas to the Seas under one sovereign sway.

The day when the Horse of Victory returned to Ayodhya unchallenged and unchallengeable, the great white Umbrella of Sovereignty was unfurled over that Imperial throne of Ramchandra, the brave, Ramchandra the good, and a loving allegiance to him was sworn, not only by the Princes of Aryan blood but Hanuman, Sugriva, Bibhishana from the south-that day was the real birthday of our Hindu people. It was truly our national day: for Aryans and Anaryans knitting themselves into a people were born as a nation. It summed up and politically crowned the efforts of all the generations that preceded it and it handed down a new and common mission, a common banner, a common cause which all the generations after it had consciously or unconsciously fought and died to defend.

Other Names

A synthetic conception gains in strength if it finds a term comprehensive enough to give it an eloquent expression. The terms Aryawarta or Bramhawarta were not so suitable as to express the vast synthesis that embraced the whole continent from the Indus to the sea and aimed to weld it into a nation. Aryawarta as defined by the ancient writers was the land that lay between the Himalayas and the Vindhya. Although it was best suited to the circumstances which gave it birth, yet and therefore, it could not serve as a common name to a people that had welded Aryans and non-Aryans into a common race and had carried their culture-empire far beyond the bending summits of Vindhyadri. This necessity of finding a suitable term to express the expansive thought of an Indian Nation was more or less effectively met when the House of Bharat came to exercise its sway over the entire world.

Without entering into speculation as to who this Bharat was the Vedic Bharat or the Jain one or what was the exact period at which he ruled it is here enough for us to know that his name had been not only the accepted but the cherished epithet by which the people of Aryawarta and Daxinapatha delighted to call their common motherland and their common cultural empire. Thus as the horizon opened out to the South we find that the centre of gravity had very naturally shifted from the Sapta Sindhus to the Gangetic Delta and the name Saptasindhu or Aryawart or Daxinapath gave way to the politically grander expression Bharatkhanda which included by the definition of our Nation attempted at a period when the vast conception must have been drawning over the minds of our great thinkers. We have met with no better attempt to define our position as a people when the vast conception must have been drawning over the minds of our great thinkers. We have met with no better attempt to define our position as a people than the terse little couplet in the Vishu Puran, 'The land which is to the north of the sea and to the south of the Himalaya mountain is named Bharata inhabited by the descendants of are Bharata.

How Names are Given ?

But this new word Bharatavarsha could not altogether suppress our cradle name Sindhus or Hindus nor could it make us forget the love we bore to that River of rivers-the Sindhu at whose breast our Patriarchs and people had drunk the milk of life. Our frontier provinces which bordered the course of Indus still clung to their ancient name Sindhu Rashtra. And throughout the Sanskrit literature we find Sindhu Sauveers recognized as an integral and an important part of our body politic. In the great Mahabharata war the king of Sindhu Sauveer figures prominently and is said to have been closely related to the Bharatas. Although the limits of the Sindhu Rashtra shifted from time to time, yet the language that the people speak did then and does even now mark them out as a people by themselves from Multan to the sea, and the name 'Sindhi' which it bears is an emphatic reminder that all those who speak it are Sindhus and are entitled to be recognized as a geographical and political unit in the commonwealth of our Indian people.

Although the epithet Bharatakhand succeeded in almost overshadowing the cradle name of our nation in India, yet the foreign nations seem to have cared little for it and as our frontier provinces continued to be known by their ancient name, so even our immediate neighbours-the Avestic Persians, the Jews, the Greeks and others clung to our ancient name Sindhus or Hindus. They did not merely indicate the borderland of Indus by this term as in days gone by, but the whole nation into which the ancient Sindhus by expansion and assimilation had grown. The Avestic Persians know us as Hindus, the Greeks dropping the harsh accent as Indos and through the Greeks almost all Europe and later on America as Hindus or Indians. Even Huen-tsang who lived so long with us persists in calling us Shintus or Hintus. Barring a few examples as that of Afganisthan being called as Shweta Bharat by the Parthians, very rarely indeed had the foreigners forgotten our cradle name or preferred the new one Bharat to it. Down to this day the whole world knows us as 'Hindus' and our land as 'Hindusthan' as if in fulfilment of the wishes of our Vedic fathers who were the first to make that choice.

But a name by its nature is determined not so much by what one likes to call oneself but generally by what others like to do. In fact a name is called into existence for this very purpose. Self is known to itself immutable and without a name or even without a form. But when it comes in contact or conflict with a non-self then alone it stands in need of a name if it wants to communicate with others or if others persist in communicating with it. It is a game that requires two to play at. If the world insists that a teacher or a wit must be handed down as an Ashtawakra or a Mulla Dopyaja well then he, in spite of his liking, is very likely to be remembered as such. If the name chosen by the world for us is not directly against our liking then it is yet more likely to shadow all other names. We might bear witness Page, Mujumdar, Peshawe. But if the world hits upon the word by which they would know us as one redolent of our glory or our early love then that word is certain not only to shadow but to survive every other name we may have. This fact added to the circumstances which brought us first into contact and then into a fierce conflict with the world at large, soonenabled the epithet Hindu to assert itself once more and so vigorously as to push into the background even the well beloved name of Bharatakhanda itself.

International Life

Although Indians were by no means cut off from the outside world before the rise of Buddhism and although their world activities had already assumed such dimensions as to give a just occasion to our patriotic poet lawgivers to claim [Let all the people of the world learn their duties from the elders born in this land]; yet as far as the present argument is concerned, the international life of India after the rise of Buddhism, requires chiefly to be considered, because it was about this time when political enterprise having exposed or exhausted all possibilities of expansion in our own land naturally began to overflow its limits to an extent unevidenced before and the communications with the outsiders began to knock at our doors more impudently and even imperatively than they ever had done.

In addition to these political developments the great and divine mission that set in motion 'the wheel of the law of Righteousness' made India the very heart-the very soul-of almost all the then known world. To countless millions of human souls from Misar to Mexico, the land of the Sindhus came to be the land of their Gods and Godmen.

Thousands of pilgrims form distant shores poured into this country and thousands of scholars, preachers, sages and saints went from this land to all the then known world. But as the outside world persisted in recognizing us by our ancient name 'Sindhu' or 'Hindu' both these incoming and outgoing processes helped mightily to render that epithet to be the most prominent of our national names.

The necessity of political and diplomatic correspondence with various states, who knew us as Hindus or Indus, must also have, by making it incumbent on our people to respond to it, revived the use of this epithet first side by side with and then at times even instead of the name Bharatkhand.

But if the rise of Buddhism has thus enabled this epithet to grow in prominence throughout the world and made us more and more conscious of ourselves as Hindus, then strange to say the fall of Buddhism only carried this process further than ever.

Fall of Buddhism

We fear that the one telling factor that contributed to the fall of Buddhism more than any other has escaped that detailed attention of scholars which it deserves. But as the subject in hand does but remotely involve its treatment here we cannot treat it here in full. All that we can do here is to make a few general remarks and leave them to be expounded and detailed out to a more favourable occasion if the work be done by others better fitted to do it. Can it be that philosophical differences alone could have made our nation turn against Buddhism? Not wholly: for, these differences had been there all along and even flourished side by side with each other. Can it be the general inanition and demoralization of the Buddhistic Church itself? Not wholly: for, if some of the Vuharas sheltered a loose, lazy and promiseous crowd of men and women who lived on others and spent what was not theirs on disreputable persuits of life, yet on the other hand the line of those spiritual giants of Arhat and Bhikkus had not altogether ended: nor had such scenes been peculiar to the Buddhistic Viharas alone! All these and many other shortcomings would not have attracted such fierce attention and proved fatal to Buddhistic power in India had not the political consequences of the Buddhistic expansion been so disastrous to the national virility and even the national existence of our race.

No prelude to a vast tragedy could be more dramatic in its effect in foreshadowing the culminating catastrophe than that incident in the life of the Shakya Sinha, when the news of the fate of the little tribal republic of the Shakyas was carried to their former Prince when he was just laying the foundation stone of the Buddhistic Church. He had already enrolled the flower of his clan in his Bhikkusangha and the little Shakya Republic thus deprived of its bravest and best, fell an easy victim to the strong to the strong and warlike in the very life time of the Shakya Sinha. The news when carried to him is said to have left the Enlightened unconcerned. Centuries rolled on; the Prince of the Skakyas had grown into the Prince of Princes-the Lokajit-the great conqueror of worlds. The confines of his little Shakya State expanded and embraced the confined the confines of India; and as if to give a touch of poetical precision and poetical justice, the woeful fate that had overtaken the tribal republic of Kapil-Vastu befell the whole of Bharatvarsha itself and it fell an easy prey to the strong and warlike-not like Shakyas to their own kith and kin-but the Lichis and Huns.

Of course the Enlightened would perhaps remain as unaffected as ever, even if this news could ever reach him like the first. But the rest of Hindus then could not drink with equanimity this cup of bitterness and political servitude at the hands of those whose barbarous violence could still be soothed by the mealy-mouthed formulas of Ahimsa and spiritual brotherhood, and whose steel could still be blunted by the soft palm leaves and rhymed charms. We do not mean to underrate-much less accuse the services of the great brotherhood and its divine mission. We have only to point out the concomitance that is too glaring to escape the attention of any student of history. We know that it could easily be pressed against this statement that the greatest and even the most powerful Indian Kings and Emperors known, belong to the Buddhist period. Yes, but known to whom? to Europeans and those of us who have unconsciously imbibed not only their thoughts but even their prejudices. There was a time when every school history in India opened from the Mohammedan invasion because the average English writers of that time knew next to nothing of our earlier life. Lately the general knowledge of Europe has extended backwards to the rise of Buddhism and we too are apt to look upon it as the first and even the most glorious epoch of our history. The fact is, it is neither. We yield to none in our love, admiration and respect for the Buddha-the Dharma-the Sangha. They are all ours.

Their glories are ours and ours their failures. Great was Ashoka, the Devapriya, and greater were the achievements of Buddhistic Bhikkus. But achievements as great if not greater and things as holy and more politic and statesmanly had gone before them and indeed enabled them to be what they were. So, we do not think that the political virility or the manly nobility of our race began and ended with the Mauryas alone or was a consequence of their embracing Buddhism. Buddhism has conquests to claim but they belong to a world far removed from this matter-of-fact world-where feet of clay do not stand long, and steel could be easily sharpened, and trishna-thirst-is too powerful and real to be quenched by painted streams that flow perennially in heavens. These must have been the considerations that must have driven themselves home to the hearts of our patriots and thinkers when the Huns and Shakas poured like volcanic torrents and burnt all that thrived.

The Indians saw that the cherished ideals of their race-their thrones and their families and the very Gods they worshipped-were trampled under foot, the holy land of their love devastated and sacked by hordes of barbarians, so inferior to them in language, religion, philosophy, mercy and all the soft and human attributes of man and God-but superior to them in strength alone-strength that summed up its creed, in two words-Fire and Sword! The inference was clear. Clear also was the fact that Buddhistic logic had no argument that could efficiently meet this new and terrible dualism -this strange Bible of Fire and Steel. So the leaders of thought and action of our race had to rekindle their Sacrificial Fire to oppose the sacrilegious one and to reopen the mines of Vedic fields for steel, to get it sharpened on the alter of Kali, 'the Terrible so that Mahakal -the 'Spirit of Time' be appeased. Nor were their anticipations belied. The success of the renovated Hindu arms was undisputed and indisputable. Vikramaditya who drove the foreigners from the Indian soil and Lalitaditya who caught and chastised them in their very dens from Tartary to Mongolia were but complements of each other. Valour had accomplished what formulas had failed to. Once more the people rose to the heights of greatness that shed its lustre on all departments of life. Poetry and philosophy, art and architecture, agriculture and commerce, thought and action felt the quickening impulse which consciousness of independence strength and victory alone can radiate. The reaction as usual was complete even to a fault. 'Up with the Vedic Dharma !' 'Back to the Vedas! ' The national cry grew louder and louder, more and more imperative, because this was essentially a political necessity.

4

Savarkar's Writings: On Board the Ship S.S. Persia

INSIDE THE ENEMY CAMP

Savarkar started to write his Autobiography in the 1930s, but British Administrators forbade such writing. He therefore started to write it after the Indian independence in 1947. First part, dealing with his childhood and reviewing the political situation in India from 1857 to 1906, was published in Marathi in 1952.

The second part of the autobiography dealing with his work in London (1906-10) was published in Marathi in 1965. It has been translated below into English (by VS Godbole, London). This book should be read in conjunction with another book 'Newsletters from London sent by Savarkar'. Savarkar shows us how the Indian freedom struggle moved through the following phases.

(1) Prayers, petitions and deputations of the Moderates

(2) Swadeshi or sponsoring of indigenous Indian industries and boycott of British goods, by the Militants.

(3) Home Rule movement of Shyamji Krishnavarma

(4) Armed revolution of Savarkar.

Savarkar reviews movements of other leaders and tells us how he changed the minds of Indian youth and also of the elder Indians in London. The following are two well-known examples:

** Mr C D Deshmukh stood first in the ICS examination in 1919. But he was not sure whether he should join the Civil Service or join the Indian freedom struggle. He sought advice of Tilak (father of the Indian unrest), who was in London at that time. Tilak told Deshmukh, "Everyone is not cut out for politics. After independence, we will require capable and experienced administrators. So, do join in the Indian Civil Service."*

Deshmukh became Finance Minister in Nehru's cabinet in 1952.

** Subhashchandra Bose stood 4th in the ICS examination in 1920. He expressed his anguish; "I have been getting heaps of congratulations on my standing fourth in the competitive examination. But I cannot say that I am delighted at the prospect of entering the ranks of the ICS. If I have to join this service I shall do so with as much reluctance as I started my study for the ICS examination with. A nice fat income with a good pension in afterlife (i.e. in retirement)-I shall surely get. ..... But after all is service to be the be-all and end-all of my life? The Civil Service can bring one all kinds of worldly comfort but are not these acquisitions made at the expense of one's soul?" (Netaji: Collected Works, page 208)*

Eventually Bose decided NOT to join the ICS, but to take part in India's freedom struggle.

[Note-In June 1940, after the Dunkirk episode, Bose called on Savarkar in Bombay and on his advice, he slipped out of India, first to Germany and then to Japan. Bose formed the Indian National Army and recruited Prisoners of War held by the Japanese. Unfortunately Japan surrendered after atom bombs were dropped on its cities by the U.S in August 1945 and eight days later Bose himself died in a plane crash. But it became clear to the British rulers that the loyalty of the Indian Army could no longer be taken for granted. They had no choice but to leave India.]

Savarkar gives a glimpse of how; numerous unknown individuals had helped in his armed revolutionary movement. One should remember that his scholarship was not sufficient even to cover cost of boarding and lodging in England, let alone for other expenses. He had to seek help from his father-in-law, to make ends meet.

Following is the English translation of Shatruchya Shibirat; Samagra Savarkar Vangamaya (Complete works of Savarkar)

Volume I (Autobiography part I), part 4 -Editor's Name-Vinayak Damodar Savarkar Place of Publication-Mumbai (Bombay), India, Publisher-Veer Savarkar Prakashan Date of publication-1993

ON 9 JUNE 1906, I BOARDED THE SHIP S.S PERSIA AT BOMBAY TO TRAVEL TO LONDON.

Very soon, the ship left the shores of India. My friends and relations had gathered to see me off. I could no longer see them. I said to myself, "How sorry I am to say good bye to them. Is it possible that I will return to India in three years time and meet them again?" The ship gathered speed. The seashore could not be recognised any more. I was still looking at the direction of the shore. But the other passengers, who had also seen off their relatives, had already moved on and were busy finding their rooms and arranging their bags. Most of them were Europeans or Anglo-Indians. Some were returning to England with their families. All of them seem to be used to sea travel.

There were some who were travelling for the first time, but they were with their friends. They were happy and were laughing. But for me it was my first travel over such a long distance and I had no friends with me. In those days very few Hindus travelled abroad and Europeans looked down on Indians as 'Natives'.

I could feel this contempt in their eyes. It was the first time; I faced a crowd of Europeans alone.

I soon realised that I must find where my room was, but whom should I ask? All the staff, white and black were busy in looking after the European passengers. No one was bothered about me. Eventually I found courage to approach a European officer. I showed him my ticket and asked how I should find my cabin. Luckily he was employed by my travel agents, Thomas Cook and Sons. It was his job to deal with such requests. He realised that I was travelling for the first time. He said, "Here is my assistant. He will help you." The assistant was from Goa and he took me to my cabin. As I entered the cabin, I saw a young Sikh, some three years younger than me, who was busy arranging his bags. He was smart, with fair complexion and wearing a turban. He asked me, "Are you Mr Savarkar?" I said Yes and he was delighted. He said, "I was waiting for you. There are places for two passengers in this cabin. This is mine that one is yours. I am so delighted that my companion is Indian. But the time was passing by and I wondered if you had changed your mind. I am travelling for the first time by sea. There are two or three Punjabis, but they have their cabins further down. I am so delighted that you are Mr Savarkar."

When faced with staying away from our kith and kin in a foreign land, one feels isolated and sad. However, when we meet a fellow countryman, how delightful the meeting becomes. I said to the Sikh youth, "I am also delighted to make acquaintance with you. What is your name?"

He said, "Harnamsingh."

Over the next two to three days we met those Punjabis mentioned by Harnamsingh. There were also a few more Indians and soon we formed a small group of about ten. Rameshchandra Dutta, well-known retired ICS officer was also travelling in the same ship, but in First class. The readers are going to come across the name of Harnamsingh hereafter. I therefore give some details about him.

Harnamsingh was born in a respected Sikh family near Amritsar. He lost his father at young age. His mother loved him dearly and got him married by the age of eighteen. He soon passed his B A examination. Maharaja of Nabha state was impressed by Harnamsingh and decided to send him to England to become a Barrister. He offered him suitable scholarship for the studies. In those days, there were hardly any Sikh Barristers. Many Sikhs felt that Harnamsingh would not only become rich but also become a boon for the Sikh society. They therefore heartily supported the idea of Harnamsingh going to England. But his mother? She had no other children. She was worried stiff-my boy is going to stay in England for three or four years, how will he manage? How can I stay without him for so long? She said, "You become a lawyer here. We are not short of money, even if you do not work. What is the need for going overseas?" Moreover, most people considered going overseas as objectionable, a dangerous adventure. In the end, a few respected men suggested that Harnamsingh should come home once a year and his scholarship should be increased accordingly. The mother agreed grudgingly. We will see later what happened in reality.

Among my fellow travellers I must mention one person in particular (later on Savarkar called him Mr Etiquette). He was a rich youth from Punjab, aged about thirty. He had travelled to Europe many times. He, like many others, had adopted western way of life and as a result, people like him felt that they were equal to foreign rulers. So, even at home he behaved as if he was an Englishman. Maharaja Shinde of Gwalior has named his son as George. In Bengal and Madras, people styled their surnames to sound like English ones like Ray. Thus, for example, Chattopadhya became Chatterjee, Bandopadhya became Banerjee. Fathers were called Papa, Mothers became Mummy. Though this person on our ship had not been anglicised to that extent, he felt that unless our people and especially students adopt European customs and manners in dress, having lunches and dinners, even going to the extent of smoking a pipe and drinking; we would not be considered as equal to Europeans. He and many of his age sincerely felt the same. Many Indian students who had gone to England for the first time were also of the same opinion.

MAZZINI (1805-1872)

At that time, I had with me an English biography of Mazzini. I do not remember the author, but probably he was Bolton King. I gave it to some to read. I had deliberately underlined the passages relating to the underground organisation (Young Italy) of Mazzini and his programme of action. Four or five of them read it. But even today (*i.e.* 1965) they feel that their names should not be disclosed. So, let us call them Keshavanand and Mr Etiquette. I knew that they had been deeply impressed. During our discussion, I bluntly asked, "Is it not our duty to start an underground society on the lines of Young Italy for the liberation of our country?"

"Of course! That is the first thing to do." They said. "But what is the use of a few ordinary youngsters like us starting such an organisation? Persons like Lokamanya Tilak, Lala Lajpat Rai or Maharaja Sayajirao of Baroda should take a lead. When they do, we should join them. Until that happens we should wait."

"Few handful of youths?" I said, "When Young Italy was started, who started it? A few unknown youths!!. Mazzini had used the same words. He said ' when we started 'Young Italy', we were only a handful of unknown youngsters. But time came when our very name struck terror in the hearts of politicians.' I further said," and how do you know that our well known leaders had not started any secret societies? You see, if a society is secret, will it broadcast its existence by advertising in newspapers? Suppose for the sake of argument that no Indian leader or Maharaja has so far come forward to start a movement for Absolute Political Independence for India. Is it not up to us to make a start? We need to do this precisely because no one is doing it."

"Suppose your mother is seriously ill and your brothers are reluctant to get help because of laziness or ignorance or fear. You know what medicine is needed. What would you do? Would you blame the brothers? Or would you do your duty? If you wish to know what a handful but determined young men can do, we have the example of Chaphekar brothers."

"I then narrated the story of Chaphekars. During the outbreak of Bubonic Plague of 1897 in Pune, The British Administration in Bombay Province resorted to harsh, oppressive measures. People were insulted and humiliated. Women were molested. When Chaphekar brothers saw that no one would punish the arrogant British officers, they shot and killed Collector Mr Rand. They went to the gallows for that, but taught a lesson to the British who realised that their barbarity would not go unpunished. Chaphekar's deed inspired me. We can harm the British at least to the extent of our numbers, whether or not others follow us. But, in most cases, one spark ignites another spark and eventually a fire ensues."

'Are you then prepared to take an oath (pledge) of such a secret organisation?' Keshavanand asked me. "I said, "Of course."

"Then I am too ready to take the oath," said Keshavanand.

I looked at Mr Etiquette. He said, "I will let you know definitely tomorrow." I said, "Take two days if needed. After all I want your full commitment." That night Mr Etiquette called me to his room. He raised some questions. I answered them all. He said, "in that case we must start the secret society right now, but what should we name it?"

I said, "Abhinav Bharat. Keshavanand has liked the name."

"Very good." He said and called Keshavanand also to his room. I showed him the oath in English and said, "Please read this carefully, but don't get carried away by emotions. Our aims are noble but they also involve enormous sacrifices and hardships. You may decide not to join in, but if you do, you must carry the mission all your life." He read it and agreed to take the oath.

"Very well then." I rose and started to read the oath.

Keshavanand took the oath after me. Mr Etiquette followed. After testing them both for trustworthiness I told them, "You were saying earlier that we should join in a strong society once it is formed. I did not say much because I wanted to test your resolve and sincerity. But now you have taken the oath, you will be delighted to know that hundreds of youth have already taken this oath and are seeking to overthrow the British Raj. There are branches in towns and villages, schools and colleges; even government servants are our members. You agreed to the name Abhinav Bharat, that is precisely the name by which it has already been active. Now you too have become its sworn members."

"On behalf of the society I am going to England to become a Barrister. That is true, but it is only an excuse. At present highly intelligent Indians go to England and try to reach positions of authority by passing examinations like ICS, IMS or Bar-at-Law. If we persuade some of these to our side, our propaganda will spread to India. Moreover, if a revolutionary act takes place in London, it draws attention of Englishmen far more than a thousand lectures in India. Such an act will draw attention of Europeans too. They will be aware of our demands."

"Our leaders are tongue tied. The Moderates always emphasise their loyalty to the British. Even the militants say that they are loyal subjects. They do want the British Raj to continue. All that they want is reforms. This creates an impression in Europe and in America that Indians are happy to be ruled over by the British.

"We on the other hand are going to proclaim in England and Europe that it is not the question of reforms here and there, we do not want British rule at all. We want to be independent."

"Thirdly, we have heard that, in Europe, some cheap but effective instruments like hand-bombs are easily available and their use can be learnt. This is impossible in India. Many such activities are only possible in England. We also want to establish contacts with enemies of England and with their help raise a banner of revolt in India to coincide with a war in Europe. At present it is only a dream, but many times such dreams become a reality."

After such discussions I also tried to persuade some other Indians. I gave oath to one or two who sounded reliable.

A few words about the oath. I am purely writing from my memory. Such oaths were taken by hundreds of youth in many languages and the papers would have been destroyed for the sake of secrecy. But I still remember its contents, language and spirit behind the oath.

Bande Mataram

The Oath of The Abhinav Bharat

In the name of God,

In the name of Bharat Mata,

In the name of all the Martyrs that have shed their blood for Bharat Mata,

By the Love, innate in all men and women, that I bear to the land of my birth, wherein lie the sacred ashes of my forefathers, and which is the cradle of my children,

By the tears of Hindi Mothers for their children whom the Foreigner has enslaved, imprisoned, tortured, and killed,

I, ... Convinced that without Absolute Political Independence or Swarajya my country can never rise to the exalted position among the nations of the earth which is Her due,

And convinced also that Swarajya can never be attained except by the waging of a bloody and relentless war against the Foreigner,

Solemnly and sincerely Swear that I shall from this moment do everything in my power to fight for Independence and place the Lotus Crown of Swaraj on the head of my Mother;

And with this object, I join the Abhinav Bharat, the revolutionary Society of all Hindusthan, and swear that I shall ever be true and faithful to this my solemn Oath, and that I shall obey the orders of this body;

If I betray the whole or any part of this solemn Oath, or if I betray this body or any other body working with a similar object, May I be doomed to the fate of a perjurer!

As I said earlier, Keshavanand signed the oath as first member and later it lighted the spirit of freedom struggle in the hearts of many youth. They were knowledgeable, orators, freedom fighters and martyrs. Many, inspired by its Mantra, gave their lives for our freedom struggle.

Thus began our European branch of Abhinav Bharat. It soon became well known throughout Europe. It would have been seditious even to become a member of our organisation. I know how difficult it was to recruit members. What questions and objections I faced. I have given above examples as an illustration. It is impossible to state all the other cases. You can get an idea from the above.

MR. ETIQUETTE

I will mention Keshavanad later, but now we must say good-bye to Mr Etiquette. At his own request, while I was in England, I did not entrust him with any political work. So his name did not appear in any news. But the work he did behind the scene was superb and worthy of a dedicated revolutionary. My work extended from publishing revolutionary literature and its distribution to buying of arms.

Whatever funds I expected from Mr Etiquette he never said no or disappointed me. If any disturbance was expected at a public meeting he would arrange a group of ten to twenty men to protect me.

So clever was the arrangement that anyone hardly noticed these men. He was well-known among Indian merchants and sent regularly to India large consignments of cloth and machinery. But he concealed my revolutionary literature and my books in them and even organised their distribution at ten to fifteen centres in Punjab.

He got my articles translated into Gurumukhi and Punjabi and distributed among soldiers in Punjab. I wrote-'You ask where are the arms? But my friends, the arms in your hands are yours. Why not use them?' Such leaflets were distributed among soldiers in various military camps. British administrators in India became aware of these leaflets and that caused uproar. Some sympathetic military officers warned us and we abandoned that route in time.

British rulers were kept in the dark and Mr Etiquette was not disturbed in any way. Throughout my stay in England he drew no attention of the Police in London. When I fell badly ill and moved to Paris for convalescence in 1910 January I heard that he had returned to India. On my return to London I was arrested and sent to India to face trial. There was lot of commotion due to my trial in Bombay and many men were arrested on suspicion of being associated with me, but Mr. Etiquette was not one of them. I did not hear his name even afterwards. May be he remained safe, may be not. Whatever the case, once he took the oath of Abhinav Bharat he never faltered and performed his functions superbly. There were many others like him, who were known only to me. They were too many to mention due to shortage of space and even today I am not in a position to disclose their names. I am sincerely grateful to them all and take this opportunity to pay homage to them.

TRANQUILITY AT NIGHT TIME

My days on the ship were thus very busy with the work of enlightening our youth, but things changed at night. I would go to the deck to enjoy fresh air and sit alone for hours. It was the first time I was seeing the might of forces of nature. What a superb sight it was! At the bottom there was vast, endless sea and over the head was vast, endless sky. Our ship was crossing the sea. It looked like an adventure of a crocodile wandering on water. It was as if we were challenging the shining stars in the sky. But then I thought-what if the nature wishes differently? It can shatter the whole world with a big bang and even the human race may be wiped out. Still it is worth admiring the adventure of man in crossing the seas.

For a week or two I would be deeply engrossed in thoughts. What is the purpose of Creation? What is going to happen in future? Is it a game of hide and seek? The ocean contains many huge snakes and crocodiles. On the land also there are similar creatures. The stronger ones eat the weaker ones and each live in fear of some one more powerful. There are volcanoes, earthquakes, comets, snow storms-are we to say that this is a game of God? Or is this an act of the Devil? And how long is this game to go on? It seems that the whole world will vanish at the will of the creator, followed by regeneration of life and the human and animal activities all over again. The creator never gets tired. And where does Man fit in all this?

I would spend hours engrossed in such thoughts, recite all the philosophies that I had learned. I also composed some poems in those days.

SUEZ AND MARSEILLES

Eventually our ship crossed the Red Sea and we entered the port of Suez. What I saw was wonderful. Many goods were being sold and bought. Asia, Europe and Africa meet here. It was a unique exhibition, a gathering of humans of all colours, shapes and sizes, Africans, Chinese, Japanese were all there. And under such circumstances a working language develops in which people conduct their transactions.

From Port Suez, we came to Marseilles in France. From here, we were going to take a train to London. I was particularly interested in Marseilles. It was from here that the contingent of French Army travelled to Paris spreading the message of the great revolution of 1789. It was here that the famous French national anthem was composed by Rouget de L'Isle. The song called Marseillaise provided undeniable inspiration to the French during their battles against England, Prussia, Spain and Austria.

Marseilles had another attraction for me. My hero of Italian freedom struggle, Mazzini (1805-72), when deposed, came to Marseilles to seek refuge. He had no friends or acquaintances, no food, no shelter. Still he was undeterred and founded his secret society Young Italy. Later, Austrian authorities in Italy sentenced Mazzini to death in absentia, but it could not be carried out in France. So Mazzini stayed in Marseilles. Austrians put pressure on France and the French ordered Mazzini to leave France. He went underground and continued to stay in Marseilles. At a later day, he left Marseilles to take part in one of the uprisings in Italy. It was only then that he left Marseilles. Therefore the city was of great reverence to me.

I went to the city with a tourist guide. He showed me buildings of local importance, gardens, ancient remains etc. I asked him to show me the house where the great Italian freedom fighter once lived. He was perplexed and replied, "I know the city well, but I have never heard of Mazzini. I can make enquiries if you have any address."

I said to myself, 'after all, this man is merely making a living. How would he know the detailed history?' I suggested that he should contact a newspaper editor or a local teacher. Luckily, we came across the office of a newspaper. My guide went inside and made some enquiries. When he came out, he said-The editor says, 'we do not know the house where Mazzini of Italy once lived. Please make enquiries in Italy. Perhaps the Italians would know the place.'

I laughed and said to myself, "when Mazzini came to Marseilles some sixty or seventy years ago, hardly a single Frenchman knew him. Today hundreds of passengers from many nations are coming here. No one is bothered about me-an Indian revolutionary. Similarly, when a few Italian revolutionaries were once wandering the streets of this town the Frenchmen hardly bothered. When Mazzini founded his secret society here, the position and strength of that society was no different to our Abhinav Bharat. The French could not care less about the fate of Italy. Mazzini became famous only in later years and after he had left Marseilles. It was but natural that the French kept no record of stay or movements of Mazzini in Marseilles. In any case, Mazzini was a destitute. He had no fixed abode. How could my guide know where Mazzini lived?'

My guide took me through what I presume to be the old city. It bore striking resemblance to lanes of my hometown Nasik in India. It was surprising that both towns had streets of cobbles, firmly set in just as they were some two hundred years ago.

By the time I returned from my guided tour, it was nearly time for the train to England. I, along with other Indians, sat in our compartments and as the train started to move, I saluted the great city of Marseilles.

No one would have imagined the turmoil that was to come in just four years time. Today, no Frenchman knows me here. And yet in four year's time many Frenchmen would ask-who is this man Savarkar? The issue of Indian freedom struggle would be discussed throughout Europe. And as a coincidence, the name of Marseilles will make headlines throughout the world at least for one year. No one had the slightest idea that this will happen.

On 13 March 1910, Savarkar was arrested in London. The next day he was brought in front of Magistrate Sir A D Rutzen of Bow Street and charged under the Fugitive Offenders Act 1881. He was refused bail and later committed to High Court. Finally, the Court of Appeal decided on 17 June that Savarkar should be sent to India to stand for a trial.

Savarkar was being taken to Mumbai (Bombay) by ship to stand a trial for waging war against the King Emperor. When the ship s s Morea anchored off Marseilles in France on 8 July, Savarkar jumped through a porthole and swam ashore. Unfortunately, British police chased and caught him and with the complicity of the French policeman they took Savarkar back to the ship. His trial began in Mumbai in September 1910.

This however caused a sensation in Europe and resulted in the court case at the International Court of Justice at The Hague. The judgement was delivered on 14 February 1911. Though Savarkar was not handed back to France, this case was later referred to in international treaties, *e.g.* between Great Britain and the USA, and between France and Italy.

The names Marseiiles and Savarkar were in the headlines throughout the World for at least one year.

EXPERIENCE OF THE PREVIOUS TRAVELLERS

Late Mr Surendranath Banerjee had described in his biography, how difficult it was to go to England in his younger days and what was the mental attitude of those who dared to go to England. He wrote:

> *"As I have observed I started for England on March 3rd 1868. Romesh Chandra Dutt and Beharilal Gupta were with me. We were all young in our teens and visit to England in those days was a more serious affair than it is now. It did not only mean absence from home but the grim prospect of social ostracism. We all three had to make arrangements in secret, as if we were engaged in some nefarious plot of which the world should know nothing. My father was helping me everyway but the fact had to be carefully concealed from my mother and when at last on the eve of my departure the news had to be broken to her she fainted away under the shock of what to her was terrible news". (p10)*
>
> *"A visit to England, however, was a new form of heterodoxy to which our country had not yet become accustomed. The anglicised habits of some of those who had come back from England added to the general alarm". (p26)*
>
> *"Some of our best men had fallen victims to the curse of drink. It was considered to be an inseparable part of English culture. A man who did not drink was hardly entitled to be called educated. The saintly Raj Narayan tells us how he himself meeting other friends called for a drink and how they were found all lying on the floor in a state of more or less inebriety." (page7).*

What happened after Banerjee returned from England? Banerjee says, "Although I was taken back into the old home by the members of my family, the whole attitude of Hindu Society, of the rank and file, was one of unqualified disapproval. My family was practically outcasted. We were among the highest of Brahmins, but those who used to eat and drink with us on ceremonial occasions stopped all social contacts and refused to invite us." (page 26).

Mr Surendranath also mentions how majority of "England Returned" leading gentlemen took to the European style of eating and drinking at home and some of them went to the length of throwing the leftovers of their meals, bones and flesh and all over their wall into the compounds of their orthodox neighbours just to spite their religious feelings."

[Note-Suez Canal was opened only in 1869. Surendranath Banerjee had to travel to London via Cape of Good Hope at the southern tip of South Africa, a journey of some 8,000 miles!!]

WE NEED TO CHANGE WHEN WE GO ABROAD

Now let us return to my voyage to England.

Apart from the misconceptions in the mind of my friend on the ship (who advocated adopting English customs), there was some truth in it. I always maintained that when we need to stay in a foreign country like England for a number of years, we need to adopt the customs, manners and daily routine of the host country, as long as these do not involve any humiliation on our part. The reason being that we go to foreign countries for specific purpose, which is best served by adapting to changed circumstances. Moreover, we can compare their traditions with those of ours and decide if we need to make any changes for our benefit.

Though these were my opinions, my departure to England was so sudden that I could, not only, not get accustomed to eating habits of the English but also did not have time to get sufficient clothes made for my stay in England. In India I had no idea of how to dress like an Englishman (collar, trouser, suit, boot etc). I did not even have any curiosity. In the eyes of my friend on the ship (later called Mr Etiquette), I was totally unsuitable for independence. Well, in the end I surrendered to him and learned from him how to dress like a European. It was much more difficult to learn how to eat with fork and spoons. At times, the situation became dangerous. I had no qualms about meat eating but I was always a vegetarian. But on the ship most of the dishes were non-vegetarian. My friend had warned me-knife in right hand, fork in the left. When meat pieces are cut they are to be put in the mouth with the fork. But while observing how others eat, I forgot the lesson and like Hindu custom put forward the right hand in my mouth. It had my knife and my lips started to bleed. I bent down and held handkerchief to my mouth and got up so that others would think that I had become seasick. Eating fish was just as difficult. I did not know where the bones were and how to separate them from the flesh. This led to some embarrassing incidents. I cut a fish and put the piece in my mouth and started to chew. All of a sudden I hit the bones. I had no option but to throw it away. I was very embarrassed and decided not to eat fish, but then, what was I supposed to eat? Other vegetarian friends were also in the same situation. Ultimately we sought help form our experienced friend. He ordered some cooked fish to our room and demonstrated how to cut open a fish, where the bones are located etc. and how to eat fish. He also told us that there was a special knife to cut fish.

I sincerely thanked our experienced friend. I had nicknamed him Mr Etiquette and will refer to him by that name. Later, he changed his views and joined our secret society -The Abhinav Bharat, but on the condition that his name should never be mentioned. Today (*i.e.* 1965) I do not know where he is or even if he is alive.

HARNAMSINGH

Harnamsingh was a Sikh, a Keshadhari, which means that he would not cut his hairs and had to tie them above the head like ancient sages. It was therefore impossible for him to wear a cap of any kind. He had to wear a turban. Even though he wore a collar, necktie etc. like a European he wore turban also.

In those days (*i.e.* by 1906) very few Sikhs had travelled abroad, therefore he presented a sight of some clumsiness, or an eccentric. Therefore, to the Europeans, especially to their women and children, a man with a turban was a sight of fun. It used to make them laugh.

At times, our group of Indian youth used to go on the deck to enjoy fresh air. Harnamsingh, who shared a cabin with me also used to join us. Europeans pointed at his turban and laughed. At first, we ignored them. But one day their children pointed to the turban and said, ' what a funny hat ' and came very close to him. Their parents, instead of controlling the children, also began to laugh.

Harnamsingh moved on, Mr Etiquette pushed a white boy aside. As a result, the rest of the children went away and their parents too did not make a fuss. But after we returned to our cabin, Mr Etiquette said to me, ' Savarkar, tell Harnamsingh not to wear the turban. Why should we dress that makes the Europeans laugh at us and ridicule our behaviour? Though they laughed at Harnamsingh, I felt that it was an insult to all of us. In future, if he insists on wearing the turban, I will not go on the deck.'

I reacted, "My friend, I will never tell Harnamsingh to abandon the turban. Some of our customs are out of date and harmful. I am ahead of all of you in proposing their abandonment. I am far more reformist when it comes to that. However, it is sheer cowardice to abandon certain customs merely because the Europeans laugh at them. Apart from convenience, if we look at it aesthetically, our turbans are far more appealing and colourful than the European hats, which look like dustbins. We should use hats when they are suitable for the occasion. Moreover, wearing a turban is essential to the Sikh way of life. To stop wearing it, simply because Europeans laugh at it, is a national insult to us. I say, ' Why don't WE ALL wear turbans and go on the deck for a walk. When Europeans see that we are all united, their ridicule will subside."

Mr Etiquette sprung up and said, "You said the right thing. From tomorrow, I too will wear a turban and accompany

Harnamsingh." Thus I had been successful in kindling his self-respect.

I used to argue in many ways with Indian youth, who were suffering from inferiority complex and try to teach them self-respect. I led this course of action to change their outlook, to make them aware of current politics and to induce them to join the Indian freedom struggle.

In short, I used to say, "Today, the English are ruling over us. We therefore have to learn their habits in detail. And while doing that, if we make mistakes, we feel so shy and guilty. I also used to feel the same way. But that is wrong. When we were masters in our land and Europeans came to our land for trade, they too had to learn our customs and manners, they too made silly mistakes and our forefathers too laughed at them in those days."

"Today, in the streets of London, Indians are teased as blackies. But we must remember that when the English came to Pune in the days of Maratha Peshwas, in the 18th and 19th century they too were called, 'Red faced' (topiwale ingraj). The English could not walk without shoes. But in our courts they had to remove their shoes and walk barefoot. They must have felt very awkward indeed. They were also not used to sitting on the floor, as it was not done in England due to cold climate there. But they had to sit cross-legged in our courts and must have felt very uncomfortable in sitting that way. No doubt, our forefathers must have laughed at them too. That is natural human reaction."

"There are interesting stories of experiences of the English in the 18th century. A Maratha Sardar (Knight) invited an officer of the East India Company for dinner. But the seating arrangement was in Indian style, i.e. no tables or chairs, no knifes and forks. With great difficulty, the English officer sat down. He was not sure which item of food, he should start with. So, he picked up karanjee, which looked like a cake. It had desiccated coconut inside. He was surprised and said, "How come coconut pieces went inside? "There was a great laughter among the participants."

"Such events happen all the time, when people of two different cultures meet. However, there is nothing to be ashamed of them. It is all to be taken as simple fun."

"But these English men and women do not laugh at us merely as a matter of fun. They laugh out of arrogance and to despise us. They thereby imply that they are ruling over us, and therefore all their customs and traditions are superior to ours. That lies behind their laughter."

"Our own people who believe that if we learn the manners and customs of the English, they will respect and consider us worthy of political reforms should think a little. Look at the thousands of Indian Christians. They have adopted the customs and manners of the English, including their religion. Of course they cannot change their colour. But have they been given any political rights? None whatsoever!!"

"Consider the Irish. They do not even have problem of colour (they are white like English). Why are they not granted the Home Rule in their affairs? Why are the English ruling over them with fixed bayonets? So, my friends, adoption of customs and manners of the English is not the criterion for the political advancement."

"Now look at the Japanese. They inflicted a smashing defeat on the Russian Navy in 1904/05. And immediately these flat nosed, short fellows became worthy of friendship of the English. Customs and manners are of secondary or even of tertiary importance!!"

On board the ship 's.s. Persia', I met some young Indian students. No matter what the topic of discussion with them was, I always tried to connect it to the Indian freedom struggle, as can be seen from the above example. Thus, the youth were awakening to the Indian politics and so political debates began to take place.

At first, most of them were either uninformed or were not interested in the subject. Some even said that it was one of the conditions for their scholarships that they must not take part in any political movement

I used to say: 'Fair enough. You cannot take part in political movements, but that does not prevent you from taking part in political discussions. So, why not join in?' How such small beginnings eventually led them to join in the freedom struggle is explained later."

I CHANGED THE MIND OF HARNAMSINGH

Those who travel a long distance across the seas have to face two reasons for sorrow from day one. First is seasickness and the second is homesickness. Seasickness makes one vomit often. Luckily, even though it was my first sea travel, I did not suffer from seasickness. But homesickness was severe. I lost my parents at young age, and having experienced the horrors of bubonic plague, we three brothers and my elder brother's wife were very close. Even otherwise I used to feel affinity to any friends or relations. I used to feel restless at the loss of their company. However, now I had to do my duty and to control my sorrow. I had to hold back my sorrow and tears. That was harsh but without it, my aim would not have been achieved. I had to pay the price. Other Indians suffered from seasickness. They could not take food for three or four days, but they did not suffer from homesickness. They had dreams of becoming Barristers and later making money or joining the ICS and enjoying high authority. They were therefore smiling. The only exception was that of Harnamsingh.

Harnam soon became seasick. He was bedridden and could not eat. I nursed him as much as I could. But he also became homesick. He wanted to go back to his family. He could not stand the separation and the thought of being away from home for so long worried him. Finally he said to me, ' Savarkar, you are the only close friend I have. You will laugh at me, but I cannot bear the pain of being away from my family. We are not short of money at home. I wish to see my relatives right now. It takes fifteen days even to hear from one's relatives. How can I stay for so long in a foreign land? I do not want to become a Barrister. Once we reach Aden, I will purchase a return ticket and go back to India. In a way, I feel ashamed that I am so weak, so fickle, but..'

I interrupted and said, ' You love your family so much. You should not be ashamed of that. It is but natural that you should feel restless and homesick. However, if we love our kith and kin so much, should we not be prepared to suffer for the sake of the very same people? At times, one must suffer separation from one's family for a higher aim in life. I feel just like you. I too wish to meet my family right now, but I am controlling my urges, for achieving higher things in life. We must resist such temptations. It is our very love of our people that should give us strength to survive through the period of separation.'

I then reminded Harnam of Guru Govind Singh (1666 -1708), the 10th and the last Guru of the Sikhs, who organised them into a fighting force and raised the sword to protect Hindus from the onslaught by the Mughals. His eldest son Ajit Singh aged 17 was killed in the battle of Chamkour. Then, his second son Juzar Singh aged 13 went out in the battlefield. He too died fighting the Mughals. The next day, Guru Govind Singh escaped the siege with his family. However, he got separated from his remaining two sons who were captured by the Mughal Subedar of Sarhind on 27 December 1704. When they refused to embrace Islam, Jovar Singh aged 8 and Fateh Singh aged 5 were bricked up and left to die by the Mughals.

I continued, "Both of us revere Guru Govind Singh. Was that warrior a heartless person? Of course not. He was an ocean of affection. When he heard that Jovar Singh and Fateh Singh were bricked up and left to die, he exclaimed

> *"My great heroes! They died for the Hindu dharma.' Suppose, those youths had been tempted by love and had stayed away from the battlefield, or that Guru Govind Singh himself had embraced Islam out of fear, would we have considered them worthy of our respect? Guru Govind Singh's family may perhaps have lived longer but would have been despised the same way as many Hindu families had been despised because they embraced Islam for similar reasons. They would have never become immortals to Hindus."*
>
> *"If we say that we are the disciples of Guru Govind Singh, then we must be prepared to suffer the separation from our beloveds for the betterment of our people, our nation, our religion. We must not budge even an inch. So, what should be our aim? Should it be to earn money by becoming a barrister or passing the Indian Civil Service (ICS) examination? Nay. Our aim must not be so low; it must be the freedom of India. We are going to England to work for that very reason and any other reasons must be secondary."*

"Just like you, I also think that each time it would take at least a month to receive a reply from India to my letters. But my mind takes me back to the days of the East India Company. It used to take six months for their ships to travel from England to India via the Cape of Good Hope in South Africa and the same time for the return journey. And yet, Englishmen came to India on successive voyages. They fought with our forefathers and established their rule in India. If we want to defeat them, we must be prepared to suffer hundred times more than they did."

"There were times when our ancestors established huge colonies from Indochina to further east up to Mexico and up to Iraq in the west. They too travelled extensively on the high seas. However, after the Muslim invasions in Northern India there was a break in the seafaring adventures. But now we must dream of flying the Indian flag all over the world once again. This zeal will give us the courage to bear the individual sufferings."

"After listening to such discourse, Harnam Singh abandoned his plan to return to India from Aden. I changed his viewpoint completely. In the end he asked me, ' Tell me, what can I do for my motherland?"

[Note-In 1908, Indian students used to wear badges honouring the heroes of the 1857 war against the rule of the British in India. There were skirmishes in England between Indian students and British authorities. Harnamsingh wore such a badge. But he refused to remove the badge. He also did not apologise for wearing the badge. He therefore had to leave the Agricultural College at Cirencester. British authorities put pressure on the Maharaja of Nabha and forced him to withdraw the scholarship of Harnam. His Principal Mr John McClellan wrote to the India Office, 'It is a great pity that Harnam has not apologised and returned to the college for continuing his studies. He was about to be given a gold medal.' This just shows how much Savarkar influenced and transformed Harnam Singh.]

5

Savarkar's Writings: Indian Politics

WHEN I REACHED LONDON

After leaving Marseilles, I did not stop to visit famous places like Paris and headed straight for London*. I left Bombay on 9 June 1906 and reached London on 2 or 3 July 1906. At the railway station, some representatives of Shyamji Krishnavarma's India House had gathered. Harnamsingh, for the sake of my company, changed his plan and came to India House with me. Other Indians went to their relevant destinations as planned.

When I arrived at India House, I did not know anybody there. When we go to foreign countries like England we have to change our habits of daily life-from answering call of nature, bathing, dining and dressing, to language and etiquettes. Many are not only different but also contrary to ours and we are reluctant or embarrassed to adopt them. If we stay in the house of Englishmen, we are treated as idiots. Luckily I did not have to stay in the house of an English family or an English boarding house. Residents in India House were fully sympathetic and friendly. I soon got acquainted with them and also with Indians living in surrounding areas. Within a week, I started my political propaganda.

In my mind I already had the outline of my propaganda. In Maharashtra, our local revolutionary organisations like 'Rashtra Samuha', 'Mitramela' were all amalgamated into one association

Abhinav Bharat. The name encompassed them all and facilitated its spread all over India. My going to London made this spread very easy. That was one of the reasons of my going to London. There, people from all provinces, businessmen and merchants, Rajas and Maharajas and a selected few hundred students, could meet. It was possible to arrange such meetings far more conveniently and with ease than was possible in India.

In a foreign country, we feel lonely and isolated. If we see a fellow countryman we suddenly feel attracted to each other. This soon develops into friendship, which crosses barriers of caste, province and status. In London, if some one organises a tea party, people of all Indian provinces, grades and prestige can participate. Back home, one would have to arrange an all India conference costing hundreds of rupees. Such gatherings were much more easier in London. Accordingly I started my meetings and spread my message of Abhinav Bharat. However, it is appropriate to review the activities of Indians in London that took place before my arrival. We need to know what their objectives and programmes were, what was the strength of the British Empire and attitude of British people towards India. This evaluation will also illustrate my starting point.

** Note-Savarkar travelled by train from Marseilles to Paris and then Calais, crossed the English Channel by boat, arrived at Dover and then travelled by Train again to London (Charing Cross) or London (Victoria).*

DADABHAI NAOROJI THE GRAND OLD MAN OF INDIAN POLITICS (1825-1917)

The honour for an organised and consistent political activities, after the 1857 war, undoubtedly goes to Dadabhai Naoroji. He was born in Bombay in 1825. According to the customs of the Parsee community at that time, he was married at the age of fifteen. Noticing his progress in High School, his relatives thought of sending him to London to become a Barrister. But his mother and some other relations strongly opposed the move. The reason being that the few Parsee boys, who were sent to England with similar intentions, had been tempted to embrace Christianity. Therefore there was strong objection in the Parsee community to sending young men abroad. Slowly Dadabhai started to take part in social reforms, and educational activities. In 1852, Bombay Presidency Association was founded in Bombay. Dadabhai was one of the smart speakers. He said, "Under the British Government, we do not suffer any great zulum (oppression or injustice). We are comparatively happier under this kind of Government than we are likely to be under any other Government. Whatever evil we have to complain originates from one cause alone namely the ignorance of European officers coming fresh from home (*i.e.* England)."

Just see how ignorant Dadabhai was. When crafty Governor Generals like Dalhousie were expanding their empire in India by the most unscrupulous and hideous means, Dadabhai was praising the British Raj!!. How absurd and foolhardy but how sincere he was!! *[Note-It is astonishing that Moderate leader Motilal Nehru also believed in such propaganda. See his speech at the First Provincial Conference of U.P held at Prayag on 29 March 1906, just a few days after Vande Mataram was banned]*

Dadabhai's lecture reflects thinking of a great many educated Indians at that time. In 1852, he had not taken active part in politics and did not do so until several years later. But from the time he entered politics till his death in 1917 his mental outlook had changed very little. He ended his speech in 1852 with the words, "Let us appeal to the British sense of justice and fair play and take it for granted that England would do justice when she understands."

Soon after this speech (*i.e.* in 1855) Rango Bapu, an agent of deposed Maharaja of Satara and Azimulla, an agent of Nanasaheb Peshwa, returned to India from visit to England* with plans for an armed uprising against the English in India. Dadabhai also went to England at that time, but only for commercial transactions of his business. For next ten years, he was busy with his business, but due to financial difficulties he shut it down. However, he had amassed enough wealth to settle in England with comfort. Slowly he got into politics.

Note-* It should be remembered that until 1869 the journey from Bombay to London was via Cape of Good Hope in South Africa, a voyage of more than 8,000 miles!

London Indian Society

The honour for an organised and consistent political activities, after the 1857 war, undoubtedly goes to Dadabhai Naoroji. He was born in Bombay in 1825. According to the customs of the Parsee community at that time, he was married at the age of fifteen.

Noticing his progress in High School, his relatives thought of sending him to London to become a Barrister. But his mother and some other relations strongly opposed the move. The reason being that the few Parsee boys, who were sent to England with similar intentions, had been tempted to embrace Christianity. Therefore there was strong objection in the Parsee community to sending young men abroad. Slowly Dadabhai started to take part in social reforms, and educational activities. In 1852, Bombay Presidency Association was founded in Bombay. Dadabhai was one of the smart speakers. He said, "Under the British Government, we do not suffer any great zulum (oppression or injustice). We are comparatively happier under this kind of Government than we are likely to be under any other Government. Whatever evil we have to complain originates from one cause alone namely the ignorance of European officers coming fresh from home (*i.e.* England)."

(Life of Dadabhai Naoroji by R P Masani, page 55)

Just see how ignorant Dadabhai was. When crafty Governor Generals like Dalhousie were expanding their empire in India by the most unscrupulous and hideous means, Dadabhai was praising the British Raj!!. How absurd and foolhardy but how sincere he was!!

[Note-It is astonishing that Moderate leader Motilal Nehru also believed in such propaganda. See his speech at the First Provincial Conference of U.P held at Prayag on 29 March 1906, just a few days after Vande Mataram was banned]

Dadabhai's lecture reflects thinking of a great many educated Indians at that time. In 1852, he had not taken active part in politics and did not do so until several years later. But from the time he entered politics till his death in 1917 his mental outlook had changed very little. He ended his speech in 1852 with the words, "Let us appeal to the British sense of justice and fair play and take it for granted that England would do justice when she understands."

Soon after this speech (*i.e.* in 1855) Rango Bapu, an agent of deposed Maharaja of Satara and Azimulla, an agent of Nanasaheb Peshwa, returned to India from visit to England* with plans for an armed uprising against the English in India. Dadabhai also went to England at that time, but only for commercial transactions of his business. For next ten years, he was busy with his business, but due to financial difficulties he shut it down. However, he had amassed enough wealth to settle in England with comfort. Slowly he got into politics.

Note- It should be remembered that until 1869 the journey from Bombay to London was via Cape of Good Hope in South Africa, a voyage of more than 8,000 miles!*

East India Association

The London Indian Society was mainly run by Indians and was meant for propaganda. But Dadabhai also started another association, which involved both Indians and British. The British were officers who had worked in India on fat salaries and were then enjoying hefty pensions in London. They were commonly known as Anglo-Indians. The intention was that these retired officers, presumed to be sympathetic to Indian cause would discuss what administrative reforms were needed in India and make presentations to the British Parliament and also raise questions there. Lord Livedon was its first President. Former Governors, Commissioners, M. Ps and prominent politicians soon joined this association. At first, Dadabhai was just an ordinary member, but he soon became its secretary. British Administrators were supposed to pay attention to opinions of this association. Dadabhai wanted the association to have branches in India too. He visited Bombay with that intention. He collected funds from Rajas and Maharajas for the running of this association. The money was of course spent on the Anglo-Indians.*

* *John Bull-Term used to denote a typical English gentleman, in those days.*

* *Anglo-Indians-This means British Officers who had served in the Indian Civil service*

Through this association, Dadabhai used to state that according to official statistics, Britain is draining away wealth from India annually to the tune of 1,500 million rupees under various headings (at prices in 1901). And this has been going on for hundred years. As a result, India is becoming poor. The reason behind recurring famines and early deaths of people in India is this enormous financial exploitation. The ICS officers are recruited only in England. From Collectors to the Governor General, they were paid huge salaries. Their pensions are also huge and have to be paid in pound sterling causing a severe burden on India's reserves. Therefore, if the examination for the ICS is conducted in India, many Indians could pass it and, as a result, the money spent on these officers will remain in India.

Over a period of thirty years, Dadabhai delivered hundreds of lectures and wrote hundreds of articles. The more he appealed to British humanity, British generosity, British sense of fair play, instead of having the required effect, even many Anglo-Indian members of the East India Association started doubting loyalty of Dadabhai.

Let us see how he used to react on such occasions. In a speech he said, "No native from one end of India to the other is more Loyal than myself to British Rule. Because I am convinced that the salvation of India, its future prosperity, civilisation, political elevation, all depend on the continuance of the British Rule in India. It is because I wish that British Rule should long continue in India and that it is good for the rulers that they should know native feelings and opinions that I come forward and speak my mind freely and boldly."

But the Anglo-Indians knew that supporting Dadabhai's demands was contrary to their own interest, they opposed them. In the end, the association funded by thousands of rupees of money from India went in the hands of opponents of Dadabhai and he had to say goodbye to it.

DADABHAI FAILS TO GET ELECTED IN THE ELECTIONS OF BRITISH PARLIAMENT

As I said earlier, The Indian National Congress was founded in 1885. Dadabhai took part it its formation. In his speech he said, "Our battle must be fought in the British Parliament and we must therefore educate the British Public." And he propagated this view vigorously. Encouraged by the retired ICS officers like Sir Hume, Sir Wedderburn and some Congress leaders, Dadabhai stood for election to British Parliament from the Holborn constituency in London in 1886. He got financial support form India, but the Conservative British did not elect Dadabhai. Another leader Lal Mohan Bose also stood as a candidate for the same elections but failed to get elected. However, the second session of the Congress was to be held in Calcutta and Dadabhai was honoured by being elected as its President. In his speech he reiterated, "What is it for which we now meet? Is this Congress a nursery for sedition or rebellion against the British Government? (Cries of No! No!) Or is it another stone in the foundation of the stability of that Government? (Cries of yes! Yes!). Let us speak out like men and proclaim that we are loyal to the backbone!" (Ref-Dadabhai's Life by Masani)

Dadabhai's main demand was that the examination for the ICS should be held in England and also in India so that Indians could enter in the service and rise to higher ranks. He laid emphasis on it. Some British M Ps promised to propose a suitable Bill in the British Parliament. But even in 1886, Dadabhai faced united opposition from Muslims. 'Congress is a Hindu organisation and does not represent Indian Muslims'-that was the theme of Sir Sayyad Ahmad who had founded The Patriotic Association (in India). The background information on this has already been given in my autobiography. This association and the likes of Islamia Anjuman complained -"If the examination for the ICS was to be held in India, it would benefit only Hindus. We Muslims are educationally backward and would not be able to compete. We Muslims are happy to live under British ICS officers, but NOT Hindu ICS officers." Even the Nizam supported this Muslim demand. They sent petitions and leaflets on these lines to the M Ps of British Parliament. At heart, Dadabhai was furious at this agitation of the Muslims. He was a Parsee and not a Hindu, but was a true nationalist.

He felt especially grieved to know that Mr Shahabuddin, the Muslim, whom he had always described as a Nationalist, had also joined the cries of opposition to his proposal. In a letter to Shahabuddin, dated 15 July 1887, Dadabhai wrote, "How your action has paralysed not only our own efforts, but the hands of the English friends and how keenly I feel this, more so, because you have based your action on selfish interests that because the Moslems are backwards, you would not allow the Hindus and all India to go forward. How you have retarded our progress for a long time!" (Ref-Dadabhai's life by Masani)

But, though Dadabhai wrote this strong letter in private, he did not criticise the Muslim attitude in public. Because it was the stance of the Congress to bow to Muslims, whenever they raised their eyebrows. That is what was considered 'Nationalist' attitude by the Congressmen.

DADABHAI'S NEW WORKS-POVERTY AND UN-BRITISH RULE IN INDIA

By 1901, Dadabhai published in England an important treatise running into 500-600 pages. It consisted of his political speeches and articles so far.

It was written with the intention of enlightening the British public about British rule in India, but I wonder if hardly ten in a million of them read it. Dadabhai had showed how the British were systematically looting wealth from India every year, and Indians were not given any rights to rectify the defects in administration. And though India had the benefit of British Raj, it was still suffering from famine, poverty and misery. This argument was fully supported by statistics and made any reader uneasy. It helped many Indians in their arguments and thoughts. But the title of the book was important-'Poverty and Un-British Rule in India.' meaning that such misrule and exploitation should not happen under the British Administration, as it is contrary to the British character.

British and Unbritish

From the title of Dadabhai's book, it was clear how the Indians (moderates as well as militants) used the words; 'British' to indicate divine and honourable and 'Un-British' to indicate satanical and unjust. It was just like detailing "Daivi" and "Asuri" qualities as described in Geeta, Chapter 16. Of course, the leaders implied that British meant divine. Therefore they had no objection to its perpetual rule. At times, the faults were made by British officers by mistake. Once these were removed, India would get rid of poverty, famine and desolation. The only exception was that of the revolutionaries who rejected this argument.

British Liberals and Conservatives

Indians had the same misconceptions about the difference between Liberal and Conservative politicians and the Liberals benefited financially from it. In my autobiography I have distinguished between 'autocratic' and, 'crafty and shrewd' administrators. The Conservatives were 'autocratic' while the liberals were 'crafty and shrewd'.

Both were British imperialists. Conservatives like Lord Salisbury had openly said, "The liberals preach that under the British Empire, the British and Indians have equal rights, that is a political hypocrisy. "Conservative papers like The Times openly wrote, "The Queen's declaration of 1858* simply states that we will treat all the citizens of British Empire equally so far as it may be possible. Indian leaders conveniently forget the proviso 'so far as it may be possible'. To be frank, we the British are the rulers, you Indians are our subjects. That is the reality of our relationship. We don't care whether you are loyal to us or not. We won over you, by force of arms, and would rule by force."

That was the stark reality, but it was unpalatable and frightening. So, the Indian leaders assumed that the Conservatives were Un-British and went on to please the Liberals whom they regarded as real British. Moreover, Mr Morley had published books praising freedom, equality and justice. British veterans of the Congress also belonged to the liberal wing. And how promising was their name-Liberal! Indian leaders were under the illusion that whenever the true British like Mr Morley and their liberal party would win elections in Britain we would enjoy equal rights as ordained in the Queen's declaration of 1858.*

* *Queen's declaration of 1858.-After the break out of 1857 war in India against the rule of the (English) East India Company, Queen Victoria made a Declaration to pacify public opinion in India (published in Calcutta Gazette on 1 November 1858). Once, she had refused to listen to the grievances of Rajas and Maharajas whose states were annexed by Dulhousie, on the grounds that she could not interfere in the affairs of East India Company. Now she was compelled to take over the entire administration of India from the hands of the East India Company.*

DADABHAI ENTERS BRITISH PARLIAMENT (1893)

And suddenly what a surprise! As if it was a divine blessing, in 1893 the Liberals came to power in England and more surprisingly even Dadabhai was elected as an M P from Finsbury constituency in London. Lord Salisbury, the conservative leader strongly campaigned against Dadabhai and had said, "Don't vote for that Blackman. Liberals like Gladstone said that the British voters should vote for Dadabhai. Indians realising the importance of the election spent large amount of money. Dadabhai was formerly Divan (Chief Minister) of Baroda state where Malharrao Gaikawad was the Maharaja. Acknowledging this relationship, the then Maharaja Sayajirao helped in all possible ways and also gave his set of horse carts for the use of Dadabhai. Eventually he won, though by a small margin.

The news created wild excitement in India as if a major war was won. There were processions, and public meetings of rejoicing. To some extent that was natural. Many were under the impression that Indians were incapable of running public administration; there was no doubt about it. How can we run a democratic and 'up to date' state? That gloomy attitude was set aside by Dadabhai's victory. If the British voters are confident that Dadabhai has the ability to be elected to be their representative in their Parliament, then our leaders like Surendranath Banerjee and others also must have the same ability. This was the confidence that waved across the whole of India. It was good so far.

Wave of Loyalty to the British

But there was other side of the story. There were a large number of Indians who were proud to be 'loyal citizens' and their hopes were unduly raised. They kept on prophesying that today we have one M. P, tomorrow there may be ten or even twenty. And when this happens the English M. Ps will listen to our men who had become British M. Ps and eventually the administrative reforms that we have been clamouring for, will take place. (they did not want anything more). But we must never abandon the Liberal party. The Conservatives were no less crafty. They too supported the candidature of Mr Bhavanagri, a Parsee who had opposed many policies of the Congress. He too got elected as an M.P in the British parliament. This of course severely jolted the liberals. But the Congress leaders behaved as if the election of Mr Bhavanagri did not count. They kept on saying that Dadabhai was the only Indian who had become an M.P in the British parliament.

An Ineffective / empty Gesture

In practice, the election of Dadabhai was only a subtle tactic by the Liberal party. It was an empty gesture, merely a delaying ploy. And yet our Indian leaders got carried away so much.

The Irish Example

Dadabhai had in front of him the example of Irish M. Ps who realised that they could not achieve much through British Parliament. Moreover, the Irish were White, Europeans. Britain had granted them right to send their own representatives to House of Commons. The elections were held on the basis of fighting for demands of the Irish people. Despite all this, they could not achieve any reforms beneficial to them. Their leaders like Parnell got exhausted. In the end most Irish M. Ps boycotted the British Parliament. They abandoned the right to send their representatives to British Parliament. Many turned to the Irish Home. Rule Movement or Sinn Fein. Many went underground to carry out revolutionary activities.

These events were unfolding in front of eyes of members of the Indian Congress Party. It is said that one should be wiser from affairs of others. But what can you do if someone does not wish to wake up at all.

[Note-Ireland was forced to become part of United Kingdom by the Act of Union of 1800. In the U.K. parliament in London, Ireland was allocated 100 seats out of 660 seats. But Catholics, who were in majority in Ireland, were given right to become M. Ps only in 1829. Irish Protestants, who were descendents of Scottish Protestant settlers, of course did not want independence for Ireland.]

Personality of Dadabhai

Of course, this does not in any way affect the greatness of Dadabhai. His efforts were continuous. He had a strong personality, which resulted in his election victory. In the Parliament too he behaved at par with the British Ministers. He was enthusiastic about his idea of the Parliamentary Front. But soon he realised that whenever he put forward any proposals of administrative reforms in India, Liberals M. Ps shied away. There was Liberal Government in power. Years went by. But Dadabhai could not stop any wealth being looted regularly by the British. He could not get any Indians appointed to high posts in India. His only success was getting his demand that the ICS examination should be held in India and England, accepted and passed in the British Parliament. Even that was declared 'impracticable' by the Executive officers of the Administration in India. Had this happened elsewhere the entire administration would have been sacked for contempt of Parliament. Dadabhai thus returned empty handed when the term of the Liberal government was completed.

Dadabha unkowingly Paid Tribute to Indian Revolutionaries

Faced with failures after failures in his attempts, Dadabhai became angry and even started to threaten the British. He once said, "Do not invite a catastrophe by being too obdurate. The Government should recollect how such obdurate conduct on the part of the British Government led to 1857."

But did he realise what he was saying? Suppose the Great War of 1857 had not taken place, with what would have Dadabhai and others threatened the British Government? So, even their Parliamentary Front movement needed support of the revolutionaries.

BRITISH COMMITTEE OF THE INDIAN NATIONAL CONGRESS

In around 1888, the Indian National Congress had established a committee in London. The purpose was to spread knowledge in Britain about aims, resolutions and loyalty of the Congress. It also published a paper entitled 'India'. Dadabhai was a member of this committee also. But the real activists were again persons like Sir Hume, Wedderburn and others who were also pioneers of the Congress. Thousands of rupees were raised in India for the running of this committee. In addition, the editor, supplier and servants were all British. Their expenses too were born by Indian supporters. Though this committee considered it to be London representative of Indian political opinion, it was never awarded that status by the British Government who did not acknowledge receipts of various resolutions and petitions sent by this committee.

At times, commissions like the Welby Commission (1897) were appointed to inquire into administration of India, at the insistence of likes of Dadabhai. The British Committee would invite Indian leaders such as Surendranath Banerjee, Wacha or Gokhale to testify in front of such commissions and also to enlighten the British about the true state of affairs in India. The British Committee would also arrange public lectures by such leaders.

Despite such efforts however, most British papers did not publish any news about the activities of the British Committee or about any resolutions passed in India. The committee even purchased some shares in a paper so that it will give publicity to its activities. At times it paid the papers to publish its activities. But even then, would the readers be interested in reading news about India? Hardly ten in a million bothered.

Then Came 1897

In 1897, Queen Victoria completed 60 years of her reign. There were plans for great celebrations throughout the British Empire. The British Committee invited a deputation of leaders from India and arranged their lectures in British Towns and Cities. To conclude these lectures, a Conference of Indians in Britain was held under the auspices of Dadabhai, Wacha and Gokhale. The following resolution was passed unanimously:

> *"Unless the present unrighteous, un-British system of Government is reformed into a truly righteous and truly British system, destruction of India and disaster to the British Empire are inevitable..... We Indians believe that our highest patriotism and best interests demand the continuance of the British Rule."*
>
> *(Ref-Dadabhai's life by Masani, p396)*

The British people did not pay the slightest attention to this resolution. They were busy celebrating the Jubilee.

But in a Far away Place called Pune?

On the day of Jubilee, *i.e.* 22 June 1897, Chaphekar brothers shot and killed Mr Rand and Lt Ayhurst to avenge the atrocities of the British during the outbreak of bubonic plague in Pune. And all of a sudden it made headlines in British papers. The editors started asking question-who was responsible for this deed? Who is this Chaphekar? His shot resembles the outburst of Mangal Pandey of 1857!

In India, especially in Bombay Province, British officers were furious. I remember the situation described in a song of 'Sanmitra Samaj', which was sung at public functions:

> *There were arrests of public figures like Tilak, Natu and others.*
>
> *People used to say:*
>
> *First the Poonaite, then Brahmin and Kokanastha at that.*
>
> *One of them killed a White man.*
>
> *Arrest someone of them.*

Resolutions of the Congress and Sparks of Revolutionaries

The purpose of this chapter is only to review the movements of Indians in Britain until I reached London in 1906. In that context only, I have mentioned killing of Mr Rand and Lt Ayhurst by Chaphekar brothers. But even that event illustrated that it was the activities of revolutionaries that drew the attention of the British public rather than the resolutions of the Congress. Conservative papers naturally justified the mass arrests in Bombay Province after the Chaphekar episode. But even the liberal papers wrote series of articles on India and claimed that the rebellion must be crushed. It was even strange that the Loyal members of the Indian Congress were also labelled-disloyal and responsible for the rebellion!!

Mr. Hyndman

There was only one exception who gave a fitting reply to the comments in British Newspapers at that time. He was not one of the leaders of the Congress Party, but editor of The Justice paper, Mr Hyndman. As usual he said that he condemned the action of Chaphekar but then retorted, "You say the rebellious tendency is on the increase in India. But you have imposed harsh rule over India. If the Indians are now prepared to overthrow your tyrannical rule by armed revolution, it is not a great surprise. The astonishing thing is that, that revolution did not take place before."

Mr Hyndman was a leader of the new political party-Social Democrats. Its leaders were British. Their main aim was opposition to the British Empire. And because of this basic stand, the Liberals were naturally against them, but even the newly founded Labour Party also kept aloof and called them 'Extreme Socialists.' The reason being that the Social Democrats were propagating dissolution of the British Empire for the benefit of the British workers. The Labour Party did not support this theory. The enormous wealth being looted by the British rulers benefited not only the middle class but also the working class, *e.g.* soldiers, naval ratings, workers in factories. And therefore the British people fully supported the British Raj. The Social

Democrats therefore had very little support in England. However, the personality of

Hyndman had its impression on public life. Social Democrats were more active in Europe. Mr Hyndman was respected as a European leader. He criticised the British Administration so severely that though Indian leaders liked it at heart, they were afraid of supporting him in public.

Dadabhai sincerely loved Mr Hyndman. They were good friends. In his public meetings Dadabhai arranged for speeches by Mr Hyndman. Once at a public meeting Mr Gokhale shared the same platform as Mr Hyndman. British members of the British Committee of Congress party, like Wedderburn reprimanded Dadabhai and Gokhale. On the other hand Hyndman criticised the Indian leaders for being under the thumbs of British Liberals. Angered by criticism of British Administration in India at the time of Chaphekar episode, British Liberals took Dadabhai and Gokhale to task. With the hope of becoming a candidate for the Liberal party in the forthcoming elections and possibility of its support in election campaign, Dadabhai broke his relation with Mr Hyndman. He wrote:

> *"I remain of the same view that after reading your article in 'Justice' I cannot any more work with you and the Social Democratic Federation on Indian matters. My desire and aim have been not to encourage a rebellion but to prevent it and to make the British connection with India a blessing to both. Unfortunately it is not the case as yet in so far as India is concerned but it is owing to evil system of Government by the executive authority in spite of the wishes of the sovereign, the people and the parliament of England to govern righteously."*

At the same time, Mr Gokhale withdrew his statements about atrocities committed by British soldiers in Pune during the outbreak of the plague, which resulted in the Chaphekar episode. He apologised without reservation to Lord Sandhurst, the Governor of Bombay province.

By the time I reached London, London Indian Society, East India Association and the British Committee of the Indian National Congress were the main instruments of political activities in London. I have reviewed their work. But just 1 ½ years before my arrival in London, yet another movement was taking place and would soon replace the above three as main sources of Indian political activity. It was Indian Home Rule Society of Shyamji Krishnavarma. It is time I introduced him.

Shyamji Krishnavarma (1857-1930)

In 1950, Shyamji's biography in English by Indulal Yadnik was published.

It has been thoroughly researched and written. One should really read it to understand Shyamji's work. I am briefly giving the following information:

> *On 4 October 1857, Shyamji Krishnavarma was born in Mandavi in the state of Cutch (Gujarat). He was born in Bhansali community. By the age of ten, he lost both of his parents. With the help of his relatives he came to Bombay for his education. At the same time his relatives wanted him to learn Sanskrit in the traditional way in a Pathashala. He soon became proficient in Sanskrit. He had to leave his education before passing Matriculation examination. Swami Dayanand Saraswati, Founder of Arya Samaj came to Bombay and was impressed by Shyamji's command of Sanskrit. Shyamji soon became a member of Arya Samaj.*

In 1875, Shyamji was married to Bhanumati, daughter of a rich person, Sheth Chhabildas Lallubhai.

In 1877, Shyamji visited the cities of Nasik, Poona, Karnavati, Kashi and Lahore to deliver his lectures in Sanskrit. He was given presentations by various scholars. In Poona, he was commanded by Prof. Kunte, Mr Joshi, secretary of Sarvajanik Sabha, Krishnashastri Chiplunkar, Prof. Kathawate and Justice M G Ranade. Raobahaddur Gopal Krishna Deshmukh had developed a liking for Shyamji.

In 1876, Prof. Monier Williams of Oxford University came to Bombay and was looking for an assistant to work in Oxford, who was proficient in English and had learnt Sanskrit in traditional way. Shyamji was just such a man. Swami Dayanand was pleased with the prospect of Shyamji going to England. But he insisted that he should learn Vedas first from Swamji. Shyamji was more interested in going to England than devoting to the work of Arya Samaj. Swamji was displeased. But Shyamji went to Oxford just as an ordinary Indian.

In the meantime, though Prof. Moiner had agreed to take Shaymji with him to Oxford, he suddenly departed to England as arrangements for Shyamji could not be made in time. But Shyamji was determined to go to England. He borrowed money from his in-laws. In March 1879, he left Bombay for London. He registered for B.A degree with Balliol College, Oxford. He continued to impress British professors with his command of Sanskrit. He had also learnt Greek and Latin. Sir Richard Temple, Governor of Bombay recommended that Maharaja of Kutch should offer a scholarship to Shyamji. This was granted.

In 1881, Shyamji delivered a lecture at the Royal Asiatic Society of London. He emphasised that the art of writing was known in the Vedic times. For this paper he was elected a Member of the Society.

In the same year he was honoured to be sent as India's representative for the fifth Oriental Congress in Berlin by Marquis of Harlington, the then Secretary of State for India. Shyamji emphasised there that Sanskrit was not a dead language like Latin but a live one.

In 1883, he was again sent as India's representative to the Oriental Conference in London, by the Earl of Kimberley, the then Secretary of State for India.

With such high level contacts Shyamji became a member of the prestigious Empire Club. Its members included former Governors, Governor Generals, and Commanders in Chief.

In 1883, Shyamji obtained his B.A degree from Oxford University. Some say that he was the first Indian to graduate from Oxford. He had letters of recommendations from Prof. Maxmuller, Prof. Morrison, Dr Jawet and former Viceroy Lord Northbrook. The last one stated-He (Shyamji) is eminently qualified for a high post in Government Service. That is exactly what Shyamji wanted.

He had also had some correspondence with British Prime Minister Gladstone. His letter dated 11 April 1883 is an indication of his intention. Shyamji wrote to Gladstone, "You have appointed Lord Rippon as Viceroy of India and I have received many letters commending your choice for this appointment."

It seems that Shyamji was also in touch with Dadabhai Naoroji, but did not take part in his political activities. Shyamji became a Barrister in January 1885 and returned to India permanently.

On reaching India, Shyamji was highly recommended for a high administrative post by Gopal Krishna Deshmukh and along with similar recommendations from high British Officials he soon obtained the post of Divan (Chief Minister) of state of Ratlam. He soon impressed the Maharaja and the Political Agent with his work. When he left his post due to ill health Maharaja offered him a sum of 32,000 Rupees in gratitude.

Shyamji then started his practice as a Barrister in Ajmer. He invested money in stocks and shares of Mills to ensure regular income. But apart from money Shyamji wanted high post of administration. He was making efforts to secure such a post. He got elected to Ajmer Council and took advantage to further his business career.

After four years in Ajmer, he was offered the post of Divan of Udaipur in December 1892. He pleased the Maharaja with his work. It needs to be emphasised that he did not take part in any political, educational, or religious reform movements. He just maintained his status. However, he did not affect the reputation of Udaipur in any way. He laid sound foundation for economy of the state. He was praised by the British Political Agent as a good administrator. As an individual he proved to be a great person.

After serving the Maharaja of Udaipur for two to two and a half years he was offered the post of Divan of Junagad state. Financially that post was very attractive. Maharaja of Udaipur agreed to Shyamji leaving his state and said that Shyamji could come back as a Divan any time.

In 1895, Shyamji accepted the post of Divan in Junagad. But soon he realised that there were some dubious affairs going on. Either he had to acquiesce to these or leave to maintain his own standards. However, there was no religious conflict. There were Hindus and Muslims on both sides. The real reason was selfishness. Worst was the fact that an Englishman named Mackonacki, whom Shyamji had done favour in getting a job for him in the state, had started the intrigue. They were both studying in Oxford at one time. Shyamji wanted someone to support him in the state. However, he soon became Shyamji's opponent and poisoned the mind of the British Political Agent and the Nawab. So much so that within a matter of eight months the Nawab asked Shyamji to leave his state for his misbehaviour. He was dismissed from the post of Divan. No specific charges were made.

Shyamji was stunned. He had no option but leave the state. However he told his opponents, "Be warned. I know many British officers from the level of Resident to Viceroy and even the Secretary of State for India. This is not the dark ages. This is British Raj-based on rule of law and justice. If the Nawab insists, he may lose his own throne. "Shyamji demanded forty thousand rupees as compensation from the Nawab. He refused. Shyamji took his case to the Political Agent, but he took the side of Mr Mackonacki. Shyamji then appealed to all the British officers right up to Secretary of State for India. But no one raised a finger against the decision of the political agent. Shyamji decided to wager one by one all the commendations he had received in the past, to see if this would influence the British authorities to his point of view, but of no avail.

In September 1895, after being driven out of Junagad, Shyamji went back to Maharaja of Udaipur who was glad to accept Shyamji as his Divan, as promised before. But the appointment needed the approval of Political Agent who happened to be Curzon Wyllie. We will meet Wyllie again later in the episode of Madanlal Dhingra. Wyllie wrote to Shyamji, "You were dismissed from the state of Junagad for bad character and as long as you cannot prove to be of good character, I cannot agree to you becoming the Divan in Udaipur again." Trapped on all sides, Shyamji now realised that the British were all the same and would support each other. That was the truth, which Shyamji had not come to accept before. It was miss-belief that the British Raj was not in dark ages. After the bitter personal experience, his confidence in the British character was shattered.

Shyamji did not know whom to turn. Someone should put forward all the facts in front of the public and seek redress. Times of India had justified the action of the Nawab of Junagad. There was just one person left-Tilak. He was well known to be a fighter for justice for people. This was evident in the old case of an adopted son of Maharaja of Kolhapur (1882) and recent case of Mr Bapat in the state of Baroda. Shyamji thought that Tilak might help him in exposing injustice done to him. It seems that either he met Tilak before going to Junagad or had some correspondence with him. He was in the habit of keeping in touch with such persons of importance and getting their commendations. It seems that he wrote a letter to Tilak in 1896 seeking redress. Tilak replied, "Please send important documents relating to your case." Shyamji had obliged.

There is another letter in January 1896. Tilak asked, "A Brahmin youth wishes to get military training. Is it possible for you to use your influence and get him recruited to army of the state?"

Shyamji had come back to Udaipur as Divan.* It is not clear if Shyamji obliged. It seems that he did not. One can presume that this youth was Chaphekar. Shyamji had established contact with Tilak for purely personal cause. He was not interested in taking part in any political or public activities of Tilak.

Shyamji Suddenly Moves to England (1897)

But the whole country was shattered by the killing of Mr Rand and Lt Ayhurst in 1897. Tilak was arrested and later charged with sedition. Natu brothers of Poona were detained without trial and charge. For many days people did not know where they were kept. Shyamji got worried. He had already become unpopular with the British Administrators. He had no faith left in their justice system. True, he had not taken part in any political activity of Tilak but had some correspondence with him for his help in his personal injustice. He got worried that if Tilak's house was searched, their correspondence would come to light and the British would not hesitate in detaining him without charge. Instead of waiting for any action by the authorities he decided to leave India and move to England, which was a safer place as far as Law was concerned. So he suddenly resigned as Divan of Udaipur state and moved to England with his wife.

MOVE MADE BUT NOT FOR ACTIVE POLITICS

The real reason behind Shyamji's move to London has been given above. Some believe that he wanted to devote the remainder of his life to politics and become a fiercer fighter than Tilak in the free atmosphere of England. There is no reason to believe in that assumption. When I got acquainted with Shyamji and raised the question of his sudden departure to London, he never pretended that he wanted to devote entirely to the service of India.

In 1905, Shyamji started his paper named The Indian Sociologist. In its July 1907 issue he explained. "It is folly for a man to allow himself to be arrested by an unsympathetic government and thus be deprived of action when by anticipating matters he can avoid such results. Just ten years ago when our friend Mr Tilak and the Natu brothers were arrested, we decided to leave India and settle in England."

Even after his arrival in England, Shyamji did not take part in any political or social activity directly or indirectly for eight years.

Shyamji's Transformation

However, after coming to London, Shyamji started to develop his ideas. He had earned enough money to live like a rich person and also invested in stocks and shares in England and France. So, financially he was independent. He was not therefore afraid of the Anglo-Indians. He felt relatively safer in England as it respected personal liberty and there was rule of law.

In his young age, he was a disciple of Swami Dayanand Saraswati. So some seeds of independent thinking were sown then which now started to show fruits. He was greatly influenced by the philosophy of Herbert Spencer. Spencer had severely criticised the economic exploitation of India by Britain. The criticism was fully justified and supported by evidence.

Sometimes minor or trivial events transform lives of many great persons. Surendranath Banerjee was forced to resign from the ICS for a minor reason. But as the result, his personal ambition changed and he devoted his life for the betterment of fellow Indians. In 1879, Vasudev Balwant Phadake was denied leave even to attend the cremation of his mother and that transformed his attitude and he resolved to overthrow the British Raj. This has happened in cases of Saints also. They faced some personal difficulties and as the result they turned to God and changed their frame of mind. Shyamji had been shattered with his experience in Junagad. His loyalty to the British took a severe shake up and he saw light.

Shyamji was disgusted with the British Administration and therefore he did not join British Committee of the Indian National Congress or the London Indian Society, both were started by Dadabhai. He started to propagate his views to Indian leaders, his friends and especially Indian students. Slowly a group was being formed and by 1902 they had their own ideas of how to liberate India from the yoke of the British.

Death of Herbert Spencer (1903)

All of a sudden, in December 1903, the British philosopher Herbert Spencer died. He was affectionately called Harbhat Pendse in Maharashtra. Many of his works were translated into Marathi. Young leaders like Tilak and Agarkar were greatly influenced by his philosophy. In my school days I read all the Marathi translations of his works. And at a later date, I studied all his works with deep interest. Shyamji was deeply devoted to Spencer and was present at his funeral in London. Shyamji made a small speech and as a token of his gratitude, he declared a donation of 1,000 pounds (some 15,000 rupees in those days).

This was accepted by Oxford University and through this fund they used to arrange lectures annually on the philosophy of Spencer by well-known scholars. British people were much impressed by generosity of Shyamji and he became well-known overnight.

FIRST POLITICAL ACT OF SHYAMJI

On 8 December 1904, fell the first anniversary of death of Spencer. On that occasion Shyamji declared his intention to award 'Herbert Spencer Travelling Fellowship' of Rs 2,000 each to five graduates from India. There were two conditions:

The first one being -. The recipient should study in England, which will allow him to follow his chosen profession.

We will discuss the second condition very soon. One of the fellowships was to be given in the name of Swami Dayanand.

Shyamji wanted to emphasise the importance of these fellowships through the Indian National Congress. It was going to hold its annual session in December in Bombay. Shyamji therefore wrote a detailed letter to Sir Wedderburn outlining his plan and pleaded that his letter should be read in the session of Congress. It read, "Details of my fellowships will be published later. But one condition must be specifically stated. Namely that on return to India the recipient must never accept service of any kind under the British Administration in India as it is unjust and uncontrolled. The recipient therefore must maintain his independent standing in the society. Socrates has said, "One, who has to oppose honestly acts of uncontrolled and unjust repressive regime and fight for truth, must maintain his independence."

"Indians must show respect for Herbert Spencer. For many years he had condemned the British Raj, which uses Native Indian troops to enslave Indians, to impose heavy taxes on essentials like salt, and to impose heavy taxes on poor people. He had shown quite clearly that the English have conquered India for England's own benefit. He further maintained that if the Indians were to overthrow the yoke of British Raj, they could not be blamed in any way. Every Indian should cherish memories of such a person." It was obvious that such a letter was not going to be read at the annual session of the Congress. Veterans like Sir Hume, Wedderburn and Cotton were from the class of exploiters.

Congress was maintaining that more and more posts, services, and positions under the British Raj should be accepted by Indians. There was no way Shyamji's letter would be read at such a Congress. They have been maintaining that the British Raj was meant for the benefit of Indians. How could they support overthrow of the same? The letter was thrown in waste paper basket. Later, when Shyamji insisted on a reply, Mr Wedderburn wrote, "The second paragraph (of your letter) contained such a severe denunciation of the Indian Government that it seemed inexpedient for me to read that part publicly in the Congress, considering how important it is for the congress to maintain its character for loyalty and moderation."

The Paper Indian Sociologist

Thus, Shyamji did not succeed in propagating his views through the Indian National Congress and felt the need for starting an independent publication of his own for propagating his views. Accordingly, on 1 January 1905, he started his monthly paper The Indian Sociologist. Its objective was clearly stated on the front page-An Organ of Freedom and of political, social and religious reform. Thus the intention was not just political, but also all round progress of the Indian society. It was not a magazine. It merely reflected views of Shyamji. But it was far more forthcoming and effective for a number of years to come. More about it later.

On the very first issue, words of Herbert Spencer were printed-Resistance to aggression is not simply justifiable but imperative. Non-resistance hurts both altruism and egoism.

One has to add however that Shyamji was not proposing an armed revolution or complete independence. His thoughts had not advanced that far. He wrote,

"Considering the political connection between India and Britain, time has come for someone in England to state the true position of Indians in India to the British public. Until now Indians had not stated their sufferings, sorrows, demands and expectations in front of the British people. We therefore wish to carry out that function. It will be our duty and privilege to plead the cause of India before the Bar of Public opinion in Great Britain and Ireland."

Thus, indirectly, Shyamji had been suggesting that The London Indian Society, The British Committee of the Indian National Congress and its publication 'India' were not representative of Indian masses, because they were controlled by the Anglo-Indians like Sir Hume and therefore did not reflect Indian opinion.

The Indian Sociologist, on the other hand was free from such influence and therefore the true mouthpiece of Indians.

The astonishing thing was that if the British Committee of the Indian National Congress was not a true representative of Indians, as it was guided by retired British ICS officers, should not, by the same token, we regard the Indian National Congress also as not representing Indians, as it was under the influence of the same retired British ICS officers?

After all they insisted on making it a 'Loyal' organisation. It was surprising that Shyamji did not appreciate this line of thinking and assured his readers that he would support the aims and policies of the Congress Party.

We must also remember that as explained above, Shyamji conferred on the British people the honour of becoming Judges to the sad plight of Indians!!

As if the only thing that was remaining was for a true representative of Indians to explain sufferings of the Indian people to the British people.

And then by a magic wand the British people were going to remove all the injustices in India!! One can say that at start Shyamji was not determined enough or clear in his mind and thoughts. But he was rapidly getting away from being a 'Loyal to British crown subject' to becoming an anti-British person.

FOUNDING OF THE INDIAN HOME RULE SOCIETY

Shyamji was disgusted with 'Loyalty to the British Crown' attitude of Congress leaders. For a number of years the Irish were demanding Home Rule for Ireland. It was natural that Shyamji should be interested in a similar movement for India. Of course, such a demand or agitation was risky and dangerous at that time. Congress leaders wished to remain aloof from Irish Home Rule movement as it was openly seen to be not loyal to the British crown (and loyalty to the British Crown was the cardinal principle of Indian Moderates). But Shyamji had no such inhibition. He established contacts with the Irish Home Rule agitators. And taking a cue from them, he suggested that unlike the Congress leaders, we should not merely demand administrative reforms but go further and say-hand over the administration of India to us. Give us 'Home Rule'. Shyamji felt the need of a new political party for achieving this aim.

One must admit that this thinking was many paces ahead of the aims of the Congress. But it was still short of 'complete independence.' May be, Shyamji was not that advanced in his thoughts. Moreover there were legal constraints in England. However, the demand for home rule for India was perfectly legal in England. On 18 February 1905, Shyamji invited about twenty selected Indians to his house (now 60 Muswell Hill Road, London N 10) to start Indian Home Rule Society. The invitees included, Barrister Rana, Dr C Muthew, Barrister Parekh, J C Mukherjee, M R Jayakar and Suhravardi.

The reason put forward for starting this new society was this-The associations in England, which are meant for advancement of people in India, are under the influence of former British bureaucrats and therefore an independent association run entirely by Indians has become necessary. Our aim is-Government for the people, of the people and by the people in India. It is 'natural right' of all Indians and it has become necessary to establish an association in England for this purpose. We will strive to achieve our goal of Home Rule for India by all practical means. We will propagate our views throughout Britain and Ireland. We will make efforts to impress on the minds of

Indians the benefits of our movement, namely unity and freedom. Having established the aims and objectives and set a programme, an executive committee was chosen.

Establishment of India House

Shyamji decided to further the cause of Home Rule. He therefore started a hostel for Indian students, visitors and leaders. He purchased a big corner house in the Highgate area of London (now 65 Cromwell Avenue, London N6). This area was the healthiest in Great Britain and Ireland. It was named India House. Tram, Underground and Bus connections were conveniently at hand. There were huge parks nearby-Waterloo Park, Highgate Woods and Queen's Woods. In the back garden of the house was a large area for taking exercises or playing games like Tennis. There was accommodation for 25 people. In the basement, there was a library and enough room for reading, and arranging lectures. Administration was kept in the hands of Indians. Drinking was forbidden. Rest of the routine was on the lines of Ruskin Institute of Oxford. Those who were offered scholarships by Shyamji, had to pay 16 shillings a week for board and lodge. Others had to pay bit more.

The inauguration took place on 1 July 1905. The ceremony was attended by some British and Irish gentlemen who sincerely wished well for the cause of Indian emancipation. This included leader of Social Democratic Party Mr Hyndman, Mr Sweeny of the Positivist Society, Editor of Justice paper Mr Swelch and some members of Irish Home Rule movement. Among Indian leaders present were, Dadabhai Naoroji, Lala Lajpat Rai and Madam Cama. Some Indian students were also present. After introduction by Shyamji, Mr Hyndman did the inauguration. His speech was strong not only for moderates like Dadabhai but even for Shyamji. He said:

Loyalty to British means disloyalty to India : "As things stand, loyalty to Great Britain means treachery to India. I have met many Indians and the loyalty to British Rule, which the majority have professed, has been disgusting. Either they were insincere or they were ignorant. But, of late, I rejoice to see that a new spirit has been manifested. Thus there are men and women here this afternoon from different provinces of India and of different schools of thought, but the ideal; namely, the final emancipation is the same with all."

"Indians have until now hugged their chains. From England itself there is nothing to be hoped." "It is the immoderate men, the determined men, the fanatical men who will work out the salvation of India by herself. The institution of this India House is a great step in that direction of Indian growth and Indian emancipation." "Some of those who are here this afternoon may live to see the first fruit of its triumphant success."

But What is Your Programme?

Shyamji caused a sensation in the political circles in England, because of his Home Rule movement. Indian militants welcomed it. Indian Moderates ignored it. But Anglo-Indian papers like The Pioneer (of Prayag) and their societies were furious and warned, "If anyone dared demand Home Rule in India and make violent speeches like the one by Mr Hyndman and wrote articles with the same intention, he would have been sent to the gallows or sent to transportation. Therefore the coward editor of 'Indian Sociologist' ran away to England and is spreading sedition among Indians by taking advantage of the liberal atmosphere there. Those demanding Home Rule should remember that they have to face the military might of the British. Do they want to spill blood? If not how are they going to achieve their object?"

Moderates also used similar but milder language and asked, "It is easy to say that our methods of petitions and presentations are useless, but apart from those what means have you got? It is easy to demand Home Rule. One can even demand heaven. But apart from outrageous words, what is your programme?" This question was also in the minds of supporters of Shyamji. It was essential that a fitting reply was given. He did not have to go far. He had in front of him

Sinn Fein who had declared a programme of Passive Resistance. Shyamji based his programme on similar lines and within a period of three months he produced a document. It was published in the October 1905 issue of The Indian Sociologist. "Now, in order to put an end to the pernicious system of the government of one country by another, such as obtains in the case of India, there seem to be only three ways in which this can be accomplished, namely,

(1) The voluntary withdrawal of English occupation.
(2) A successful effort on the part of Indians to throw off the foreign yoke.
(3) The disinterested intervention of some Foreign power in favour of India.

The last expedient is obviously out of the question in the present political and moral condition of the world.

"As to the second expedient, Mr Meredith Townsend in his work 'Asia and Europe' asks 'Will England retain India?' Although he haughtily believes that 'the British dominion over the great peninsula of Asia is a benefit to mankind!' he holds that 'the empire which came in a day will disappear in a night.' In his opinion it is not necessary for Indians to resort to arms for compelling England to relinquish its hold on India. He neatly expressed himself and enforces his argument in the following words: "There are no white servants, and even grooms, no white postman, the Empire would collapse like a house of cards, and every ruling man would be starving prisoner in his own house. He would not move or feed himself or get water."

"If anyone refuses to buy or sell any commodity, or to have any transactions with any class of people, he commits no crime known to law. It is therefore plain that Indians can obtain emancipation by simply refusing to help their foreign master without incurring the evils of a violent revolution."

Commenting on above article of Shyamji, Pioneer the Anglo-Indian paper (of Prayag) said, "In reality, Shyamji is sponsoring an armed revolution." Shyamji replied, "We have never advocated the use of Force as a part of our political programme!

We are thoroughly convinced that the existence of the feeling of common nationality creating a notion that it was shameful to assist the foreigner in maintaining his dominion-to quote

Professor Sir J R Seeley-is the best remedy for the existing evils, and that Indians have no need to take up arms in order to free their country from the present foreign domination."

Furthering his idea of Passive Resistance, Shyamji proposed,

(1) No Indian should invest money in Government stocks.

(2) India should denounce the public debt imposed by British administration.

(3) Indians should boycott civil and military services.

(4) Indians should boycott Government sponsored schools and colleges as they invariably produce 'Loyal' students.

(5) Indian Barristers, Solicitors and Lawyers should boycott British courts and set up Civil courts to settle their differences.

The purpose of this chapter is to review the political movements run by Indians in London until I arrived there. Therefore I stated that Shyamji sponsored the idea of Home Rule for India and that Passive Resistance as the weapon for achieving the same. But it has to be stated that it was Bipinchandra Pal who proposed these measures first.

BIPINCHANDRA PAL (1858-1932) PUT FORWARD ABOVE PROGRAMME FIRST

There was great anger in India after Lord Curzon arrogantly proposed partition of Bengal in 1903. 'Loyalty' to the British of Lala Lajpat Rai and Bipinchandra Pal was burnt to ashes. Bipinchandra Pal had even been to England to study the possibility of approaching the British public to seek redress and also to follow the Parliamentary Front*. He had realised that begging bowl attitude of the Congress was bound to fail. A new movement had to be based on self-confidence. He had studied the example of Sinn Fein and their Passive Resistance and produced his own programme of action. It was published in his weekly paper New India and in the daily Vande Mataram. In short this is what Pal said: "Time has now come to say good bye to the British. The question no longer is whether you should partition Bengal or not; or whether you should make some administrative reforms for our benefit or not. We want the right to administer ourselves. We want Autonomy. We know that you are not willing to accede to our demands. We will no longer beg favours from you. We have to make it impossible for you to govern. And therefore we will resort to Passive Resistance."

Afterwards, Bipinbabu had outlined his programme on the same lines as proposed by Shyamji. The only exception was of the armed revolutionaries. They laughed at the 'invincible weapon' of Passive Resistance. However, until then no political leader or newspaper had set such clear cut, uncompromising forward looking aim. After the partition of Bengal, next to Surendranath, Bipinchandra Pal impressed Indian youth with his speeches and writings.

Now, let us return to Shyamji's work in London. Naturally, he wished that all leaders in India should support his demand for Home Rule and start a programme of general dissociation from the British. But not only the Moderates, even the Militants shied away and did not come forward for opening a branch of Home Rule movement. The only exception being that of Bipinchandra Pal, who had pioneered the idea. But he did not have any organisation behind him. Even, in later life, he was not an organiser. The only person who had that skill was the militant leader Tilak. Shyamji had started to correspond with Tilak and informed him of his political movement. Tilak, in his paper Kesari, published details of Shyamji's Home Rule movement in London and wrote an article expounding Shyamji's programme without in any way suggesting his support. In a letter dated 14 July 1905, Tilak explained to Shyamji why he could not undertake Home Rule movement at present. He said, "I wished that you had more active members in London. Then lot more could be achieved. I congratulate you for the work you are carrying out with self-sacrifice. Unfortunately I still cannot come to London. Moreover, it is impossible that we in India will enjoy the freedom of thought, expression and propagation that you find in England.

BUT DADABHAI WAS ALREADY TALKING OF SELF GOVERNMENT IN 1904

Shyamji started his Indian Home Rule society in 1905. But Dadabhai was also demanding Self Government for India through his lectures. In India the atmosphere was charged on account of the arrogant and autocratic rule of Lord Curzon (1898-1905). Dadabhai must have been delighted by the increased public awareness. He would have hoped for reaching the next goal. In 1904 a deputation of Congress under leadership of Gokhale was sent to London for explaining to the British public the growing unrest in India due to the arrogant attitude of Lord Curzon. Lala Lajpat Rai was also a member of the deputation.

They delivered lectures at various towns and cities in England. On this occasion, Dadabhai had said, "Time has passed for making administrative reforms here and there, in India. It is in the interest of both Britain and India that like Australia and Canada, India should also be granted Self-Government." Gokhale also said that Self Government for India within the British Empire is our political aspiration. Lala Lajpat Rai was even more forward looking. He was present at the inauguration of the India House. Not only that, he was the first paying guest there and he used to state this proudly. Anglo-Indian members of the British Committee of the Indian National Congress. Like Sir Cotton and Wedderburn became furious at such demands of Dadabhai and Gokhale. They said that when even the Congress party itself has not been sponsoring 'Self -Government' why are you proposing the same when you are on delegation from the Congress? Moreover, why are you maintaining contacts with Shyamji who is working against Congress? Dadabhai and Gokhale made their excuses but Lala Lajpat Rai bluntly replied, "I came as a member of the deputation, because I was asked. But that does not mean I have no independent opinion of my own. I will abide by my conscience. If need be, I will resign from the deputation."

Why the Word 'Home Rule' was not Used?

It may sound strange that though Dadabhai implied nothing different from Shyamji's 'Home Rule' he declined to use the word 'Home Rule'. Why?

Bipinbabu's 'Autonomy', Shyamji's 'Home Rule' or Dadabhai's 'Self Government', all meant the same, namely, internal freedom to rule within the British Empire.

Still most Indian leaders were scared to use the word 'Home Rule'. The reason was simple. The British had experienced enough trouble with Irish Home Rule movement and activities of those Irishmen. Some Irish were elected as M. Ps to British Parliament. They tried all kinds of tactics of obstructions in British Parliament to achieve their aims. Some even came to physical blows and skirmishes.

The British had started to say, " Oh, give them Home Rule." That was not out of love or affection, but out of utter despair. Therefore Congress leaders did not want to show any similarity between their own movement and that of the Irish. Otherwise they thought that the British will be angry with them and would not accede to our demands.

And British sympathy was their trump card. Therefore Dadabhai did not support the demand for Home Rule by Shyamji.

Time Seeks Revenge

As discussed above, for various reasons, neither the Militants like Tilak nor the Moderates such as Dadabhai supported Shyamji's demand for Home Rule for India in 1905. But the funny thing was that, just nine to ten years later, there was competition between Tilak and Dadabhai to demand 'Home Rule' for India. In 1915, Anne Bessant started her Home Rule movement and Dadabhai became its President, while the Nationalists also started Home Rule League* with Tilak as its President.

Thus, in a funny way, Time sought its revenge. If Shyamji had said, " Others come around to my viewpoint some ten to fifteen years later. It will take them another ten to fifteen years to understand my policies of today. I pioneered the Home Rule movement in 1905, therefore Congress leaders now feel safe to demand the same today." He would have been fully justified.

The programme of Passive Resistance put forward by Shyamji and Bipinbabu was taken up by Gandhi in 1920 and given the name of 'Non violent non-cooperation'. Gandhi behaved as if he had thought of the programme himself. And he even promised Swaraj within one year.

Looking back, let us remember that those Indians who were tired of and fed up with the activities of the British Committee of the Indian National Congress and London Indian Society, now joined Shyamji's Indian Home Rule Society and thus within a year those two societies faded away.

BARRISTER SARDARSINGH RANA

One of the prominent members of Shyamji's Home Rule society was Barrister Sardarsingh Rana. He was born in Kathiawad (Gujarat) in the family of a Maharaja. In 1898, he came to London to become a Barrister. He wanted to take part in politics. So, he joined as a life member of London Indian Society. He also started to take part in the British Committee of Indian National congress. He became acquainted with Shyamji. Later, he started his business dealing with diamonds and precious stones in Paris. He used to look after his business and visit London from time to time. He became interested in Shyamji's Home Rule movement and accepted the position of its Vice Presidency and took part in the activities of the society.

In December 1905, his letter was published in The Indian Sociologist. He declared his intention to offer three scholarships of Rs 2,000 each on the same conditions as Shyamji. One was in the name of Maharana Pratap, one in the name of Shivaji, yet one more was in the name of a Muslim benefactor. In his letter he said, "For completing my studies in England some Indian friends had offered financial help. Now it is my turn to do the same for my other countrymen."

The Shivaji Scholarship of Rana was offered to me. I was recommended by Tilak, editor of the paper Kesari and Mr Paranjape, editor of the paper Kal. I was supported by the blessing and financial help of Maharaja of Javhar. This will be fully explained in the next part-My life in Poona/ Bombay.

END OF DADABHAI'S PARLIAMENTARY FRONT (1906)

Elections to the British Parliament were held in January 1906. As discussed before, Dadabhai had realised that not much could be achieved through British Parliament even as an M.P.

Still at the age of 80 he again stood for election on ticket of the Liberal Party. There were many even among the Liberal voters who were saying that they should not vote for Dadabhai. They had enough nuisance from the Irish M. Ps and did not want to add to their woos by voting for a black man. Dadabhai was defeated. Indians in London had spent large amount of money and most had supported Dadabhai, irrespective of their personal opinions. It was astonishing that the Liberal party won the election. Mr Morley was elected; even Sir Henry Cotton got elected as an M.P (from Nottingham). The exception was that of Dadabhai.

Both factions of Indians in England felt sorry at the defeat of Dadabhai and expressed their feelings in public meetings. Shyamji however, was delighted. He declared that it was not the question of an individual. It showed how the Indian leaders were misguided. That was the main benefit. He wrote,

"Recently, Indian hopeful candidates had spent at least 1.5 to 2 million rupees during last twenty years. What a waste! With the same amount of money hundreds of Indians could have been sent for further education in Europe and America and would have received training in Scientific, Technical and Mechanical skills. Or the money could have been spent on some useful national purpose."

MORLEY BECOMES SECRETARY OF STATE FOR INDIA

But despite the defeat of Dadabhai came a startling news that the New Liberal Government had appointed Mr Morley as Secretary of State for India. He considered himself to be a disciple of philosophers Spencer and Mill. He had written treaties on liberalism. He had condemned the repressive policies of the Conservative government. Indian leaders therefore forgot the sorrow of defeat of Dadabhai and held new hopes. They thought this was the opportunity of getting their aspirations fulfilled. They dreamed that Indians would be appointed to positions of high authority, injustices like the partition of Bengal will be removed. However, the militants kept on increasing their agitation. They were determined to continue with their activities of Swadeshi, Boycott of English goods, National education etc., until their demands were met. People were following the trio- Lal / Bal / Pal. Lal means Lala Lajpat Rai of Punjab, Bal means Bal Gangadhar Tilak of Maharashtra and Pal means Bipinchandra Pal of Bengal.

The revolutionaries were least worried and could not care less whether Morley came or went. They wanted to expand their organisation. In 1905-06 my secret revolutionary society The Abhinav Bharat spread quickly in Maharashtra and had branches even in Bengal and Punjab. Mr Arvind Ghosh and Barrister P. Mitra were its leaders. They ran papers like Yugantar. Work of Revolutionary organisation Anushilan Samiti is well known. These are briefly mentioned here as a background.

First Annual Meeting of Home Rule Society

Shyamji, in his paper Indian Sociologist criticised the Indian Moderates for holding high hopes from Mr Morley becoming Secretary of State for India. The first annual meeting of their Home Rule Society was held on 24 February 1906. They said that it is absurd to say-good men like Mr Morley or bad men like Lord Curzon. The British rulers are all the same. They may come or go. We are not going to get Home Rule by making petitions to them but only by following a programme of Passive Resistance.

SURENDRANATH BANERJEE IS ARRESTED AND FINED (1906)

It soon became apparent that the militants were fully justified in their criticism of the moderates. Very soon after Mr Morley assumed the office of Secretary of State for India, there was a spate of arrests in Bengal. Singing of Vande Mataram was banned. On 14 April 1906 Surendranath Banerjee led a huge public procession against that ban in Barisal (now in Bangladesh). He was arrested and heavily fined. The meeting was dispersed brutally by the police. This incidence showed how justified was the criticism by the militants of the hopes of moderates. It was surprising that Banerjee was a Moderate and Loyal to British Crown. He said so openly on many occasions. He was elected a

President of the Congress twice in the past. So, really the British Committee of the Congress should have arranged a protest meeting in London. But the Indian moderates still felt that since Mr Morley had become Secretary of State for India, Indians were bound to be appointed to high posts. Hence, even Dadabhai did not join in such a protest. He and others hoped that if any high posts were given to Indians they were bound to go to Loyal Moderate Indians and not to Militants like Tilak. With this hope the Moderates did not raise their voice against the arrest of Banerjee.

Shyamji's Home Rule Society, however organised a public protest meeting on 4 May 1906. Shyamji was in the chair. Most Indians attended. Among them were, Vitthalbhai Patel and Bhai Paramanand. Shyamji said that not only the British Committee did not organise such a protest meeting, but also even after invitation, Dadabhai and Gokhale were not present at this meeting.

FIRST MEETING OF INDIANS IN PARIS: BEGINNING OF INDIA'S ROLE IN INTERNATIONAL POLITICS

On 5 May, in Paris, a similar protest meeting was organised by Barrister Rana and Mr Godrej. Many Indians attended and there were strong condemnations of the Police action in Barisal. This meeting was important. Until this time, the Congress Party used to look after politics in Britain. But they regarded the British Empire as 'their own empire'. They considered it disgraceful to raise voice against the British Raj, in Europe, which would be something un-becoming of 'Loyal' subjects. They felt that such actions would draw wrath of the British rulers. Therefore grievances of Indians against the British were never publicised in Europe. But the members of the Indian Home Rule movement in London had no such qualms. They were not controlled by Anglo-Indians and therefore established contacts with opponents of the British Raj and also with other European nations. They openly sided with the members of the Irish Home Rule movement and members of Social Democrats like Mr Hyndman. The protest meeting in Paris was a great step forward.

Though it was held by the Home Rulers, Paris soon became a centre of propaganda of Indian revolutionaries for next ten to fifteen years. Persons like Barrister Rana, Shyamji, Madam Cama and Lala Hardayal worked from here. Only when the First World War broke out in 1914 and France and Britain became allies that the Indian revolutionaries had to move to Berlin. My connection with Paris will be dealt with later.

In those days most Indians staying in Paris were merchants. Among them those who were dealing with diamonds and precious stones were rich. They stood aloof from the politics of the Congress. However, as Barrister Rana and Madam Cama became active in Paris, they enlightened the Indian merchants. I met Cama later in London. Let me introduce her.

6

Savarkar's Writings: Peak of British Empire

Let us now turn to the British people with whom we had to fight a bloody war, in detail. I give the outline of the situation at that time. In those days, the British public was firmly of the opinion that Britain must continue to rule over India. There were several reasons for this.

British people, from the Buckingham Palace to huts in villages, were aware of the enormous flow of wealth from India to Britain. Thousands of men were recruited into British Army, Navy and reserve forces. Workers in British factories knew that British Rule had forced India to become a supplier of raw materials and importer of British goods. The livelihood of these workers depended on this situation continuing. Apart from the farmers, workers and merchants, British administrators from Viceroy downwards got their salaries from the Indian exchequer and even after retirement their pensions were also paid in pounds by Indian treasury. Thus, continuing rule of the British over India was a question of daily bread for hundreds of thousands of men and women. Therefore they all supported the British Raj.

British Empire reached its peak towards the end of 19th century. No other empire in the history of mankind compared with the British Empire in the extent, wealth, discipline or control. Sun does not set on the British Empire-we may not like it but that was the reality. They had borrowed the phrase from the Spanish whom they defeated in 1588 in the days of Queen

Elizabeth I. They ruled over the countries that the Caesar had not heard of. Enormous amount of wealth was flowing into London from all parts of the world. British Army had proved to be invincible on land. Britain was mistress of all the seas. It was said-Napoleon could do everything but cross the English Channel.

Britain had gone through the stages of amalgamation of its various sections (tribes) into becoming a powerful nation. There had been many wars between England, Scotland and Wales. There had been religious wars too. There were wars between feudal power and King's power then, between feudal power and people's power in Britain. On the other hand, Germany, Russia and other European countries were going through those stages of formation of a nation. Britain had been far advanced and could concentrate on becoming a world Power. Every citizen of Britain was well aware of this status and they considered it essential to hold down India by force of arms to maintain that world power status.

There was one more cunning twist. British politicians wanted to brainwash its people into thinking that looting wealth from India was not a sin, but a duty. From school children to Parliament, they had been told that they were ruling India for its own benefit. They offered peace and stability to the millions affected by poverty and famine. Instead of saying that they had imposed their rule, they propagated the view that Indians have willingly invited the British to rule over them.

If we read British papers or books on the subject, one would find this line of thinking clearly evident. The British people too were so carried away by this propaganda that they sincerely believed in it. If a Herbert Spencer or Hyndman were to expose the British exploitation of India, he would be regarded as an eccentric or despised as an anti-national.

What was worse was that every church, every missionary who set foot on Indian soil had been preaching that the British must rule India for the benefit of Indians themselves-material and spiritual. Those pagans who worship stones were sinners who must be taught the truth of the Bible and spread its message.

Christianity must have a firm hold on India for the stability of the British Empire. There are plenty of extracts to support this, let just take two:

* *When the East India Company got control of whole of India, Mr Maugles, one of its Directors gave evidence to House of Commons and explained the Company's policy of rule in India. He said, ".. Providence has entrusted the extensive empire of India to England in order that the banner of Christ should wave triumphant from one end of India to the other. Everyone must exert all his strength that there may be no idolatrousness on any account in continuing the grand work of making all India Christ."*

* Now let us see what Reverend Kennedy said in 1856: *".. Whatever misfortunes come on us, as long as our empire in India continued, our chief work is the propagation of Christianity in the land. Until Hindusthan from Cape Camorin to the Himalayas embraces the religion of Christ, we must use all power and all the authority in our hands until India becomes a magnificent nation, the bulwark of Christianity in the East."*

Letters of Prof. Maxmuller and Macaulay whom our people had regarded as liberals had the same dreams. This is evident from their letters recently published. For further details, readers should refer to my book

Indian War of Independence 1857-chapter entitled Adding fuel to fire.

One must stress that the Christianity here was not the one of 'turning the other cheek, but the ' Christianity' to stabilise British power. When the British went around the world to conquer, they had Rifle in one hand and the Bible in the other. They knew from experience that a Hindu once forced to become a Christian, becomes lost to Hinduism forever. His progeny too automatically become Christian. They in turn became enemies of Hinduism and supporters of the British rule in India. They considered the British Raj as their own.

The position of the British people was like the drunken monkey. They would send its representatives to the House of Commons, only those who would keep a firm grip on British power in India. It was the British Parliament thus elected by

British people who would be responsible for sending administrators to India from Viceroy to Collectors. These administrators (ruling class) were called-Anglo-Indians. They were not independent, but mere puppets of the British people. If any one of them had behaved in a way not liked by the British people, they would have insisted on sacking of such officers-even Viceroys. If need be, they would have even toppled their own government. When examples of repression, torture, and injustice in India were known, the British people showed no concern. They always honoured barbarians like Robert Clive, Dalhousie, Canning or Curzon. Thus, in reality, the British people and the Anglo-Indian ruling class in India were no different. Lord Curzon had declared on many occasions in 1904-05, "We will not relinquish our power to the last drop of our blood." And he dismissed the Queen's declaration of 1858, which the Congress leaders worshiped, as 'an impossible charter.' Though the words were spoken by Curzon, they reflected the thinking of the British people.

(Notes-1 Times (of London) says on 18 February 1930, page xi, col A, "Up to 1909 or so there was no doubt what sort of Government India had..... Constitutionally speaking, the supreme power rested with the electors of this country, who made and unmade Ministries, and therefore called the Secretary of State for India and the whole Cabinet to account if unacceptable things were done in India."-That is exactly what Savarkar was saying in 1906. 2 One should remember that statue of General Havelock, who was involved in barbaric suppression of Indians during the 1857-59 uprising in India, was erected in London, Trafalgar Square in 1861, by public subscription. 3.Savarkar's views were also fully justified by what happened at the time of Jalianwala Bagh massacre in 1919. Readers of The Morning Post (London) collected funds totalling £20,000 and honoured Brigadier General Dyer with a sword publicly!)

That was the stark reality of life, which was understood by the Indian revolutionaries. The reality was frightening. We were insignificant as compared to the mighty British Power. We were convinced that it was cowardice NOT to accept the facts. It was suicidal and self- deception to deny them. May be because the situation was so fearful, that Moderate leaders from Dadabhai to Gokhale had conveniently deluded themselves in the following terms: "The British people are just and honourable. They do detest injustice and the suppression practised by the imperial administration and are therefore not responsible for the suppression in India."

The Moderates therefore, attempted to convince the British people of the real situation in India. We have already seen how futile their efforts were.

For the purpose of this chapter, I need to add a few words. Though I have criticised the methods and efforts of the moderate leaders, as individuals, I held them with deep respect for their patriotism and service to our nation. Our criticism was of their ways and NOT of personalities. They however, always cursed the revolutionaries, but we never did the same to them. The same comments apply to the activities and methods of Bipinchandra Pal and Shyamji who preached non-cooperation. It is true that they did not believe that the British People were innocent and just, and that something practical must be done which will force the British rulers to take note of demands of Indians. However, they insisted that the methods of resistance MUST be nonviolent! They believed that the British people would not tolerate any use of force against un-armed protesters; they would not allow any illegitimate or unlawful means to be adopted against Indian agitators. Shyamji's writings fully support this belief of his. In other words, even the most militants depended on the British people being just and believing in rule of law!! It was still 'loyalty to the British' but in a different way.

In reality, the British rulers were never ashamed of or hesitant to or incapable of resorting to use of force. Their rule was based on the Bayonet. We revolutionaries were fully convinced of it. We supported all the efforts of the militants and had extremely friendly and warm relations with all the leaders (Moderates and Militants). We only criticised their false hopes. That is all.

We fully co-operated with the Militants in their activities such as Swadeshi and our relations were like those between Guru and Disciples.

ONLY THE REVOLUTIONARIES WERE AWARE OF THE MILITARY MIGHT OF THE BRITISH

In the Indian politics of those days (*i.e.* 1906) there were two factions, the Moderates and the Militants. The first one wanted to appeal to the better nature of the British, while the second felt that Passive Resistance would achieve their aim. Neither party therefore was much concerned about the military strength of the British. Large volumes of lectures and articles by leaders from Dadabhai Naoroji to Bipin Chandra Pal are available. But, even for a curiosity, there is no mention of any doubt, ' what if, the British use their military might?' They were determined that there should be no secrecy in their movement. Military strength of the British was never considered a factor in their programme.

Revolutionaries, on the other hand, had to start with an armed struggle. Their leaders, if not each follower, had to consider the military strength of the British. They had no choice. They were not only aware of that strength; they were also concerned about it. Because it was they who were going to fall victims to the bullets and bayonets of the British. They were going to the gallows. It was their households, which were going to be utterly destroyed by the British. There was no way they could ignore or underestimate the military strength of the British.

The Moderates tried armchair politics and considered it to be appropriate and honourable. Militants went as far as Passive Resistance. Moderates and even some militants attacked the Revolutionaries in scathing terms. Their attacks were more acrimonious than attacks in the British Newspapers. In their public utterances and private conversations they said, ' How are these handful of youngsters going to achieve independence? They are fools. Do they have the faintest idea of how powerful the British are? Do they really think that the British will be scared with few sticks and revolvers and run away? If the British wish, they can blast off the whole country with guns.'

Referring to the revolutionaries openly they would say, " You will totally ruin your lives, and you may even go to the gallows!! You consider us Moderates as mild. Just you wait. Once you are flogged, you will lick the boots of the English. If you really want to serve the country, follow our path." The Moderates therefore said that we (the revolutionaries) should follow their suit.

Militants said that we (Indians) should practise nonviolent non-cooperation. The British, the Moderates and even the Militant newspapers always cursed us and called us ' of perverted minds, murderers, terrorists, fanatics.'

But, these remarks merely proved that our critics were ignorant of the fact that the revolutionaries were NOT unaware of the might of the British. And who told them that the revolutionaries believed that the British could be driven out of India with a handful of revolvers? The funny thing was that if the English were capable of blasting off the whole country with guns, would they pay any attention to the prayers and petitions of the Moderates? Would they pack their guns and leave India by the mere declaration of non cooperation? One must therefore conclude that only the Revolutionaries were acutely aware of the British character and their formidable military strength.

"Speaking for myself, I can vouch that I never dismissed strength of the British. Right from the start, whenever I administered the oath of Abhinav Bharat, I used to make the newcomers aware of what sacrifices they would have to make."

"I made it clear to them that they would have to forego their houses, property, pleasures of life, reputation, affections of the beloved and even face death. From the days of Mitra Mela in Nasik (in India) to our weekly meetings in London, while discussing the histories of revolutionaries of many countries, I used to emphasise this point."

Even before leaving for London, I preached to my friends, 'Any nation who set out to establish a world empire needs certain qualities. The British do have the necessary attributes. Of course, they are brave. They are also cruel and deceptive. It is not for nothing that they have established an empire over us. I say to you, time and again, that their Military power is their Bible. And also no one can match their craftiness today. Therefore they are administering their rule over this huge country systematically like clockwork.'

'The trained officers who come from Britain (members of the elite Indian Civil Service) know every minute detail about us, our geography, our languages, castes, history and other characters. From the office of the Governor General's Council to the office of the village chief they are functioning like a clock with eternal vigilance. First, they defeated us on the battlefields and the name of

'Sahib' has created fear in our hearts. And now they are ruling over us by their intellectual power through their specially trained staff (the Indian Civil Service) and Indian assistants as if it the whole thing is a perfectly working machine.'

For this important reason, the British people were least interested in how India was administered. All that they wanted to know was that it was being run firmly and without any risk. They were least interested in whether Indians faced injustice, or starvation. They were least bothered if the British administrators were harsh or liberal. They were more interested in cricket matches or industrial accidents than the annual sessions of the Indian National Congress or severe famines in India. If at all they were worried it was because of some revolutionary outbreak, be it by Phadake (1879) or Chaphekar (1897).

My Records in London C.I.D

British authorities kept a close eye on the Indian revolutionaries. I can testify from my own experience.

I came to London in July 1906, but would not have believed that Bombay C.I.D would have sent a report about me, detailing all the political activities in which I had taken part. I learnt about it in 1910 when I was arrested and was being sent to India to stand for a trial. So it means that ever since I was 20 the British (in India and Britain) had started a secret file on me and had compiled reports of my activities (true or false). This went on till 1947 (when India became independent). In my active life, I had forgotten many details, but the British kept records of my activities. Their tenacity is worth praising. Some of the details were published in Government reports. These are now useful for writing my autobiography.

Reports by Mr. Montgomery, I.C.S.

Out of the secret files, the report by Mr Montgomery is now made known. It was prepared in 1906. He compiled it from information collected by officials in Nasik, Pune, Bombay and other places. He added his own remarks and the report was sent to Home Office in Bombay. This probably happened in March to May 1906 because it states "Mr Savarkar is studying for the L.LB examination at Bombay University." Just a few months after this report, I went to London, and I was introduced as a 'revolutionary suspect' to London C.I.D probably based on this report. It is interesting to see what the British Authorities had recorded. I am quoting from papers that have now been made public.

Mr Montgomery says : "Mr V D Savarkar is from Nasik. He had been interested in public debates since childhood. He is hardly 22. But he has already grown into an accomplished orator of an enviable rank. He has been impressed by thoughts of Mr S M Paranjape. However, it is said that all that glitters is not gold. I think the same will be true in case of Savarkar. At present he is studying for L.LB degree in Bombay having obtained B.A degree from Fergusson College in Poona. The students of this college are generally dissatisfied with the current state of affairs."

"While in College, Savarkar had a group of his own that shows his attitude. Savarkar speaks very quickly. He is also very courageous. His speeches are very effective and as he gets response from the audience, he gets carried away and is not aware of the C.I.D officers that are present."

"His classmates are not devoted to him, because there is discrepancy between his preaching and his behaviour. He is very proud of his religion, but keeps hair on his head, wears shirt and a short coat."

"He sponsored Swadeshi while in College. On the day of Dussehra, he organised a public bonfire of English clothes. For this behaviour he was fined but his friends made a collection for him. So much money was raised that after paying the fine large amount was left. This he donated to Paisa Fund of one Mr Kale.

From this day, people started to look at him as a Martyr. Wrangler R P Paranjape (Principal of Fergusson College who fined Savarkar.) does not have much following. He is respected only among the social reformers."

"Mr S M Paranjape supported Savarkar and through his paper KAL obtained public sympathy for Savarkar. His public life began at this stage. In my opinion, Savarkar is childish and is spoiling his career. He does not know what he is preaching. Not only that he is spoiling the lives of other students. He has contacts with 'Sanmitra Samaj' of Nasik. This society organised tours in support of Swadeshi."

"On 23 February 1906, Savarkar had organised and chaired a public meeting in Poona. Some students of Poona had gone to see Agamya Guru. This guru wished that students of Poona should start a society on lines of the one in Jabalpur and through it freedom movement of India should start. (Agamya Guru had started an Indo-European movement.) Students of Poona agreed to start such a society and asked the Guru for further guidance. He asked them to set up a committee of 'seven' and he would meet the 'selected seven'."

"These students sent a telegram to Savarkar asking him to come to Poona. He did and met Agamya Guru. Afterwards he addressed the students as a chairman. He said, "My friends, the situation of our country is very bad. This puts a heavy responsibility on our shoulders. Therefore we need to unite and form a society. It is not possible for the Guru to meet you individually and therefore I have come here."

"Now let us start a committee of seven and then he will tell us what to do. So, you choose the members of this group of 'seven'." "Afterwards, one Mr Pangarkar read a boring essay describing the importance of the society. In the end, Savarkar made a forceful and inspiring speech. This was like the speech of a general addressing his soldiers about to go into a battlefield. He spoke for 35 minutes and said, "My friends, it is futile to depend on the older generation. I have already told you how precarious our situation is. We cannot tolerate it any longer. It must be changed. People of older generation have no dynamism left. I do not think they will be able to do anything." "Those who have experience of the world need to teach the young."

"Mazzini was old, his followers were young. He inspired his followers and induced them to become revolutionaries. He carried out his mission." "Old men have experience of life but the goddess of freedom needs fresh flowers. It does not like faded flowers, which have to be discarded. Therefore we must unite and be prepared for sacrificing our lives."

'What does the saint Ramdas say?-collect many people. Inspire them with thoughts. Then fall on .... I do not remember the last word." "I can see secret police in front of me. I am glad that they have come. If they co-operate with us that will be great. We can achieve high goals."

"We should always remember the teaching of Ramdas. We must obey his orders. We have lost everything. Continuing efforts is the only way. There is no point in crying for what we have lost but to regain our glory we need to sacrifice our blood. We have lost our Dharma (way of life) we need to re-establish it. etc." The above report is full of misinformation and just as in any secret police reports; it is full of false statements and inconsistent details. For example, it has been said that I had a separate group of mine own, but later on it says his fellow students did not have faith in him.

It has been said that I did not behave as I preached, because I kept hair on my head, used shirt and a short coat. If Mr Montgomery wishes to say that the 'entire group of students did not follow me' the same can also be said about any public figure. If the leader were a 'reformer' the conservatives would not have respect for him.

But if Mr Montgomery wishes to imply that my contemporary students had no faith or affection for me, it is proved to be false by the first statement.-Savarkar had his own group and because of their faith and love for him, other students and professors called it the 'Savarkar camp'. It is interesting to note that Mr Montgomery has declared me not having faith in our religion, because I wear a short coat. His definition of a 'religious person' is funny.

The report further says that as suggested by Agamya Guru, students had to chose their representative. A meeting of students was held, and though many were not in my group or even in my college, they chose me as their representative. They sent me a telegram and requested me to come to Poona and when I arrived in Poona, the students made me the chairman. Is this an indication that my contemporaries had no love for or faith in me? But such statements are made without any checks.

There are also many un-excusable loose ends. For example, someone reported-Sanmitra Samaj of Nasik conducted many tours in support of Swadeshi. Now, this society was in Poona and not in Nasik. It never conducted any tours for spread of Swadeshi. Their only programme was at the time of Ganesh festival and they organised a musical programme (Mela) once a year, and that used to be on a big scale. Their poems were very inspiring. But the society was not a political society in any sense. Moreover, I had no connection with it, even remotely.

The fact is that I was associated with the society-Mitramela. Its members did conduct tours in support of Swadeshi and took part in Ganesh festivals. The magistrate is confused between our Mitramela of Nasik and Sanmitra Samaj of Poona. And therefore he made up his statement. It is astonishing that the C.I.D of Bombay province had no knowledge of our secret society Mitramela or Abhinav Bharat. They certainly had no detailed knowledge of either society.

Later, Mr Montgomery says-According to Savarkar, Mazzini was old but his followers were young. True, I had delivered many speeches on Mazzini and his association called Young Italy. Some were open, some in secret. But I always emphasised that Mazzini was young.

It is impossible that I would have made remarks about Mazzini being old. Either Mr Montgomery did not know of my lectures delivered in secret or had not read the biography of him. It is even possible that both were true. Perhaps he believed what he was told. When Mazzini was old, Italy was liberated and there was no need for his society to remain secret. Poor Mr Montgomery did not know this history.

Despite these drawbacks, the Bombay C.I.D have noted correctly two of my speeches and used them here. The police had noted how clever I was in ensuring that I do not get caught in breaking any law of sedition. In the above speech I had referred to saint Ramdas. His preaching was-Gather many people together, get them induced to your cause and let us all make a determined attack on ....I pretended that I did not remember the word (foreigner). So I used the word-'our calamities'. The audience appreciated my cleverness and applauded loudly.

Two more lines in the report are also an indication of my cleverness. I said, "I am aware that the secret police are present in the audience. I am glad that they are listening to my speeches. After all they are our brothers. They are bound to change and join us one day. "I said this openly but then added-"We have to regain what we have lost." To give a religious aspect to my speech I said, "But do we know what we have lost? We have lost our Dharma (way of life). I did not say-we have lost our freedom. Thus, though I was within the law, the audience got my message.

Mr Montgomery says-'Savarkar gets so excited that he forgets that secret police are present at his public meetings.' Above explanation proves Mr Montgomery wrong.

I criticized the report not just for the discrepancies. Some 12 years later the same report was used to compile another comprehensive report, indicating how Indian revolutionaries carried out their activities and how they can be curbed. It was the Rowlatt Report.

ROWLATT REPORT

British administration in India had appointed Mr Rowlatt, a senior British judge to enquire into activities of Indian revolutionaries. The committee also included senior judges of Bombay and Madras high courts. It was named 'Sedition Committee' and worked 'in camera'. It examined all the reports of C.I.D officers and proceedings of court cases of Indian revolutionaries. The Government of India published its findings in 'Sedition Committee Report' towards the end of 1918. It ran into some 250 pages. Despite the fact that it contains mistakes and false statements, it still provides a thorough, detailed, chronological history of the Indian Revolutionaries from 1890 to 1918. As for the mistakes, as the report is based on C.I.D reports of various officers, it has the same drawbacks. For example, it says about me on page 5: "Before leaving India, Vinayak Savarkar had been drawn into a movement initiated early in 1905 by a person styling himself as Shri Agamya Guru Paramahansa. As a part of this movement a number of students early in 1906 started in Poona a society which elected Vinayak Savatkar as their leader."

I have already explained how wrong it is to think that my political activities began after my meeting with Agamya Guru in 1905. I had started my secret society in 1899 and also I and my other members had carried out a lot of open and secret activities. These are not mentioned in Rowalatt Report at all. Second mistake is to state that I was drawn to the movement of Agamya Guru.

Third mistake is to say that I started a branch of Agamya Guru's movement in Poona, as there was no such movement by Agamya Guru. My public speech of 22 February 1906 was noted by Mr Montgomery. And he writes-'The Mahatma Agamya Guru at this meeting advised the raising of funds.'

This is the fourth mistake because Guru did not attend the meeting at all. Further information in the Rowlatt Report is even more absurd. It says:"After Savarkar left India in June 1906, the Society (started by Agamya Guru in Poona) subsequently joined Abhinav Bharat Society, founded by Ganesha, Vinayak Savarkar's elder brother. At the time of his departure from India Vinayak Savarkar and his brother were the leaders of an association known as the Mitra Mela, started in around 1899, in connection with Ganapati Celebrations."

There are several serious mistakes in it:

* There was no movement by Agamya Guru.
* It did not have a branch in Poona.
* Abhinav Bharat was there from the start and was not started by my elder brother.
* Mitra Mela was not started for Ganapati celebrations.

Thus, the Rowlatt Report is full of mistakes and inaccuracies. After reading it, an uninformed reader or researcher would think that my political work started after I came in contact with Agamya Guru in February 1906 and that he was my first Political Guru, and that I joined his society. From then on and with his blessings I became a Revolutionary. Until then the organization called Mitra Mela was merely celebrating Ganapati Festivals!!

The Story of Agamya Guru

There is some element of truth even in the twisted facts. The same applies to Rowlatt Committee Report and the report of Mr. Montgomery. There was one Mahatma Shree Agamya Guru Paramhansa. He came to Poona in 1906. In the beginning he delivered lectures that would suit the Militants. He used to say, "Those who wish to carry out some patriotic work in an organized way, should see me." When one calls himself a Mahatma or a Swami, he invariably gathers some followers. He even talked like a Militant. So students started to go to him with expectations. Some members of Abhinav Bharat also joined them to see, if the person had some verifiable qualities. But the Guru always kept quiet about any political activities. He always insisted on the students to collect some funds, appoint a committee and send their leader to him. Then he would guide the student's leader. Having created a mystery around him, some students were carried away.

They pleaded with my friends and asked them to send me a telegram, which they did. Accordingly I came from Bombay to Poona. Until that time, I had not heard of Agamya Guru. Students of schools and colleges decided to have a meeting. Accordingly a big gathering was arranged on 23 February 1906. I talked about organizing the youth for obtaining our freedom. This is the meeting Mr. Montgomery was referring to. Many students suggested that a committee should now be appointed. Accordingly seven members of a committee were selected with me as its leader. I then approached Agamya Guru with members of the committee and asked, "Can you now tell us what plans of action have you got?" But he did not respond properly. At times he spoke about Yoga and Pranayam (breathing exercises), at times he talked about God and religion. I interrupted and asked, " Will you please talk about your programme of action and your guidance for us?"

The Guru said, "What guidance can I give to this group of students? What can you achieve? I told you to collect some funds. Even that you have not done. Go away and collect some money." I realized the true worth of the Guru. Students dispersed. I asked my friends 'why did you send me a telegram?' There are many bogus Gurus. They tremble at the very thought of an armed revolution. I will never see this Agamya Guru again."

I do not know what happened to him afterwards. I did not bother. My contact with the Guru was very short. I would not have mentioned his name in my autobiography. But the Rowlatt Report and the report of Mr. Montgomery had made a mountain out of a mole. After serving eleven years in prison on the Andaman Islands and further three years in Indian jails, I was released in 1924 on the condition that I would live in Ratnagiri. It was at that time that I came across the Rowlatt Report and laughed at it for the above reason.

When I was interned in Ratnagiri, I met Dadarao Karandikar, a follower of Tilak. This is what he said about Agamya Guru. "I met Agamya Guru in London in 1908 and later he was sent to prison for trying to molest an English girl."This information is contained in Mr Karandikar's book 'Letters from England.' He adds, 'I met Agamya Guru after he had served his sentence and that was the end of it.'

Had the Guru not met me briefly, his name would have never been mentioned in the British Administration reports.

Other Mistakes : Rowlatt report also contains some more blunders. On page 4 it has been said-"Another paper edited by Chitpawan Brahmins in Poona was the Vihari. Criminal proceedings were successfully taken against three successive editors for seditious articles, which appeared in it, in 1906/07/08 years."

Now, the paper Vihari was published from Bombay not Poona. Its Manager Mr. Phatak was not a Poonaite. Its first editor, who became a member of Abhinav Bharat, was Mr. Chiplunakar. He too was not a Poonaite. I started to write anonymously and that increased the circulation of the Paper. But I too was not a Poonaite. It is astonishing that Rowlatt Report does not know that I was anonymously running the paper. When I went to London, Mr. Phadake became editor of the paper. But he too was not a Poonaite. When he was convicted of sedition, Mr. Mandlik became the editor. But he too was not a Poonaite. When he too was convicted of sedition, the paper was closed. See what the Rowlatt Report has said. None of us was in any way connected with Poona. All that is true is that we were Chitpawan Brahmins. It is astonishing that the Rowlatt report did not know that Mr. Phadake and Mr. Mandlik were members of Abhinav Bharat.

INCREDIBLE WORK OF INDIAN REVOLUTIONARIES

From the above discussion, it will be clear that many activities of Indian revolutionaries were not known to the C.I.D. Many details have been wrongly reported or are false and twisted. There were organisations similar to Abhinav Bharat. But the information about them in Rowlatt report is sketchy, incomplete, false or twisted. This is astonishing as well as makes us proud of our revolutionary work. The main reason being that though the C.I.D had enormous resources and widespread organization, we surpassed them in our skills and carried out many missions successfully. This includes Khudiram Bose (1908), Madanlal Dhingra (1909), Kanhere (1910), Bhagatsingh (1931) right up to Udhamsingh (1940). Who would not be proud of our organizational skills?

Indian History should not be Written based Solely on British C.I.D Reports

I have discussed failings of C.I.D reports as far as details pertaining to me are concerned. The same remarks will apply to other C.I.D reports, which have not been seen by researchers. Therefore history of our revolutionary movement should not be based purely on these reports. Otherwise serious mistakes and blunders will be permanently made. Let me give an example.

Report about my activities was first made by Mr. Montgomery in 1906. In 1918, the Rowlatt Report copied it word for word. Unfortunately Mr. Yadnik, who wrote a biography of Shyamji in 1950 assumed the Rowlatt report as infallible and gave credit for my activities to Agamya Guru. It is clear how innocent writers can make such mistakes. And once they do, the mistakes become permanent. That is the danger. What applies to me personally also applies to the history of revolutionary movement as well.

However, it must be stressed that the C.I.D reports are an important but partial source of very important information. But they should not be treated as exclusive source of information. Many revolutionaries have written their biographies and histories of revolutionary movements in which they took part. These are available in Bengali, English, Hindi and other languages. For the validity of Rowlatt report we should study all these and then only accept what can be tallied.

Joseph Mazzini—Biography and Politics

I spent about a week getting used to life in India House. Afterwards I asked the Manager, one Mr Mukherjee, "I understand that Mazzini's autobiography and his articles are published. But I have not been able to read them. You know the main public libraries in London. Could you possibly borrow the works for me?"

"Mazzini's autobiography?" said Mr. Mukherjee. He thought deeply and replied, "I think we do have such a book in our collection." He came back with a book. I was delighted. But it was only a book of 300 pages. How can Mazzini's works be contained in such a small volume? I thought. I read the book thoroughly and noted that it was only Volume One. I showed that note to Mr. Mukherjee. He took me to the library in India House. He murmured-I try to tidy up, but the residents displace the books. He eventually found three volumes. I did not have all the six volumes, but I was very pleased with what I had. It was as if someone had found hidden treasure while excavating inside a house. I read the three volumes in a week and pressed Mr.

Mukherjee for the remainder volumes. He was impressed with my sincerity and studious nature. He tried hard but was frustrated at not finding them in market. Some ten days later he came straight to my room and said, "Well Mr. Savarkar, here are the rest of the books." I thanked him from the bottom of my heart and read the remaining volumes in no time.

Mazzini's Influence on Indian Politics

Just eight to nine years before the 1857 war, Mazzini and Garibaldi were engaged in battles of their freedom struggle in 1848-49. Italian revolutionaries were defeated and had to go into exile. They sincerely believed that it was their duty to help other countries also, that were trying to regain their independence from occupying forces. They heard of the 1857 war in India against the East India Company. Despite the censorship, the news of the war was filtering through. Events of Kanpur, Kalpi and especially the fighting abilities of Tatya Tope, which appeared in French newspapers, impressed the Italian revolutionaries. They felt deep sympathy with Indians and Garibaldi even wanted to go to India and fight shoulder to shoulder with Tatya Tope. Unfortunately there were plans for one more uprising in Italy itself. He therefore abandoned that plan.

After the unsuccessful war of 1857-59, there was a period of lull in Indian politics. But the next generation of English educated Indians like Surendranath Banerjee had taken inspiration from Mazzini's biography. Surendranath was forced to resign from the ICS and then decided to devote his life for the service of India. He was deeply impressed by the deeds of Mazzini. During 1875 to 1878 he delivered public speeches on the subject-Mazzini and his secret society Young Italy. By that time Italy had been freed from the yoke of Austrians just five years earlier. Surendranath inspired hundreds of Bengali youth in their twenties and thirties. And there was a wave of forming 'secret societies' though not on the basis of Mazzini. Bipinchandra Pal was one of the youth. He was around thirty at that time and though he took no part in any political movement he had been a leader in the Brahmosamaj. In his autobiography he wrote, "I was inspired by Surendranath's speeches on Mazzini and was determined to take part in political movement to achieve our freedom."

Secrecy for the Sake of Secrecy

However, Surendrnath wrote in his autobiography," I used to tell our youth that you become staunch patriots, devote your life for uplift of our motherland but avoid the revolutionary methods of Mazzini. Those methods were useful for Italy. But Hindusthan is not Italy. Mazzini's tactics will be disastrous in our country. Our efforts must be legal, constitutional and absolutely peaceful."

Bipinbabu also wrote that these were indeed the honest opinions of Surendranath. So what was the purpose of secret societies? For solving puzzles? Bipinbabu explains-

"Between 1875-1878 after Surendranath's lecture on Mazzini's Young Italy, young men (in Bengal) formed a number of secret societies, though without any revolutionary motive or plan of secret assassinations as the way to national emancipation. Surendranath was himself, I think, the president of quite a number of these secret societies. These societies had no plan or policy of political action to liberate their people from British yoke. They only gave a philip to patriotism. They never seriously meant to rise in revolt against the British. They practically did nothing and passed away like a fashion. (page 248) "

In the first part of my autobiography I reviewed the situation in Bengal and remarked that till 1895 there was no revolutionary movement there. Above information does not invalidate that statement. Of course one must say that the seeds that Surendranath had sowed did bear fruit some twenty-five years later. Though not intended by him, Bengal became a hot bed of fervent revolutionaries, which surpassed all the secret societies mentioned by Bipinbabu. But that was later on.

Having seen what effect Mazzini's biography had on Surendranath Banerjee, Pal and others of Bengal, let us now see its effect in Punjab by examining life of Lala Lajpat Rai. We already saw how he did not take any interest in politics till he was in his late thirties. Shortly before the establishment of the

Indian National Congress, Surendranath had started a National League in Bengal. In 1884, he went to Punjab to explain its work. He also spoke on Mazzini and his Young Italy.

Lala Lajpat Rai attended that speech and he was deeply impressed by Mazzini's life. He too became determined to liberate India from the yoke of the British. He says so in his autobiography. Later he studied Mazzini's life in detail, and he wrote a biography of Mazzini in Urdu to inspire the youth and to encourage them to start working on the lines of young Italians of the time of Mazzini and Garibaldi.

In Maharashtra, the revolutionary spirit was present ever since 1857, but people there learnt about Mazzini much later than Bengal. Anti-British revolutionary movement was already deeply rooted. Those feelings were not to be imported from outside. From the heroes of 1857 war, revolutionaries of Maharashtra to the members of Abhinav Bharat, our sources of inspiration were Shree Ram, Shree Krishna and Shivaji. The deeds of these national heroes were being taught with the hidden message of revolt. Despite Vasudev Balwant Phadake (1879-83) and Chaphekar (1897), Maharsahtra did no know much of Mazzini. A far as I can remember, first biography of Mazzini was written by one Mr. Ghanekar in 1900. Mr. S M Paranjape in his paper Kal also wrote histories of various freedom movements in modern Europe. He did write an article about Young Italy movement of Mazzini. I realized that works of Ghanekar and Paranjape would be useful in inspiring our youth and there was a strong parallel between situations in Italy and India. I had delivered several lectures on Mazzini. I had read a biography of Mazzini in English and had realized that Mazzini's autobiography and a collection of his articles, translated into English, were available. I was therefore very curious to read those and my desire was fulfilled when Mr. Mukherjee provided all the six parts I had asked for.

I Decide to Translate Mazzini's Work into Marathi

As I studied Mazzini's works I realized that the revolutionary tactics that I had preached to my friends, were remarkably similar to those proposed by Mazzini for Italian Revolutionaries. Secret societies must work on two fronts: Propaganda and Action.

Some work has to be done in secret and some in the open. It is impossible to regain independence without resorting to force of arms. However, it is also essential to carry out propaganda by peaceful means to prepare the masses for their part in the revolution.

It is essential to join forces with the enemies of Britain in Asia and Europe and sympathetic elements in America. Guerrilla tactics must be used to attack British sources of power, its centres, its officers; individually and in groups, to induce Indians employed by British such as soldiers to rise in revolt, to rise whenever there was a war between Britain and other foreign power, to carry out revolutionary activities one after the other-that was my plan of action.

And I used to argue my case in open but still keeping within the legal limits. I was surprised to find that Mazzini had followed the same path for liberation of his country. It bolstered my confidence hundred times.

I realized that if my friends and followers were to read Mazzini's articles that will increase their faith in our methods enormously. That was obvious. In 1906, I and my colleagues in Abhinav Bharat were hardly twenty to twenty two years of age. Our leaders, both Moderates and Militants dismissed our activities as 'childish'. They were the leaders of our society at that time. But then Mazzini and his fellow revolutionaries were similarly ridiculed as 'childish' and 'absurd' by contemporary elders in Italian society in 1830s. Mazzini had replied to such ridicule in his articles. The funny thing was that in 1906 persons like Mazzini and Garibaldi were regarded as 'great patriots' by Indian leaders without realizing that in their days Mazzini and Garibaldi too were being branded as 'foolhardy' and 'childish'.

Mazzini's articles were going to make firm our plans of action and induce faith among people of India in our methods. I was therefore determined to translate Mazzini's thoughts in Marathi.

The Method that I Adopted

But if those revolutionary thoughts were to be widely read in Marathi, I had to do this within the framework of existing laws. There were only two ways in which this could be done. Either follow the path of Surendranath who had not published Mazzini's biography or his articles, he merely delivered lectures. But even then at the end of his lectures he used to emphasise that though Mazzini's armed revolution had proved to be successful in case of Italy, we Indians must never adopt those methods, as they would be ruinous to India.

But to say that, would have been disastrous. After all I wanted people of Maharashtra to study and follow the revolutionary path of Mazzini. That was the purpose of my book. Path of Surendranath was totally unsuitable for me.

Second path was to translate Mazzini's autobiography and articles as they were and keep them in front of the readers. But I had to go one step forward. My book was not just worth reading as History, or just a readable work. I wanted to emphasise that people should follow Mazzini's example. Otherwise ordinary people would not have got the message. I therefore decided to add a preface to show parallels between Italy and India, add some suggestive lines that the readers would be thrilled and inspired to carry out armed revolution in India also.

With this intention, as soon as I completed studying all the six parts I rapidly started to translate the works in Marathi. I had to write Newsletters for Kal and Vihari papers, conduct my propaganda and look after my correspondence.

Still within about two and half months I completed my translation, which ran into some 300 pages. I added a 25-page preface to it. On the front page I put up-London, India House

Date 28 September 1906.

I completed the task of the translation, but publishing it was no easy task. I turned to my elder brother Babarao, in India. He always had to face more than half the burden of our activities but if any name was to be made and publicity was given I always benefited. Such was the division of responsibility and fame or credit. The police were already keeping a close watch on my elder brother Babarao. He received no support. Finally he approached Tilak who advised-Remember it is risky to publish such works and decide your line of action. Babarao had difficulty in finding a printer. Finally members of Abhinav Bharat had some influence with Jagadahitechhu printers who agreed to print. Babarao wanted to sell copies of the book before the police woke up.

Therefore an advertisement was put in papers promoting pre-publication sale. There was a queue of subscribers. He also wanted to show that Abhinav Bharat was not a revolutionary organization but a legal organization. He therefore had already published a series called-Laghu Abhinav Bharat Mala. It contained Sinhagadacha Powada, Baji Phabhu's Powada, (both composed by me), Afzalkhan's assassination Powada by Govind Kavi. (Powada means a Ballad) Another series was declared under the name Thorali Abhinav Bharat Mala and its first publication was my biography of Mazzini and his politics. The price of this 300-page book was kept at 1 ½ rupees. It was dedicated to Lokamanya Tilak, editor of Kesari and to Lokamanya Paranjape, editor of the paper Kal.

RAJAMANYA VS. LOKAMANYA

I need to explain the term Lokamanya. As I remember, it used to be customary to use the title Rajmanya Rajashree before surname to honour an elderly relative or a public figure. Mr. Paranjape had written a provocative article about it in Kal. One could not imagine what subjects he would choose to incite the public. He argued, " When we were independent and had our own kings it was indeed an honour to address some one as Rajamanya or Rajashree. But where is our kingdom today? We are all slaves of foreigners. It is therefore insulting to call some a Rajamanya or Rajashree. We should address each other as Deshbandhu (Patriot Brother). And when it comes to our leaders such as Tilak who bear the brunt of the rule of foreigners, we should call them Lokamanya-or people's leader. That would be most appropriate.

This suggestion of Mr Paranjape was so popular that overnight the youngsters dropped the initial words Ra Ra (Rajamanya Rajeshree) in their correspondence, in speeches and in articles. They used the title Deshbandhu before a person's name to address or mention him just as we use Shree before a person's surname today. Tilak became Lokamanya Tilak not only in Maharashtra but also all over India. That became his permanent title.

Why was the Book Dedicated to Both?

I had decided to dedicate the book to Mr. Paranjape because I was drawn to Mazzini by the articles on him published in the paper Kal. Moreover he had become a source of inspiration among the revolutionaries. If we could increase his prestige, it would also increase ours. We held Tilak with deep respect; we had deep affection for Paranjape too. So we titled them both Lokamanya. I was going to dedicate my book to Paranjape for articles which appeared in Kal and the personal encouragement I received from him and he had already agreed to this. But we felt that first honour should go to Tilak. So, I wanted to dedicate the book to both. When my elder brother sought Tilak's advice on publishing the book he said that it was risky to do so. I therefore was not sure if he would like the book to be dedicated to him. Would it not be a great hindrance to his activities?

If I was to dedicate to Paranjape alone some mischievous group would have commented, 'Look. These revolutionaries do not have much respect for Tilak.' In the end my elder brother Babarao approached Tilak who said, "You do what you like. I am not opposed to it." The problem was then solved. I dedicated the book to Lokamanya Tilak of Kesari and to Lokamanya Paranjape of Kal.

I sent the manuscript in December 1906 and the book was published in June 1907. People were so anxious that the 2,000 copies were sold out within a month. Still the book was in demand. Many asked for their copies to be reserved when the second edition would be printed. It was a record in book selling. Many papers gave favourable comments. There were editorials in Vihari and Kesari. Article in Kal (see below) reflected public reaction closely. I therefore quote form it.

"Patriot Savarkar is well known to Marathi readers. His enthusiasm, fierce patriotism, superb articles and oratory have made him well known. Having passed his B.A examination from Bombay University he had recently left for England to study to become a Barrister."

"Though he has gone abroad, he has not forgotten his country, his people and his language for one moment. It is persons like him who should be going abroad. He was not impressed by the large buildings, big factories and enormous wealth of England, but he has been all the time thinking of uplifting our country from slavery and to progress it to the level of advanced countries. If we send more persons like him abroad our country will benefit, because like roots of a tree, they absorb what is beneficial to our country."

"Savarkar has written this book in Marathi, while staying in London, heart of English language. This is probably the first literary work, which was written in London for the benefit of our people."

"There is a wonderful conflux of three-Mazzini's articles devoted to the goddess of freedom, its translation by Savarkar in the free atmosphere of England, and the anxious readers in Maharashtra. This is bound to relieve us from all the pain."

"These articles by Mazzini are streams of nectar. Like the Mantras of Vedas, they have tremendous power. If recited many times in a systematic way, they can cure any serpent bite. ..... One cannot thank Mr. Savarkar enough for making these articles available. Those who can read must study such works of literature. Those who cannot read can still benefit, if someone reads it out for them. We believe that recitation of Bhagatwat Geeta every day gives us salvation. Mazzini's articles also have similar powers."

I had already said that my preface was written to stay within the Law. So many things were implied, but still the readers got the message. I am aware that it will not have the same effect in today's circumstances. Here are those passages:

Mazzini asks, "Oh, priests, were you not born in our motherland? Did you not grow up here? So, how can you go to heaven when we are suffering from slavery? True religion is not in your camps but ours. If you want Religion to succeed join our fight. Religion and politics are intertwined and cannot be separated. If 20 million of our fellow countrymen arise to regain our freedom, they will defeat not only one Austria but three Austrias combined together."

Now, this is what Mazzini was sure of achieving with only 20 million of Italians. What would he have said if his people amounted to ten times that figure and the numerical strength of his Enemy remained the same? He would have achieved his freedom in no time.

Mazzini asks, "Italy is being ruled by Austria. 75,000 Austrian soldiers are controlling us. We have become a slave market. Whatever little princely states had remained have become puppets of Austrians. Italy has become a big prison guarded by Austrian soldiers. Our name has become extinct. We have no national flag. Do you think you will regain your freedom by begging? Austrians have enslaved us not for releasing us by mere petitions!"

Countries enslaved by foreigners resort to the begging bowl (asking for leniency from rulers etc.). Italians were no exception, but they abandoned that path. Italy knew that hundreds of years of slavery and thousands of broken promises were the stark reality of life. 'Loyalty to foreign rule' would lead to nothing. There were revolutions happening in Poland and Spain. This had affected Italians. True, there are countries in the world, which do not take inspiration from events in neighbouring countries (such as bloodbaths to achieve their freedom). But Italy was not that thick.

Swadeshi movement began in earnest in Italy. Students boycotted Austrian Tobacco. They set up roadblocks. Anyone found to be smoking Austrian Tobacco was beaten up. This movement soon led to political movement. This had also happened during American war of Independence (1776-83). History repeats itself. Swadeshi implies putting a break on foreign exploitation of one's country. Ordinary people do not appreciate freedom struggle, but they do understand how foreign trade affects their livelihood. They therefore join in the Swadeshi movement. As soon as the interests of ruling foreign power are threatened they resort to suppression.

Then ordinary people realize that it is not the boycott of foreign goods that is the issue. Those goods are inert. Therefore it is no use getting angry at those goods. Real anger should be aimed at the foreign power. It is not the Austrian Tobacco; it is the Austrian rulers that need to be driven out. It is not Tea; it is the English that need to be thrown out. Thus it is no use begging. In the end one has to resort to force of arms to achieve independence. Though most people come to that conclusion they are not sure how that can be achieved.

Mazzini says, "There is no alternative but to resort to secret societies. If truth can be openly told, it would be a crime to resort to secret societies and secret plots, but where propagation of truth has been forbidden by a foreign ruling power, when the whole country is a vast prison, secret societies are sacrosanct. Nay, that is the only path left. It is our divine right to establish secret societies. When the time comes we will break open the prison doors and start breathing again. Most European nations had resorted to this method to achieve their independence.

With secret societies people can be easily induced to fight for freedom, but the same is impossible through articles in newspapers or public speeches. Even if we use 'implied meaning' in our articles or preaching, people not being clever enough do not appreciate our stand. With secret societies, we can openly preach fighting for our freedom. Moreover, mere propaganda is not enough. Action plans are needed and obviously these cannot be discussed in the open." Therefore Mazzini started his secret society-Young Italy. They had twin programme of educating people, teaching them the need for liberation from slavery, unity, equality, principles of democracy, and teaching of military tactics, all these were taught.

Independence can never be won without a fight. But it had become impossible in Italy. Italians had no arms and were not allowed to hold any. Under these circumstances any other country would have been frightened, but not Italy. Her brave youth went to Spain, America, Germany and Poland and learned how to fight.

Thus, Garibaldi, Vicioty and others became military experts. Their secret societies purchased arms and sent shipments of them. Sometimes these did come to light. For example, once Mazzini's French sympathizer loaded a ship full of arms. But it was caught on the high seas before it could reach the shores of Italy. Such misfortunes are bound to occur in a great fight. Those who are scared of such events stay enslaved, but brave men face such disasters and win their independence.

Another ploy employed by Italians was to bring Italian soldiers to their side. No foreign power can rule other country without the help of native soldiers. If these could be turned to the side of freedom fighters, it has two advantages-The foreign rulers lose faith in native soldiers and panic. Moreover, trained and armed soldiers become available for the freedom struggle. .... When this stage is reached, you resort to guerrilla tactics. Mazzini says-"for this action, the freedom fighters do not need sophisticated military training. Fighting can start when enough fighters are ready and determined. They learn by experience, as the war progresses. With guerrilla tactics, there is no danger of facing large-scale defeats. Guerrillas can also move freely."

With the establishment of secret societies there was always at least one rebellion every year, right from 1831 to 1870. Italians faced many defeats, but they kept on fighting. Mazzini stated, "Every failure is one more step to success." There was defeat in 1820, in 1831, in 1848-every time Mazzini said-"try once more."

In Rome, in 1848, Italians were fighting French soldiers. Garibaldi took part in the fight. Suddenly he was called by the War Council. When he arrived, he was given a standing ovation. He could not understand why. Then he looked at himself and realized that his clothes were torn by passing bullets or sword marks. His sword was so bent that he could not put it back in its sheath. We salute such sword. As long as there is one such sword in the world, enslaved people have hope of regaining their independence. Later on, fighting ensued between France, Austria and Germany. France and Austria both enemies of Italians were facing life threatening crisis, Italy erupted in armed rebellion and in 1859 half of Italy was liberated. In 1866 Venice was liberated, in 1870 Rome was free and Mazzini entered the gates of Rome. Mazzini who was imprisoned in Savona in 1831 now entered Rome as Italy's liberator. Can anyone draw these two pictures side by side?

Within a year Mazzini died. Thousands of Italians lined streets for last glimpse of their great hero. Many cried. God has given a Mazzini to every country. Therefore no one should envy Italy. These are extracts from my preface to Mazzini's biography. Now I quote some of Mazzini's thoughts expressed in his articles: "Youth of my country, love our motherland. This is the land of your forefathers and therefore your own land. This is the place where you first heard your mother's lovely and caring voice. This is where you too first spoke your words. This land has been given to you by God. You should be proud of it. Devote everything you have even your blood for the motherland. Lead it to a better life. Make sure that you do not in any way demote it. Make sure that it becomes free. Our country must remain one. It must not be divided. God has given us the Alps on one side and the sea on the other to guard our land. Today it has been blotted with slavery. Let no one sleep in this state easily. Be determined to liberate our motherland."

"You love mankind. Our country is your cradle and whole mankind is your mother. Other countries too are trying to free themselves of foreign rule. Help them as much as you can. Believe in Humanity. Make sacrifices for your aim in life. Don't despair by hardships or misery. Life is not for pleasure but for performing your duty."

"Once you are determined to uphold your freedom, dignity of your nation and of humanity, then you must fight for these values. You must fight incessantly and for all your life. You must fight with any arms you can get hold of. You must be prepared to face hatred and ridicule. You must consider all obstacles as minor. Don't worry about any fruits your efforts may bear. Just do your duty." "Our first aim is to seek liberation from the yoke of Austria and France.

Secondly we will seek to unite our country. At present it has been fragmented into many tiny states. We will not be able to maintain freedom if the fragments remain. Therefore we must seek unification of all Italy.

Our third aim is Democracy. If any Prince is guaranteeing our freedom and unity, I will bow to him and abandon progress to democracy. I have said so publicly. Not only that I appeal that Democrats and Monarchists should unite first to liberate our country from the yoke of Austrians."

I had only translated those parts of Mazzini's thoughts that would be useful to our readers in Bombay province. After all, I had limitations of size of my book (300 pages). However, I had translated one chapter fully. Mazzini's secret society-Young Italy became known to authorities and was no longer a secret. This led to tremendous upheaval. Soldiers who had taken part in rebellions and members of Young Italy were arrested all over Italy. Many broke down under torture by the Police. Many committed suicide for fear of not withstanding physical torture and betraying their comrades. They considered death to be more honourable than betrayal of their comrades. Lives of hundreds of families were ruined. Many were hanged. Many were shot dead. Many went into exile-had little money or resources for survival. This applied to even Mazzini and Garibaldi.

I had described those terrible events in details. There was a purpose behind this.

By 1907/08, branches of Abhinav Bharat had spread to Marathawada on the east and Gwalior on the north. Many revolutionary groups were springing up all over the country. I used to stress to my members-"You are getting excited by the idea of achieving our freedom. But remember what lies ahead. We must be aware of terrible difficulties that lie in our way." I had given them examples from revolutions in various countries. I knew that at one stage even Mazzini was on the point of becoming insane. He had confessed to this.

I, and many Indian revolutionaries often said:

We were of course aware of these dangers.

We have undertaken this duty not lightly or blindly.

We know that it is a fiery ordeal.

We have deliberately set up on this course.

Time and again I used to stress-"Before taking oath of Abhinav Bharat, understand what it implies. Become our member only if you have the courage to stand the dangers. Otherwise join the Militants or Moderates. They too are patriots at the lower stage of our struggle for freedom."

My book was not a novel, but it was widely welcomed by the people. This shows how the background that we had prepared just a few years earlier had borne fruits. At times, the earth is parched and as soon as rains start, the earth absorbs all the water. In a similar manner the book was received by people of Bombay province. Copies were paraded through streets, as if it was a religious book. Secret police report says that each copy was read by twenty to twenty five youth. Many parents asked their children to learn by heart my Preface. Revolutionaries like Mr. Kelkar have testified to this.

Of course, this was not going to go unnoticed by the British Authorities. Before they decided to take action all the copies of the first edition were sold out. There was advertisement about the second edition in newspapers. The authorities suddenly decided to act. According to law, they had two options. They could prosecute the writer, publisher and printer for sedition and then confiscate the book. But then, they were not sure of success. I had taken extreme care not to be caught in any Law in India. I had simply translated Mazzini's biography and his thoughts. Nowhere did I preach rebellion against the British Rule in India. There was no mention of enslavement of India at all. So, the authorities were not sure that a case in court of Law would succeed. They therefore decided to proscribe the book. There was a notification in Government Gazette. Thus, I saved the publisher and printer from prosecution but not the book.

As soon as the order to proscribe the book was passed, there were searches everywhere. Houses, shops and persons were extensively searched. People too were determined to hide copies of the book. At times the papers published news of confiscation of copies by the police in such a tone as to ridicule their work.

In some cases, copies were hidden in the recesses of walls, which were bricked and plastered over. At times they were hidden in compartments in old wells. Police did find four to five hundred copies but the rest were preserved by the people for more than 40 years and they were secretly read. Later, as members of Abhinav Bharat were prosecuted, existence of this book was considered as evidence of the person being a revolutionary.

Many people agitated for the removal of ban on the book. They quoted from the book in open meetings and thus broke the law and went to jail for it. But the British did not lift the ban.

Some thirty years later we were granted Provincial Autonomy by Government of India Act 1935. Congress party formed ministries in seven major provinces. But even they did not lift ban on this book.

For they too, like the British, did not want to support an armed revolution. So, the Congress Ministers were keen to maintain the ban. The astonishing fact was that many of these ministers and their followers were members of Abhinav Bharat and taken inspiration from our activities and had recited our poems. They also included followers of Mr M N Roy (a Humanist), Socialists and Communists. But apart from members of Hindu Mahasabha, others did not support lifting of the ban.

Time marched on. Forty years after the book was published, we once again had Congress Ministry in Bombay province, after the Second World War. Its Chief Minister was one Mr Balarao Kher, who was once a member of Abhinav Bharat. At long last, in 1946, he lifted the ban on the book. It was only then that it became possible to publish the second edition. But that was possible only because the public had preserved copies of the first edition defying the Government ban. I was lucky enough to preside over the publishing ceremony of the second edition.

Mazzini, Garibaldi, Victor Emmanual and Cavour

As my book was on Mazzini, I had mentioned his work. However, there were three other personalities who must be mentioned. They too had influenced my thoughts. Mazzini was the philosopher warrior. Garibaldi was the general who fought the battles. But it was not just the revolutionaries who liberated Italy from the yoke of Austria and France. Almost all the princely states had accepted suzerainty of Austria.

Only the tiny state of Piedmont was left free. Its position was similar to that of Nepal today. But its King Victor Emanuel dared to take on the role of leadership of the Italian revolutionaries, openly. It was agreed that whatever province was liberated by the revolutionaries, will become part of Piedmont State. For this adventure, he had to fight against the Austrians. Had he been defeated he would have lost even his tiny state. But he decided to wage his entire fortune, having had the ambition of becoming King of whole of Italy. In the end the tide turned in his favour and armies of France and Austria were driven out of Italy. And in Rome, Victor Emanuel was crowned 'King of Italy'. Though the King deserves full credit, his Prime Minister Count Cavour was equally responsible for the turn of events. He obtained sympathy of England and other European nations and also their help in secret. Moreover, he isolated Austria and France and got them engaged in other wars. His diplomacy too was an important factor in the victory of Italian revolutionaries.

Therefore we salute Mazzini, Garibaldi, Victor Emmanuel and Count Cavour as the heroes of Italian freedom struggle.

When I studied Mazzini's political thoughts, I also studied biographies of others and read extensively books on history of the Italian freedom struggle.

Travelin has written a biography of Garibaldi, I read biography of Cavour. An English lady had written a wonderful book entitled Liberation of Italy (I do not remember her name)

These four Italians had become the source of our inspiration, which infused in us the ability to fight, provided enthusiasm for a long struggle, efficiency and direction not only to us the revolutionaries, but also to the Indian leaders like Surendranath Banerjee and countless other educated Indians. I therefore pay my sincerest homage to their memory.

After Italy was liberated, an Englishman (possibly Meredith) composed a small poem to commemorate the victory. He says:

Italia, to vindicate thy name
Mazzini, Cavour, Garibaldi three.
Thy Soul, thy Brain, thy Sword, they set thy free
From ruinous discord with one lustrous aim!!
- May He bless Thee and them!!

——————

Note -Mazzini lived in London (185 North Gower Street London N.W1) from 1837 to 1848 when he was in exile. In 1950, commemorative plaque was fixed on this house, by the Greater London Council (GLC) in his memory.

7

Writing of Indian War of Independence 1857

FREE INDIA SOCIETY

Before leaving for London, I had outlined my possible work there. I had already started the secret society-Abhinav Bharat. In London I started organizing our youth, started to inspire them and convert them to the revolutionary path by individual dialogue. I delivered public speeches. I was busy with writing my books. I was in search of bombs and other explosives and also arranging training for how to use them. I started all such activities. I started Free India Society for works, which could be carried out openly. We will deal with this society later in detail. One of the activities was 'weekly meetings' of Indians. I used to deliver at least one lecture at such meetings and talk about Mazzini-life and mission, heroes of the Indian War of independence 1857 and also discuss what we could do to free our country. While discussing Mazzini's life I used to emphasise, how he established his secret society-Young Italy, how he induced Italian soldiers employed by Austrian rulers to join in the freedom struggle, how he took help from people of various princely states in Italy to liberate the country. I would stress that we Indians also could do the same.

Many thought an Armed Revolution was Impossible

But most elderly and young men did not accept my thoughts, though based firmly on history. They argued, "How can you compare Italy with Hindusthan? Italy was one of the advanced countries of Europe. Winds of freedom were flowing through the rest of Europe, whose countries were free. The small princely states did have their own small armies, and the Italians did have arms like their rulers, Austria and France. The country was eager to gain independence. Therefore efforts of Mazzini, Garibaldi and others did succeed."

Later, those sceptical men would ask-"In contrast to Italy, where are the necessary arms for us to fight? How can we face the rifles and guns of the British? Indian soldiers under the command of the British are illiterate, mercenaries and loyal to the British. They would never rebel against the English. Moreover, the Indian masses are disarmed. So, how can we try an armed revolution in India? Your dream is a mirage. It will never become a reality."

These Indian students who attended our meetings in London were intelligent and selected few. Their line of thinking was the same as mentioned above. Of course, their questions and doubts were not new to me. Whenever I met young and old in India in Nasik, Pune, Bombay or other places, they had reacted in the same way and told me that armed revolution was totally impracticable, impossible, laughable and even suicidal.

I replied firmly-"The arms being borne by Indian soldiers under the British command are our arms. True, our Indian soldiers are illiterate, but they too must have some desire to make our country independent. Spread the fire of movement for freedom among them and see how the same soldiers turn against the English with the same arms and ammunitions!"

THE EXAMPLE OF 1857

I was firm on my stand and wanted to write a detailed, fully supported by evidence and inspiring account of the 1857 war. As soon as I completed my works on Mazzini, I started to gather information. I was interested to know what the contemporary British personalities had recorded. Once again I approached Mr. Mukherjee who had helped me with works of Mazzini. I said to him, " Can you please search for any books on the great revolt of 1857 in India? I will buy them if required. I intend to wrote a book on the subject." He was an elderly and experienced man. He used to attend my lectures under the auspices of Free India Society. He had even taken the oath of Abhinav Bharat. After some thought he said, "I believe I have seen a book by Mr Kaye. It is probably in our library. I will find it in a day or two." Accordingly he found the book and gave it to me. He had no idea what was in the book, as he had not read it. At that time, most Indians were ignorant of the fact that the armed revolution of 1857 was a great attempt by our soldiers to overthrow the English rule. On the contrary, many were under the impression that our soldiers made a great mistake by their uprising, they massacred innocent English women and children and they violated English women. They thought that the rebellious Indian soldiers were indeed brutes and a blot on our history, a disgrace to our culture. Their mutiny had harmed us considerably. The hard working and kindhearted English government was leading us to the path of progress. Now these stupid, ignorant, fanatical soldiers have created a great obstacle in our path. Therefore most educated Indians did not attach any importance to this great event.

Mr Mukherjee handed me the book The History of the Indian Mutiny by Sir John William Kaye and commented, "what's in that book? Why do you want to read it?" His question was true as far as the book that he gave me was concerned. When I read it I too thought, 'is that all to that war? What am I going to write about it? There was no information of any great battles, no inspiring account of our heroes. It contained some details of rebellions for sons of Tipu Sultan and other minor skirmishes. There was brief mention of 1857 war, but no mention of Nanasaheb, Tatya Tope, Rani Laxmibai, Maulavi Ahmad Shah and others. I was utterly frustrated with the thought that the war might have been just a minor affair. At last I found an important note on the last page. It said-There are five more volumes of this, which includes the works of Mr Malleson and therefore the entire works are entitled Indian Mutiny by Kaye and Malleson. I was surprised and showed that note to Mr Mukherjee and requested him, 'Please obtain those volumes, even if you have to go to a thief's market. You have been living here for some years and know a lot of people and markets. You are the only one who can help.' He was touched and within a week he obtained all the six volumes for me.

As I read them the whole picture unfolded in front of me. The battles were extensive; there were mentions of deeds of our heroes, Nanasaheb, Tatya Tope, Rani Laxmibai of Jhansi, Maulavi Ahmadshah, Veer Kuvarsingh of Bihar and others. I could imagine their bravery and audacity. Of course, since the volumes were written by English authors, Kaye and Malleson, they were not unbiased accounts. On the contrary, they cursed our heroes on every page, but even then it provided details of how extensive and widespread the revolt was. Moreover, it provided me with another important piece of information. There was an extensive bibliography at the end of the six volumes. From this, I gathered that there was huge literature on the subject. Once again I was determined to find it.

INDIA OFFICE LIBRARY AND RECORDS

I showed the bibliography to Mr. Mukherjee and said, " I am deeply interested in studying all the books mentioned in the Bibliography. My research work will be completed only if I read all the relevant references. Can you show me a way forward?" He said that he would try. He made some enquiries and in just a few days told me -'India Office' which controls affairs of India from London has an excellent library. It contains extensive papers relating to the 1857 war and also has books published after the works of Kaye and Malleson. But entry is difficult. One needs references from well known persons."

I was in a fix. It was nearly impossible to get references from Shyamji and other Indian leaders, because they too believed that the war of 1857 was a revolt of religiously fanatic and barbarian Indian soldiers and that it was a suicidal interruption. Moreover, Shyamji and others were seeking more power to Indian people and therefore not 'Loyal' subjects. So, references from them would be of no use. Once again I turned to Mr. Mukherjee. He had been living in London for a number of years, was married to an English woman and had a son by her. He was Indian, but his wife was white. He was working as Manager of India House and his wife was a teacher. He had English acquaintances. He obliged, went to India Office library, found out the rules and regulations, obtained the necessary references for me and I got my reader's pass. I had warned Mr. Mukherjee not to speak about my real purpose in going to India Office library. With that precaution, I did not have much difficulty in getting my pass.

** This was located inside office of the Secretary of state for India, now Foreign and Commonwealth Office. It is now part of British Library on Euston Road, London N.W1*

I was Surprised by Tenacity and Discipline of the English

As soon as I got letter of admission form India Office Library, I went there with Mr. Mukherjee. The librarian saw letter that I had received. I told the librarian that I wished to write a book on the events of 1857 and would therefore like to read relevant books. The librarian took to the area where the books on 1857 war and relevant files, properly indexed, were kept. I could not believe that all these related to 1857. So, I asked the librarian, "Can you please show me only those parts which are related to 1857." He replied, "All this area is full of sins of the Indian sepoys." At heart, I was furious at this remark. But I was also assured that all the papers were relating to 1857. At one time I had difficulty in getting even one book on the subject and now I was surprised at the extensive information available. I was overwhelmed by excellent skills of collection and preservation of historical documents of the English Administrators. I talked to the librarian about seating arrangements and rules and regulations and left.

The Librarian was Outwitted

The next day I reached the library at 11 o'clock. I browsed through the list of books and files. The librarian told me, which of those were of importance and asked me to read them first. I started my study in earnest. I was so engrossed that I neglected my legal studies for some time. The librarian was surprised by my studious nature and sincerity of my efforts. Whatever information I asked for he would provide. At times he would come to my desk and had discussions with me. He used to say how the Indian mutineers were disloyal sepoys. They were religious fanatics, barbarians and demons, how they mercilessly killed English women and children and created a reign of terror, bloodbath and loot and despite these deeds, they were finally defeated. He tried to create disgust and hatred in my mind about the brave soldiers, Princes and others who took part in fighting. He hoped that a young studious man like me would write a book on 1857, Indians would feel disgusted about those soldiers and their revolt. I used to listen to him quietly and never revealed my true intentions, because I wanted to gain his confidence and get as much information as possible. I got his full confidence, so much that he showed me many secret documents-discussions in British Parliament, secret letters sent by British Civil and Military officers, speeches by leaders of opposition leaders. These papers were not normally available to British readers. I was therefore able to judge what persons of various political persuasions thought of the war.

Of course, I could not find a single (so called) unbiased British writer, who would praise the efforts of Indian soldiers, who were fighting for their religion and country and wanted to overthrow a foreign rule. I found information on how and where the war was fought, how it spread, what were the reactions of British soldiers, citizens and public leaders. I was convinced that in 1857, Indian soldiers, princes and general public of various provinces came together and fought a tenacious, pre-planned war to overthrow the rule of the (English) East India Company. It did not succeed, but gave a big jolt to the British Empire. It did not hinder our progress, but left a guide for similar action in future. That was the outline of my book.

I was Banned from India Office Library

On the one hand, I was studying in India Office Library and on the other; I was talking about the 1857 war in the secret meeting being held in India House. I used to explain the heroic deeds of our heroes of 1857 and induce the youth to try a similar uprising in future and be ready for self-sacrifice. I also used to write my book on 1857 war. In May 1908, I arranged celebration of the 50th anniversary of that war, in India House. That was reported in my newsletters published in contemporary paper Kal. British Secret Service had infiltrated our organisation and the Indian traitor must have told the authorities how explosive my book was going to be. He also smuggled parts of the manuscript of my book. The British Secret Service was alarmed and warned the Librarian at India Office Library that I should not be admitted to the library. He was stunned and informed me accordingly. Once again I was in a dilemma. I had nearly completed my book in Marathi and quoted references extensively. But I wanted to confirm some pieces of information. So, I entrusted this work to Mr V V S Iyer, who was my friend in confidence, He had taken the oath of Abhinav Bharat from me. He was not known to the British C I D and therefore could finish this task successfully.

The Work was Completed but...

Thus, I completed my work Indian War of Independence 1857. We spent thousands of rupees and sent copies to many countries. Many suffered for this adventure. Many editions were later published as below. The British Administration in India banned this book in 1909. The ban was lifted 37 years later when India achieved independence and the true story was told under the title-The story of the History. And was published by Mr. G M Joshi.

English Translation

Members of Abhinav Bharat in London decided to translate the book into English. This was done by Mr Koregavkar (who later turned government witness against Savarkar), Mr Phadake and Mr Kunte.

It was of course impossible to print the book in England, so attempts were made in France. But the French were afraid of Germans and would not support anti-British activity. (In 1904, the French had signed a Treaty of Friendship with Great Britain)* So, Savarkar's friends tried German printers. Surprisingly enough, they too declined. However, they introduced Savarkar to a Printer in Holland where it was eventually printed and published. Savarkar kept on saying that the book was being printed in France to hoodwink the British C I D.

The Times reported on 11 August 1909, " The mail from India brings the following notification issued at Simla on July 23-' In exercise of the power conferred by section 19 of the Sea Customs Act 1878 (viii of 1878) the Governor-General is pleased to prohibit the bringing by sea or land into British India of any copy of the book or pamphlet in Marathi on the subject of the Indian Mutiny by Vinayak Damodar Savarkar or any English translation or version of the same."

However, in England there was no ban on Savarkar's book, and The School of Oriental and African Studies (SOAS) and India Office Library (IOL) do hold copies of the first edition. Copies of the book were available from Madam Cama at 25 Rue de Ponthieu, Champs Elysees, Paris. Price 10 Shillings.

Copies were also available from F.H Publication, 749 Third Avenue, New York. Price clothed $2, paper edition$1.50.

[Savarkar's book served as a source of inspiration to Indian revolutionaries for the next 38 years.]

Madame Cama published second edition of the book in France.

Gadr party, a revolutionary party in America published the third edition of the book. The party also published editions in Indian languages. In India, Bhagatsingh published the fourth edition secretly.

** Entente Cordiale-a friendship treaty between Britain and France was signed by British Foreign Secretary Lord Lansdowne and French Ambassador Paul Cambon in London on 8 April 1904. It ended centuries of military conflict between the two countries from Hastings to Agincourt, Trafalgar to Waterloo*

Subhashchandra Bose published one edition in Japan and another edition in Tamil was published with his blessings.

Government of India Act 1935 granted Provincial Autonomy in India and Congress Ministries came to power in seven major provinces. But Congress leaders did not lift ban on this book, as they were obsessed with nonviolence.

After the Second World War, Congress Ministries came to power again in seven major provinces of India. At long last, they yielded to popular demand and lifted ban on this book in 1946.

In 1947, while discussing Indian Independence Bill, Mr Attlee the British Prime Minister commented, " India is being granted independence because:

(1) Indian Army is no longer loyal to the British.

(2) Britain does not have enough army to hold down India by force.

Thus, Savarkar's aim of freeing India from the hands of the British was achieved.

Seventh edition in Marathi was published in 1946. It was a translation of the English version that was in circulation. Mr. Parchure published another Marathi edition, as the first one was sold out quickly.

Savarkar thought that the original Marathi manuscript must have been permanently lost. He had given it to Madame Cama in France for safekeeping. She kept it in a bank safe. However, during the First World War, it was lost. Madam Cama died in 1937. So, in January 1947 Savarkar wrote-the original Marathi manuscript has been lost. However, in November 1947 he received a letter from Ramlal Bajpayee in America. He said, "The manuscript is safe here with Dr D S Kutinho, your friend in London in 1908." In December 1947, he received similar letter from one Mr. Gohokar who was studying in Washington. On his return to India, Gohokar handed over the Marathi manuscript to Savarkar (February 1949).

But this is NOT the copy that was sent to the printers. This has notes like-'references to be added here', 'I wish to say so and so here' etc. Two or three chapters were also missing. Eventually the missing chapters were translated from English edition into Marathi and the Marathi edition was published by Mr Shankar Ramchandra (popularly called Mamarao) Date in 1965

After the lifting of ban on the book, Gujarati and Hindi translations were published. In 1967 another edition in Hindi and Malayalam was published.

Note-Who paid for the cost of publication of the English edition in Holland in 1909? In a public speech in Pune on 1 May 1938, Savarkar said that Dadasaheb Karandikar and Dadasaheb Khaparde, the lawyers working for Tilak had borne the cost. These two lawyers came to London for an appeal against Tilak's sentence of Transportation for six years.

Case of Mr. Chanderi Rao

(Note-Some light on how Savarkar carried out his work in London is thrown by the case of Chanderi Rao. The information has been taken from 'Source Material for a History of Freedom Movement in India' (collected from Bombay Government Records) Volume II 1885-1920.

Of course we need to treat evidence in such cases with caution. What is told in court of law is not the whole truth. The defendants draft their testimony because they wish their sentences to be reduced; sometimes they are forced to say certain things by the police)

CID Report

Bombay 28 January 1910-Collector of Customs wrote: *You will be interested to know that today we caught a revolutionary who had travelled on the ship s.s Sydney. His suitcase had a secret compartment. It contained a Browning Pistol, cartridges and copies of the book Indian War of Independence. On his back were leaflets of Bomb Manual, which were covered under his clothes. His shoes also carried some revolutionary leaflets.*

The person arrested is Mr Rao and he was handed over to police authorities.

Bombay 28

Deputy Commissioner of Police wrote, "I produced the accused in front of officer Mr. Drekup. He was charged with bringing into India, without license one Pistol and fifty cartridges. I had produced as evidence, reports of Mr. Larimer of the Customs and officer Mr. Fawell, and the suitcase and revolutionary literature. The accused maintained that he was innocent, as he did not know what the suitcase contained. I then said to the Deputy Commissioner that the seditious papers were tied to his back and receipt for the suitcase was also found on him. I stressed how serious the offence was and pleaded that he should be severely sentenced. He (Mr Drekup) then sentenced the accused to two years rigorous imprisonment and a fine of 500 Rupees or additional imprisonment of six months if the fine was not paid. This was the maximum permissible sentence. I then took the accused to Byculla Prison and told the Superintendent that, as further enquiries are due to be conducted, the prisoner should be kept in isolation."

Extracts from Chanderi Rao's Statement

"I was born in Erode village of Coimbatur district in 1877. My father was a landlord. He died in 1903. I was educated in Erode, Coimbatur, Trichanapalli and south Arcot. I could not pass the Matriculate examination. In 1896 I joined police force in Trichunapalli area. I also worked as jail superintendent in Insen Central Jail. I resigned and joined as a Plague Inspector in local council. I worked there till August 1909. My pay was Rs 125 plus Rs 25 house rent. I also used to get travelling expenses."

"I realized that someone who had passed English Sanitary Inspector's examination would be appointed to higher post with monthly salary from Rs 200 to 300. I therefore took six month's leave and went to England. I had saved some money during my three year's service. I borrowed Rs 1,000 from my friends, sold some of my wife's jewellery and arranged the finances. My wife used to live with me in Rangoon. I sent her and my son to her sister who used to live in Titiruvar. I was not a Nationalist and took no interest in politics. In Rangoon I was not a member of any political party." "On 23 July 1909, I travelled by the route Rangoon-Madras-Bombay and then travelled by s.s Ville de Kiotat to Marseilles and then straight to London. I had not taken any letter of introduction for my stay in England."

"One Mr V V S Iyer used to come to my residence often and discuss politics. When the question of resigning from government service arose, both Mr Iyer and Mr Swami opposed such a move. They suggested that I would be more useful to Indian revolutionaries by staying in government service."

"I was present at the political meeting at 2 Sutherland Place (London W2). The subject was-how to smuggle arms and ammunitions into India and raise an armed revolt against the English. The speakers were M/s Iyer, Rajan, Madhavrao and Gyanchand Varma. There were only six people at the meeting, one was Mr Banerjee and the other Mr Ali who was married to an English woman and lives in Sinclair Gardens."

"Second meeting was held in the house of Nitinsen Dwarakadas of 128 Holland Park (London W11). The subjects discussed were-how to fight the British with arms, how to collect money, arms, ammunitions and send them to India. I was asked to speak. I said, "public education is more important at this stage." Nitinsen rose and said in Hindusthani that I spoke foolishly. I then sat down. He then suggested means of driving the British out of India. He is not a good speaker. One Satyanand Prasad used to attend and speak at such meetings."

"Mr Savarkar was not well and was staying in a sanatorium. I met him afterwards."

"I have no idea whether arms are smuggled into India. One man does not know what the other one is doing."

"At that time both Mr Iyer and Savarkar used to live in 11 Upper Addison Gardens (London W14). After the second meeting, Mr Madhavrao took me there. I was forced to take the oath of Abhinav Bharat.* At first I refused, then they threatened me and said that one who did not listen to them has now been imprisoned in India. They were eager to enrol me, as I was in government service. They argued that in India people die of hunger, plague or other diseases. So they asked me-is it not worthwhile to die for one's motherland? In the end I gave up. The oath was as follows-

I swear by almighty God, our beloved Bharatmata and my ancestors that our nation will not gain its rightful place in the world without us gaining full independence.

Moreover, the independence is not going to be gained without the bloodshed and battles. I therefore declare that I will try my best to gain independence for my country without fearing for my life. I will stay true to this oath and should I betray it, may God strike me down.

Vande Mataram." * *Oath of Abhinav Bharat-What Mr Rao says is not true. No one was forced to take the oath. On the contrary, there was high standard to meet before being considered to become a member of Abhinav Bharat.* * *We did want our members to enter Government service.*

"I took the oath at midnight. Mr Iyer said it first and then I repeated it." "I beg the police authorities not to divulge this information about the oath and take care that it is not disclosed to anyone else. Otherwise I fear that the revolutionaries will shoot me dead."

"Mr Madhavrao then took me to Mr Iyer. There we met Mr Chattopadhya, Iyer, Banerjee and Mr Kunte-who comes from Gwalior, and gets money from the Maharaja there. Mr Iyer took me to the top floor. Now only two of us were left. He administered the oath to me. I had to take it with folded hands. If it is revealed that any un-authorised persons know about the oath, they change the words."

"As far as I know, Savarkar and Iyer are in charge of the London operations. I had to pay a sovereign (a gold coin, not in use anymore) as my contribution. I came down stairs with Mr Iyer and met others. This happened in the month of December. On 3 January I left London. I was introduced to Mr Savarkar. He said, "I am glad that you are in government service. We want persons like you.* When are you going back?" I gave him the date. I never saw him afterwards."

"When I was in London, I was asked to undertake the task of killing Mr Morley. I refused. I said that I had no wish to get hanged. I was told that I had to do this deed, otherwise I would be killed. I said that even then I would not kill Mr. Morley. It is one thing to fight a duel with pistol or sword, it is quite another to stab some one in the back. Mr Iyer and Madhavrao both were inducing me to kill Mr. Morley. Madhavrao raised this question first. I was going to see Mr. Arnold and his secretary Mrs. White for some work. Mr Madhavrao said, "Why don't you go to see Mr Morley? He lives somewhere in Hampton. Go and see him with a revolver." I did not have a revolver, Mr Madhavrao did. It was similar to the one found in my case."

"Mr Iyer then gave me a letter for Mr Tirumal Acharya in Paris. I had no idea what was in that letter. He told me that I will have to carry a suitcase with 25 pistols in a secret compartment. This was because I refused to kill Mr. Morley. On the day of my departure I left from 2 Sutherland Place. That is where Mr Iyer gave me the letter for Mr Acharya."

"From the discussions I had with Mr Iyer and Mr Madhavrao, it is quite clear that they want to kill Lord Morley and Lord Curzon. These two had been on the hit list when Dhingra killed Sir Curzon Wyllie. But at that time I was not in England. I was however told in a discussion-Lord Curzon was present at a public function attended by Dhingra whose friend pointed out to Curzon. But Dhingra could not see Curzon. I do not know who Dhingra's friend was. I also heard in London that there was a plot to kill two judges of Bombay. One being Mr Chandavarkar and the other one was the judge (Davar) who sentenced Tilak to Transportation. I do not know what happened to that plan. One more judge was on the hit list, the one who sentenced Chindabaram Pillai."

"For the next two to three years, Abhinav Bharat is going to carry out a campaign of political assassinations till total revolution is achieved in India. People are going to become seditious. High officials both civilian and in Police are going to be targeted. This will lead to general uprising. Arms will be supplied to those who will take part."

"On 4 January, I reached Paris and met Tirumal Acharya. He used to stay with a Gujarati named Govind Amin in 75 Faborg Du Temple. I stayed with them."

"On 8 January, I went to the house of Shyamji Krishnavarma. We took tea. Rana, Madame Cama, Hardayal were not present. Nitinsen was there. Shyamji requested that myself, Savarkar, Govind Amin and Satyaprasad should have dinner with him. He also said that he had promised to send 100 pistols to India and I should take 25 with me without asking any questions.* I said that it was risky. Govind Amin said that the pistols will be properly concealed so that no one will suspect. Then I agreed. I complained to Savarkar that this was a risky venture, but in the end I agreed to carry his books and pamphlets with me. Govind Amin requested me to carry one revolver for him. He said that he is going to carry revolvers to India. On 9th I was taken to the house of Madam Cama and I was forced to take oath again. Savarkar was alone with me, when I took the oath."

* *Shyamji never made such requests to any one.*

"We went downstairs. Govind Amin, Turimal Acharya, Satyanada Prasad and others were present. We took tea. I met one Mr Varma there. He is tall, slim, of fair complexion and wore glasses. I do not know his initials. They could be G.K. He had come to Paris to learn how to make bombs. I gave money for purchasing my case (trunk), that date appears on the receipt. Govind Amin took me to the shop. It was he who made all the arrangements. Cost of my case was 25 Franks. In addition, I had to pay 5 Franks extra for modifications."

"Govind Amin came to me with the case. He told what was in the secret compartment. It was probably filled in the house of Rana because the books on 1857 war are kept in that house. I was never allowed in the house of Rana, but Tirumal Acharya and Rana's son used to come and go. Most of the time, it was these two who sent books and leaflets by post. Savarkar and others told me that I should send a telegram to Rana, once I reached India safely. I was also entrusted to make observations and tell them, if any events have taken place that would lead to their arrest if they were to return to India. They all want to return within the next two to three months."

Extracts from Judgment of Nasik Conspiracy Trial

The judge says about Savarkar's activities in Europe-Let us now consider the evidence in front of us. We have testimony of the cook who worked in India House during May 1908 and February 1909,* testimony of an Engineering student* who knew Savarkar since October 1906, testimony of Mr Rao who knew

Savarkar towards the end of 1909, letters which Savarkar wrote to his friends in India, the publications which were found with him and his associates.

We found no reason to disbelieve these pieces of evidence. It amply proves that Savarkar was the leader of revolutionaries in India House. He wrote history of Indian Mutiny, which he calls War of Independence, in Marathi. It was translated into English by his colleagues in India House. He publicly celebrated anniversary of the mutiny in 1907 and 1908. He produced and circulated the leaflet-Oh Martyrs, glorifying the rebels of the Indian Mutiny. He did not stop at mere speeches and writings. He prepared Bomb manual and distributed its copies and he was in the process of doing the same. Many had reached parts of India. Two of the witnesses were given the oath of Abhinav Bharat and he told them that it has branches all over the world.

...Let us now turn to other piece of evidence. When Savarkar was arrested at London (Victoria) station on 13 March 1910, copies of the leaflet-Choose Oh Indian Princes-inciting the Princes to help the revolutionaries in overthrowing of British Raj, were found in his trunk.

* *The cook was Chaturbhuj Amin*

* *The student was Harishandra Koregavkar*

8

Savarkar's Thoughts and Theory

ASSOCIATES IN ARMED REVOLUTION SHYAMJI KRISHNAVARMA (1857-1930)

Shyamji Krishnavarma (not Shyamji Krishna Varma; his surname was Bhansali) was born on 04 October 1857 at Mandavi (Kathiavad-in Gujarat). He lost both parents by the age of 10 years. His relatives helped him to come to Mumbai for High School studies. He learnt Sanskrit in a traditional Pathshala. In 1875, he married Bhanumati, daughter of Seth Chhabildas Lallubhai (famous for Chhabildas High Schools in Mumbai). In 1876, Prof. Monier Williams (who became famous for his Sanskrit-English dictionary) visited India. He was looking for an assistant who was good in Sanskrit as well as in English. Shyamji was such a man. Shyamji organised a series of lectures in Sanskrit on behalf of Arya Samaj. Notable persons of the time like Kunte, Krishnashastri Chiplunkar, Justice Ranade and Gopalrao Deshmukh were impressed by Shyamji's scholarship. But things did not work out fast enough. Prof. Williams went back to Oxford.

Shyamji borrowed money from his father-in-law and came to England in March 1879. Prof. Monier Williams said that he had not promised any help. Shyamji then registered with Balliol College, Oxford and obtained B.A degree in 1883. When Prof. Williams realised the potential of Shyamji, he wrote a letter of recommendation to Sir Richard Temple, the Governor of Bombay province who in turn, persuaded Maharaja of Kutch to offer a scholarship of 100 pounds/ year to Shyamji. In 1881, Shyamji read a paper at the Royal Asiatic Society of Great Britain and Ireland. He emphasized that the art of writing was known in Vedic times. As a result of presenting this paper, he was elected a Member of the society.

Marquis of Harlington, the then Secretary of State for India sent Shyamji as India's representative for the fifth Oriental Congress in Berlin. Shyamji emphasized that Sanskrit was a living language. In 1883, Shyamji was sent as India's representative to the Oriental Congress, in London by the Earl of Kimberley, the then Secretary of State for India. Shyamji joined the Empire Club which had among its members former governors, governor-generals and Army Generals. He became well known to Prof. Max Mueller, Dadabhai Naoroji and former Governor General, Lord Northbrook. In 1884, Shyamji became a Barrister from the Inner Temple and returned to India in January 1885. From 1885-88, he served as Dewan (minister) of Ratlam state (salary of Rs. 700 per month plus cash of Rs. 32,000 at the end of service). From 1888-1892, he practiced as a Barrister at Ajmer. From 1892-95, Shyamji was Dewan of Udaipur (salary of Rs.1000 per month). Thereafter, from 1895-96, he served as Dewan of Junagadh state with a salary of Rs.1500 per month, when things started to go wrong. Shyamji had done a favour to an Englishman named Meconoki whom he knew in London. Shyamji used his influence and offered a suitable post to Meconoki. But he conspired against Shyamji and as the result Shyamji was dismissed from the position of Dewan of Junagadh. Shyamji was furious and fought for justice. But as soon as it was known that his fight concerned an Englishman, all the other Englishmen closed ranks and refused to listen. He appealed right up to the Secretary of State for India, but to no avail. After Shyamji's dismissal from Junagad, Maharana of Udaipur wanted him to come back as his Dewan. But Sir Curzon Wyllie who was Governor General's Agent in Rajputana refused permission. He said that Shyamji had been declared unfit to hold the office of Dewan by the British Resident at Junagadh. He cannot be appointed as Divan of Udaipur, until that Resident clears the name of Shyamji. As the British Resident himself was involved in the conspiracy to remove Shyamji, there was no chance that he would change his mind. Further details are obscure, but it seems that he did become Dewan of Udaipur.

Shyamji had burnt his fingers. He realized what the British justice meant in practice. He sought help of Tilak. However, in 1897 the two British officers Rand and Lt Ayerst, were shot dead by Chapekar brothers, for insults and humiliations suffered by the people of Pune during the recent outbreak of plague. Shyamji thought that if Tilak's house was searched by the police, they would find his letters and harass him too. He, therefore, hurriedly resigned as Dewan of Udaipur, quietly left India and came to London and purchased a house on 60, Muswell Hill Road.

On 18 February 1905, Shyamji founded Indian Home Rule Society. Indian members of the British Committee of the Congress Party were becoming disaffected with the British members of the committee. They were attracted to Shyamji's society. Among its members we find-Barrister Rana, Barrister Parekh, Dr. C M Muthu (he looked after Savarkar in Brighton), Mukundrao Jaykar, Suhrawardy and Godrej (he helped Savarkar and Cama in Paris).

Shyamji also started his monthly magazine the Indian Sociologist. It was proscribed in Britain four years later. His monthly ran from January 1905 to December 1914.

In 1905, Shyamji purchased a house on 65, Cromwell Avenue, London N6 to be used as the students' hostel. This was inaugurated as INDIA HOUSE by My Hyndman, a Scottish Socialist on 1 July 1905. Dadabhai Naoroji, Lala Lajpat Rai, Madame Cama, Mr Squelsh of the Justice paper and Mr Sweeny of the Positivist Society were present at the ceremony. (The paper Justice ran from 19 January 1884 to 22 January 1925, it was renamed Social Democrat and ran from February 1925 to December 1933. The Government of India banned the paper Justice in 1910).

In 1905, Tilak's Kesari carried an editorial about Shyamji's activities in London including his starting of the students' hostel 'India House'. In Pune, Savarkar read about Shyamji's activities in Tilak's paper Kesari. He also came across an issue of Shyamji's monthly the Indian Sociologist, which contained information about scholarships being offered by Shyamji. On the 9th, Savarkar applied for the Shivaji scholarship. Tilak gave him a reference and also assured that Savarkar had no intention of seeking government employment. On 05 May 1906, a meeting to condemn the police action at a meeting in Barisal (Bengal, now in Bangladesh) to protest the partition of Bengal was held at Shyamji's home by the Indian Home Rule Society. At this meeting, Vitthalbhai Patel (elder brother of Sardar Patel) and Bhai Paramanand were present. Dadabhai Naoroji and Gokhale were invited but did not attend. In May 1907, Shyamji left London for Paris and carried out his propaganda from there. His address was 10 Avenue Ingress, Pasey, Paris. On 01 May 1909, benchers of the Inner Temple struck Shyamji off the register of Barristers.

In 1903, Shyamji had endowed a sum of 1,000 pounds to the Oxford University in memory of philosopher Herbert Spencer who died in that year. This was returned to him in July 1909. The once venerated Sanskrit scholar had suddenly become a persona non grata because now he was seeking independence for India. Shyamji died in exile in Switzerland on 31 May 1930. His wife Bhanumati donated Shyamji's collection of Sanskrit books to the Indian Culture Institute of Sarborne University of Paris. She also donated 10,000 Swiss Francs to Geneva University and 10,000 Swiss Francs to a local hospital in memory of Shyamji. Shyamji's wife Bhanumati also died Switzerland on 22 August 1933. They were both cremated at St George Cemetery, Geneva. They had no children and like many Indian freedom fighters they never saw their beloved motherland again.

* *In August 2003, Narendra Modi, then Chief minister of Gujarat, took their ashes from Geneva to Mandavi, the birth place of Shyamji. On 15 August 2004, due to the efforts of Hemany Padhya of Milton Keynes, a plaque was placed on his house in London.*

RELIGIOUS VOWS AND OBSERVANCES

Given below is an English translation of Savarkar's assorted views on religious vows and observances.

How should vows and observances be selected? The objectives of vows and observances are self-purification, reaping the fruits of actions and obtaining blessings for the hereafter. All these objectives can be met by service to humankind. If one were to select those vows and observances which directly benefit humankind, our society and nation and which instead of reinforcing ignorance and superstition in man further his knowledge and happiness, one can obtain this-worldly fruit of benefiting our nation and humankind and at the same time obtain blessing for the hereafter by pleasing the gods. (Samaj Chitre or portraits of society, Samagra Savarkar vangmaya, Vol.2, p. 702)

Service to man is service to God : ...The righteousness of yagnas (*sacrificial fire), charity and penances stems from their ability to uphold society. Man (Nar) is the ultimate manifestation of the Divine (Narayan). Which yagna, which vow, which penance other than that of serving humankind can please the gods? (1935, Samagra Savarkar vangmaya, Vol.3, p. 338)

Advice to women: Oh women, Hinduism will live and become victorious only if this Hindu nation lives, survives and becomes victorious. Hinduism will surely die if this Hindu nation were to die, if this Hindusthan becomes ahindusthan (lit: land of the non-Hindus). If Hindu women truly wish to observe religious vows, under the present circumstances, these have to be necessarily those that directly benefit this Hindu nation.

Do such service on a regular basis! Give away riches, labour, food and if need be your honour and your very lives for this most beloved Hindu nation! That is the dharma (* righteousness) for both this world and the hereafter. Vows and observances are to be judged on this touchstone! (Samagra Savarkar vangmaya, Vol.4, p. 307)

Reinvent those vows that are based on superstitious beliefs: ...Those vows that have no material benefit and are solely popularized on the basis of Puranic fables should be reinvented and given a different form. (Samagra Savarkar vangmaya, Vol.4, p. 298)

Which vows need to be observed? ...In the present circumstances, vows should directly serve the Hindu nation or humanity. They should alleviate the sufferings of the wretched and the meek. Vows should involve physical or economic hardships and should result in direct service of the nation. These are the vows that should be observed by Hindu saints and commoners. (Ksha kirane or X rays, Samagra Savarkar vangmaya, Vol.3, p. 157)

Which vows need to be discarded? Those vows whose presiding gods and their descriptions have been rendered totally false by today's experimental science should be discarded. In ancient times, certain incidents and lifeless objects were considered as living gods purely due to the ignorance regarding the science of creation. Those vows which were popularized merely to appease such gods should be considered worthy of rejection in the present time. (Samaj chitre or portraits of society, Samagra Savarkar vangmaya, Vol.2, p. 703)

It is foolishness to say that I shall perform Satyanarayana puja if God blesses me (*Satyanarayana puja is performed by devout Hindus on any auspicious occasion, usually in the Hindu month of shravan. It is usually performed as thanksgiving for blessings received; story of Satyanarayana narrated by Sri Vishnu to the rishi Narada in the Reva khand of Sri Skandapurana)

To hope that God will do what is good for me; to say that I shall perform satyanarayana puja if God blesses me is downright silly and utterly false.

For if it is god whom we thank for saving us from a calamity, who brought that calamity upon us in the first place? The same satyanarayana, the same god! (1934, Vidnyannishtha nibandha or pro-science essays, Samagra Savarkar vangmaya, Vol. 3, p.296)

RELIGIOUS AND SOCIAL REFORM

Note: The word 'samskara' refers broadly to the deliberate and positive influences which help create deep and lasting impressions on the mind of a person so as to generate interest in him about Truth and Dharma, help bring out a positive personality and free the mind of its negativities. In this section, the word 'samskara' has been used by Savarkar to refer to the sixteen traditional Hindu samskaras. These are :

1. garbhadaan (coming together of husband and wife for purpose of conception),
2. punsavanam (ceremony to be performed after conception to seek a male child),
3. seemantonnayan (ceremony of parting of hairs of the expectant mother to keep her spirits high and positive),
4. jataakarma (the newborn is given a secret name and honey and clarified butter or ghee to taste before it is breastfed),
5. naamakarana (naming ceremony),
6. nishkramana (formal seeing of the sun and moon by the child),
7. annapraashana (ceremony wherein the child is first given solid food),
8. chudaakarana (ritual shaving of the head leaving a tuft of hair intact),
9. karnavedha (ritual piercing of the ears),
10. upanayan and vedaarambha (thread ceremony and initiation of Vedic studies),
11. keshaanta (ritual cutting of hairs and giving gurudakshina or offering to the guru),
12. samaavartan (return to the house to start the life of a householder),
13. vivaaha (marriage ceremony),
14. vaanaprastha (retirement to a life of austerities),
15. sanyaas (renunciation of all worldly ties andengagement in contemplation and meditation),
16. antyeshti (last rites after death).

Given below is an English translation of Savarkar's assorted views on this subject.

What do Religious Ceremonies Represent?

Ceremonies that have been perpetuated as dharmic in the dharmasamskaras perhaps reflect the prevailing history of those times. It is as if the wisdom and ignorance of those times have been fossilized in the form of the dharmic samskaras. (1935,

Vidnyannishtha nibandha or pro-science essays, Samagra Savarkar vangmaya, Vol. 3, p.317)

When does a custom or practice become fit to be discarded? No practice is per se self-evident and eternally valid from the dharmic viewpoint. A practice may be considered dharmic so long as it is useful to a particular society under specific circumstances. Once a practice starts becoming harmful to society, it becomes fit to be discarded. (1931, Samagra Savarkar vangmaya, Vol. 3, p.776)

Dynamism and Status Quo

While dynamism is necessary for the welfare of society, maintaining status quo is also desirable to some extent. (1936, Samagra Savarkar vangmaya, Vol. 3, p.633)

Do not raise the bogey of Sanatana dharma to stall reform : Even after a hitherto beneficial religious custom becomes harmful to the nation, it is not instantly discarded by society for fear of violating the scriptures. Even when giving up a harmful custom was in the interests of the nation and dharma, society would blindly insist that doing so would be sinful. Latter-day authors of the smritis would raise the bogey of "this is Sanatana dharma" while inserting shlokas. This proved to be a costly mistake. (1963, Sahaa soneri paane or Six Glorious epochs of Indian History, Samagra Savarkar vangmaya, Vol. 4, p.756)

When does a custom become adharma? That custom which only harms humanity instead of benefiting it even to the slightest extent is adharma. (Samagra Savarkar vangmaya, Vol. 4, p.313)

Changing a tradition is not an insult to our forefathers: A custom may have been beneficial in the past or seemed to have been correct in the light of prevailing wisdom. However, if such a custom has now become harmful or been rendered invalid by experimental science, then changing it or accepting its invalidity is not an insult to our forefathers; rather it is a tribute to both us and them. For it proves that our forefathers had extended the frontiers of human wisdom in their times to the fullest extent possible and that we in our turn have enriched human wisdom by taking advantage of their contribution. (1935,

Savarkaraanchya goshti or Short stories by Savarkar, Samagra Savarkar vangmaya, Vol. 2, p.552)

Do not wait for reforms to automatically happen with the passage of time: Though work in the social sphere may appear secondary to political activity, it needs to be taken up because both are closely related. It is incorrect to wait for reforms to happen automatically with the passage of time. For the things we take for granted today have occurred because of efforts made in the past. So it is important that we make strenuous efforts to realize our dreams. (1937, Hindu samaj sanrakshak Savarkar or Savarkar, the protector of Hindu society, p. 388)

SOCIAL REFORM-POLITICAL FREEDOM

If freedom is won without having achieved social reform, it will not last even for three days. (1941, Akhand Hindusthan ladhaa parva or The battle for undivided Hindusthan, p. 202)

Reformer

Given below is an English translation of Savarkar's assorted views on 'reformer'.

Who is a True Reformer?

He who gives up verbosity and acts as per the principle of 'irrespective of whether others do it or not, as far as I am concerned, I will practise reform on a daily basis" alone is a true reformer. (1935, Hindutvache panchapran or The Spirit of Hindutva; Samagra Savarkar vangmaya, Vol. 3, p.75)

How does Reform Succeed?

Many are those who suggest reform but few are those who practise it! Any reform succeeds primarily on the strength of those who practise it. (1937; Ksha kirane or X-rays; Samagra Savarkar Vangmaya, Vol.3, p.252)

However the key to bring about reform in any deep-rooted tradition is to put it into practice with immediate effect rather than indulging in intellectual rumination. Rather than intellectual or verbal arguments, making evident the desirable effects of reform and remove any doubts on that score. (1931, Bhasha shuddhi or purification of language, p. 84)

The future is yours: ...Reform implies a minority, tradition implies a majority! Hence a revolutionary social reformer is always alone to begin with. So if you are true reformers, it is imperative that you should hold aloft the flag of reform irrespective of whether some one else joins you or not....people will crowd before the deity of tradition; continue the festivity of reform assuming that before the deity of reform there are only five of you, the sixth being the future. (1930, Hindu samaj sanrakshak Savarkar or Savarkar as defender of Hindu society, p. 222)

A Reformer has to Renounce Popularity

'Varam janahitam dhyeyam kevalaa na janastutihi!' ('Not praise of people, public welfare alone'!). Who does not like praise from the public? In his Kumarasambhava, Kalidasa has described the doyen of ascetics Lord Mahadeva Himself thus, "stotram kasya na tushtaye" ("who is he who is not pleased by praise").

Praise is desirable, even necessary but praise that is obtained by putting the welfare of the people at stake is to be emphatically rejected! Social and religious reformers should scrupulously stay away from that temptation.

This is because those who fight for the welfare of the people in the realm of politics can easily gain the praise of the public. (1936, Vidnyannishtha nibandha or pro-science essays, Samagra Savarkar vangmaya, Vol. 3, p.414)

He who wants to truly serve the nation should champion that which is in the interests of the people irrespective of whether it is popular or not. He who embraces or rejects a principle or policy that is in national interest solely with an eye on whether he will be applauded or humiliated is not a sincere servant of the people. (1937, Hindu samaj sanrakshak parva or the phase as defender of Hindu society, p. 159)

Working in the social field is like walking on a bed of thorns. It is not for the faint-hearted! (Samagra Savarkar vangmaya, Vol 3, p.640)

Those reformers who have to wound the sentiments of the people as a matter of duty have also to face the wrath of society for some time as a matter of duty. (1937, (Samagra Savarkar vangmaya, Vol 3, p.651)

Each one has a Right to Freedom of Thought

I hold that each one has a right to form his opinions after independent thought and to express them fearlessly. (1943, Akhand Hindusthan Ladhaa Parva or the phase of the battle for Undivided Hindusthan, p.185)

How should reformers behave with conservatives? Just as we reformers have a right to reform; this class of sincere conservatives has a right to boycott us. Being their co-religionists, reformers should not berate, much less hate them because they call for a boycott. Rather they should happily put up with the inconvenience of boycott till the conservatives have a change of heart. (1936, Samagra Savarkar vangmaya, Vol 3, p.632)

A true reformer is undaunted by boycott: ...if a reformer has a right to reform, then society also has a right to boycott the reformer.

A reformer who is undaunted by boycott and continues to be a reformer in the face of odds is alone a true reformer. (1936, Vidnyannishtha nibandha or pro-science essays, Samagra Savarkar vangmaya, Vol 3, p.419)

Conservatives are also our brethren: ...If we were to search for the most devout followers of the Hindu Nation, those with single-minded pride of Hindutva and a truly burning desire for the victory of Hindutva in their hearts, leaving aside the question of whether or not they possess strength and intelligence, if we were to search for such of our co-religionists, we shall first visit our schools that impart knowledge of the Vedas and shastras and traditional centres!

Conservative or reformer, each Hindu is a brother in dharma, a brother in nation. ...Any group would have some fools, hypocrites and ill-tempered individuals. If the conservatives have hypocrites in their midst, do the reformists not have their share of them? As far as possible, I try not to be unfair in any of my writings.

(Vidnyannishtha nibandha or pro-science essays, Samagra Savarkar vangmaya, Vol 3, p.424-425)

When is the charge of hurting religious sentiments untenable?...Each one may publicly preach what he thinks to be true. Each one should have the right to make a reasoned argument against a practice that is anti-people or based on falsehood and say so. So long as that argument is civilized and inspired not by hatred but by good wishes, so long as it does not result in willful humiliation, then it should not be considered to have hurt religious sentiments. (Vidnyannishtha nibandha or pro-science essays, Samagra Savarkar vangmaya, Vol 3, p.430)

A refutation of the charge that "your social thoughts are demoralizing" Time and again, Shalya chastised Karna to demoralize him. But Karna's opponent Partha was also chastised by his charioteer (meaning Krishna). The cause and effect of the two chastisements was different. So too the cause and effect of the criticism of missionaries and the criticism of those who defied death for the sake of this Hindu Nation has to be necessarily different. (1934, Vidnyannishtha nibandha or pro-science essays, Samagra Savarkar vangmaya, Vol 3, p.375)

The Means of Propaganda of the Reformers

Those who have to draw the attention of society to the ill-effects of certain undesirable traditions without caring whether society shall rise against them will not only have to develop ways of intellectual persuasion to do their work but also vividly focus on ordinary incidents involving those who are directly and frequently affected by the ill-effects of such traditions. (1937; Ksha kirane or X-rays; Samagra Savarkar Vangmaya, Vol.3, p.153)

The do's and dont's to be followed by reformers: A rationalist should also be a utilitarian. He must know the sociological principle that bringing people together is never achieved by the individualism of each person. It will be necessarily based on a common principle binding all individuals. Hence, even if a belief or tradition is superstitious but results in a greater national good, a resourceful rationalist will not fail to use it as a temporary means of bringing people together. He will outright demolish those beliefs or traditions that in the final analysis are harmful to the nation. To the rest, he will turn a blind eye. Without remaining superstitious himself, he will refrain from demolishing in a blind craze for rationalism, those superstitious beliefs which overall add to national strength. (1935, Maharashtra Sharada periodical, September 1935)

In a Ram temple, some Hindu brethren will pray to the idol itself as God, some will worship it as an image of God's incarnation, some will worship it in the belief that it gives deliverance. While a rationalist is not bound by any of these beliefs, he will nonetheless look upon the idol as a memorial of a national hero and will worship it with nationalist feeling. That is the difference. But he will not go to the extreme of refusing to participate in the festivity of King Ramchandra as this would harm public and national organization. Such extremism is not rationalism but madness akin to superstition. Sometimes, useful superstition is not to be rejected. (1935, Maharashtra Sharada periodical, September 1935)

Unsheath those Weapons!

Discard those 5000 year old superstitions of untouchability and scripture-based caste discrimination! Unshackle the bonds that stem from literalist belief in shrutis, smritis and puranas and hinder your duty! And unsheath every weapon that is capable of destroying all calamities that strike you today! May you find that weapon in the armoury of your tradition or in that of modernity. (1934, Vidnyannishtha nibandha or pro-science essays, Samagra Savarkar vangmaya, Vol 3, p.380)

Eradication of Untouchability

Given below is an English translation of Savarkar's assorted views on eradication of untouchability.

Why should untouchability be eradicated? To regard our 70 million co-religionists as 'untouchables' and worse than animals is an insult not only to humanity but also to the sanctity of our soul. It is my firm conviction that this is why untouchability should be principally eradicated. Untouchability should go also because its eradication is in the interests of our Hindu society. Even if the Hindu society were to partially benefit from that custom, I would have opposed it with equal vehemence. When I refuse to touch some one because he was born in a particular community but play with cats and dogs, I am committing a most heinous crime against humanity. Untouchability should be eradicated not only because it is incumbent on us but because it is impossible to justify this inhuman custom when we consider any aspect of dharma. Hence this custom should be eradicated as a command of dharma.

From the point of view of justice, dharma and humanism, fighting untouchability is a duty and we Hindus should completely eradicate it. In the present circumstances, how we will benefit by fighting it is a secondary consideration. This question of benefit is an aapaddharma (duty to be done in certain exceptional circumstances) and eradication of untouchability is the foremost and absolute dharma. (1927, Samagra Savarkar vangmaya, vol.3, p.483)

The meaning of Savarkar's contention that 'eradication of untouchability is essential for Hindu consolidation and in national interest'

On many occasions, it is difficult to grasp the true meaning of religious principles. It may also be difficult to understand some abstract concepts. Under such circumstances, we need to preach differently. We therefore say, "Worship God for your prosperity, to beget children and to obtain health, wealth and other worldly pleasures." Similarly, if people have not been enlightened enough to reject untouchability for the sake of justice and humanism, it is desirable to ask them to eradicate the evil of untouchability as an exceptional if not an absolute duty; indeed asking them thus is also a justifiable and principled duty...many times, we need to tell people that if they do not believe that rejecting untouchability is justifiable, they should at the very least reject it only because it is suicidal to the nation and its eradication cannot possibly wait till they get convinced of its importance. Taking such a stand is not only inevitable but also a sacred duty under the circumstances. (1927, Samagra Savarkar vangmaya, Vol.3, p.483, 484)

Untouchability-a Political Calamity

The problem of untouchability has ceased to be merely a social question. It now threatens the very integrity of our Hindusthan. It now promises to be an important political calamity. (1947, Akhand Hindusthan ladha parva or phase of the battle for Akhand Hindusthan, p. 370)

Untouchability and Poverty are Two Separate Problems

Untouchability and poverty are two separate problems. It is not as if untouchables alone are poor. Many castes that are not untouchable, Brahmins included are poor. (1940, Hindu samaj sanrakshak Savarkar or Savarkar, the defender of Hindu society, p. 333)

No Profession is Lowly

As for profession, I consider every profession to be honourable as it is necessary for smooth functioning of society. (1930, Jatyuchchedak nibandh or essays on abolition of caste, Samagra Savarkar vangmaya, Vol.3, p.448)

...Scavenging cannot be considered a lowly profession as it is in the interests of society and inevitable. A reformer should show by his actions that a scavenger is worthy of equal treatment as other professionals provided he is as clean as them. (1935, Hindutvache panchapran or The Spirit of Hindutva, Samagra Savarkar vangmaya, Vol.3, p.73)

Drawing Water at Public Places and Entering Public Temples

The demand of untouchables to be allowed to draw water at public places and enter public temples is extremely modest and justified. Those who champion these demands will be initially boycotted but that has to be squarely faced.

An agitation would have to be launched against the boycott. Agitation should prove effective in our internecine disputes. But if need be, we should be ready to have our skulls broken. (1924,

Hindu samaj sanrakshak Savarkar or Savarkar, the defender of Hindu society, p. 52)

All important holy places, temples, holy and historical sites (such as the Ram temple at Panchavati in Nashik, Sethubandh Rameshwar etc.) should be open with the same regulations to all Hindus, irrespective of varna or caste. (1931, Jatyuchchedak nibandh or essays on abolition of caste, Samagra Savarkar vangmaya, Vol.3, p.480)

Is it not an atrocity on our part when we deny temple entry to so-called untouchables when God Himself threw His doors open to so-called untouchable saints such as Chokha and Ravidas? (1924, Hindu samaj sanrakshak Savarkar or Savarkar, the defender of Hindu society, p. 68)

He who is polluted by darshan (glimpse) is no God. (1927, Hindutvache panchapran or The Spirit of Hindutva, Samagra Savarkar vangmaya, Vol.3, p.47)

I can understand impurity but not untouchability. If a Brahmin is impure he may be denied temple entry. On the other hand, even a Mahar who is pure should be allowed temple entry. (1928, Shraddhanand weekly, 01 November)

Patitpavan is the most favourite name of God. (1927, Hindutvache panchapran or The Spirit of Hindutva, Samagra Savarkar vangmaya, Vol.3, p.44)

No Separate Temples or Schools for Untouchables

Building separate and exclusive new temples for untouchables is not the right way of eradicating untouchability...What to speak of temples, having separate schools for untouchables is also, in a sense harmful...The liberation of untouchables is not theirs alone, it is also the liberation of those touchables whose hands and minds had been soiled by this injustice. It is desirable in the extreme to build pan-Hindu temples that are freely open to all Hindus irrespective of their caste rather than build separate and exclusive temples for untouchables...While it is important to build new pan-Hindu temples, it is equally important to throw open old temples to all Hindus. (1929, Samagra Savarkar vangmaya, Vol.3, p.491-493)

Savarkar named the new pan-Hindu temple at Ratnagiri as 'Patitpavan Mandir' ('one who purifies the degraded'), so did he consider the untouchables as degraded? That race which has no strength to protect its existing temples has forfeited its right to build new ones. The objective of this temple is to build that strength. Today, it is not just the Mahar, Chamar or the untouchable community that is degraded, the entire Hindu society, slave that it has become of foreign rule is degraded. I will call Him who raises this entire degraded Hindu nation as Patitpavan. I will call only Him who restores all that we Hindus have lost as Patitpavan. (1929, Hindu samaj sanrakshak Savarkar or Savarkar, the defender of Hindu society, p. 196)

Agitation in support of just demands of untouchables: ...Henceforth if the caste Hindus deny the so-called untouchables their lawful rights, then one cannot blame the untouchables if they resort to civil agitation (satyagraha). Of course, such an agitation may be launched only if all efforts to change the minds of the caste Hindus into granting lawful rights fail. Often, it is possible to convince the caste Hindus that it is necessary to at least publicly reject untouchability in principle and practice. This I say from experience and I can vouch that in most cases the problem resolves through such fraternal love. I appreciate that on the rare occasions when the problem is not resolved; our untouchable brethren will be forced to launch civil agitation for the protection of their lawful rights. Agitation is not a permanent policy but an inevitable and bitter weapon, a last resort. (1927, Samagra Savarkar vangmaya, Vol.3, p.485)

The untouchables also consider some other caste untouchable: Each abuse that the untouchable hurls at the touchable to express the horror of untouchablity returns back to him. This is because every untouchable caste considers some other lower caste untouchable. Finding out the lowest caste is like digging deep into the bowels of the earth! (Samagra Savarkar vangmaya, Vol.3, p.519)

Criticism should be Unbiased

Just as one should expose the atrocities perpetrated by caste Hindus on untouchables, the fact that there is a rapidly increasing class of caste Hindus that is selflessly engaged in eradication of untouchability should not be brushed under the carpet...The empathy shown by these caste Hindus is not shown among the untouchables by the Mahars for the Chamars or the Dhors. It is also in the interests of the untouchables to express their gratitude. (1936, Samagra Savarkar vangmaya, Vol.2, p.670)

The seemingly impossible task of untouchability eradication can made possible by change of heart: Easy as it is, the task of eradicating untouchability lends strength to Hindu consolidation. If we destroy the belief that we should not touch our brother in dharma because he took birth in a particular caste and eradicate untouchability in the next five years by alleviating the economic and social hardships faced by our brothers in dharma, that will be an achievement as momentous as victory on the battlefield. By a simple change of heart, the seemingly impossible task can be achieved. (1942, Hindu Rashtra Darshan or six presidential addresses to the Hindu Mahasabha, Samagra Savarkar vangmaya, Vol.6, p.499)

Don't wait for others; touch and untouchability shall go: Oh Hindu! Wherever you are and perhaps alone you may be, without waiting for others, pledge that you shall touch millions and millions of your untouchable brethren, that you will accept those re-converted and be assured that the twin momentous national tasks of 'liberation of untouchables and re-conversion' have been achieved!

Say, my hand that I use to caress my dog with affection, I shall with brotherly love place on the back of he who has been called untouchable, my brother in Hindu Dharma, my brother in nation, my blood brother! Say I will touch! And lo! Untouchability shall be dead. (1927, Hindutvache panchapran or The Spirit of Hindutva, Samagra Savarkar vangmaya, Vol.3, p.29)

*When will the squalor in the Maharwada (*colony of Mahars located outside the village precints) go?* The squalor in the Maharwada (*colony of Mahars, an ex-untouchable caste; usually located outside the village precincts) will not go while you recline in your armchairs. It is only when you go there and make efforts to remove it in the spirit of 'serve man, serve God'...And what if the squalor in the Maharwada remains? In that case, it will pollute not only the environment in the Maharwada but also the pristine environment of your armchairs. We will all end up as victims of a horrendous social malaise. (1925, Balwant weekly, 29 April)

An Untouchability Eradication Programme for each Village

Gather all Hindus in the village on a few auspicious days in a month and start mass prayers for at least half an hour...On a Sunday, take along a couple of volunteers and roam around the village chanting slogans of re-conversion (* bringing back converted Hindus to the Hindu fold) and asking for handful of grain. From the proceeds of its sale, help our untouchable brethren. Open a school for them. Go to their locality, organize singing of devotional songs and teach them the importance of cleanliness. Alleviate their grievances; protect them from the evil designs of other religionists. Convince people to remove obstacles to the public use of lakes and wells. (1927, Shraddhanand weekly, 23 June)

ABOLITION OF CASTE

Given below is an English translation of Savarkar's assorted views on abolition of caste

The Basic Aim of Consolidating Hindu Society

The Hindu social jurists had based social organization on the principle of distribution of duties sans competition and mutual cooperation as means to attain earthly prosperity on the path to salvation of the soul. The duties of every individual from the shudra to the Brahmin were defined to facilitate societal development. But fighting spirit (kshaatratej) is necessary to fulfil these duties properly and to protect social life. (Samagra Savarkar vangmaya, Vol. 6, p.522)

The Practice of Caste and Consolidation of Hindu Society

Firstly, it should not be forgotten that the practice of birth-based caste division must have been responsible for the mighty consolidation and amazing stability of the Hindu society under certain circumstances and conditions. While evaluating its merits and demerits, it will be sheer ingratitude to only point fingers at the latter day ill-effects of the institution of caste.

It must also be admitted that keeping the interests of the Hindu Nation at heart, the Hindus of yesteryears gave birth to or allowed birth-based caste divisions to develop spontaneously with the aim of preserving the purity of blood ties, community life and tradition. (1963, Sahaa soneri pane or Six Glorious Epochs of Indian History; Samagra Savarkar vangmaya, Vol. 4, p. 710)

Birth-based Caste System as an Experiment in the Science of Heredity

Considering its sheer magnitude, the amazing diligence and the epochal time-frame over which this inspirational experiment was played out, the human race should be certainly grateful to this great experiment played by birth-based caste system to find out the extent to which natural laws of heredity may possibly benefit the human race. Assuming that the experiment temporarily failed due to its extreme practice or distortion, it is no mean achievement to prove that such an experiment failed in such a form and under such conditions. By thus failing in this great experiment of the caste system, our Hindu race enriched human experience and has thereby succeeded in earning the gratitude of the human race; such was the scientific outlook and thought, sheer guts and amazing diligence at the root of this experiment. (1931, Jatyuchchedak nibandha or essays on abolition of caste, Samagra Savarkar vangmaya, Vol. 3, p. 457)

The Role of Heredity in the Development of Merit

Heredity is not the sole determinant of merit; rather it is one of its many determinants.

Even if inbreeding occurs, change in other factors such as light, food, water, climate, mental makeup of ancestors, their upbringing, education, availability of opportunity and means enhance or diminish or change the innate merit of children. Even where inbreeding occurs, like good qualities, bad qualities too may get enhanced or accentuated; hence occasionally heredity may prove harmful in the extreme and crossbreeding becomes the most effective means of removing defects or disabilities in children.

Even if inbreeding occurs, the good qualities of ancestors may occasionally diminish or get distorted with passage of time. In such circumstances too, cross-breeding proves beneficial to animals. While it is possible to maintain blood purity by inbreeding in case of natural species, it is virtually impossible to maintain it if the same is ordained by scriptures or belief.

And in those Hindu castes such as the Brahmins etc. too which have strict rules regarding inter-marriages, crossbreeding has been occurring for generations past as ordained by scriptures or secretly due to sexual attraction. This will undoubtedly continue in future too and hence even if inter-marriages are strictly prohibited, the very belief that the son of a Brahmin has the innate qualities of a Brahmin or that the son of a Kshatriya must be naturally imbued with the qualities of a Kshatriya needs to be discarded. This is because of the fact that due to crossbreeding between all our castes from time immemorial, no caste can claim monopoly over a specific merit. (1931, Jatyuchchedak nibandha or essays on abolition of caste, Samagra Savarkar vangmaya, Vol. 3, p. 472)

The meaning of 'chaturvarnya mayaa srishtam' ('I have created the chaturvarnya system') Chaturvarnya means the four varnas (* the word varna is virtually untranslatable. It denotes the old Hindu idea of a four-tiered society with an intellectual or spiritual class called the Brahmins; the ruling, political or warrior class called the Kshatriyas; the merchant or commercial class called the Vaishyas and the servant or service-oriented class called the Shudras. They represent the four human tendencies of learning, fighting, trading and serving). These four varnas were determined by merit and actions and not by birth... 'Chaturvarnya mayaa srishtam' means 'I have created the chaturvarnya system'. Nowhere in this shloka (by Sri Krishna in the Bhagwad Gita) is any there any suggestion whatsoever, that He gives birth to people on basis of merit and that this perpetuates on basis of birth in a particular family... The smritis clearly say, 'janmanaa jaayate shudraha' or 'everyone is a shudra at birth'. It is only after imbibing samskaras that one attains the status of the twice-born (meaning Brahmin, Kshatriya, Vaishya). (1930, Jatyuchchedak nibandha or essays on abolition of caste, Samagra Savarkar vangmaya, Vol. 3, p. 444)

....The present-day caste division has arisen from the debris of the chaturvarnya of yore. (1930, Jatyuchchedak nibandha or essays on abolition of caste, Samagra Savarkar vangmaya, Vol. 3, p. 449)

The Sanatana Dharma will not die if the caste system goes away: Both chaturvarnya and caste divisions are but practices. They are not coterminous with Sanatana Dharma (*lit: timeless code, though the word Dharma is virtually untranslatable). The practice of caste division arose from a tectonic change in the practice of chaturvarnya.

As the Sanatana Dharma did not die due to this tectonic change, so too it will not die if the present-day distortion that is caste division is destroyed. The true Sanatana Dharma, those true philosophical ideas expounding the character of ishwar-jeev-jagat (God-individual-creation) and the First Principle can never die. (1930, Jatyuchchedak nibandha or essays on abolition of caste, Samagra Savarkar vangmaya, Vol. 3, p. 444)

Notions of 'high and low' on basis of qualities, Hindu is the caste by birth: No one should ever think that a certain Hindu caste is high or that another is low. The notion of high and low will be determined by overt merit of individuals.

Every Hindu child has but one caste at birth-Hindu. Other than that, consider no other sub-caste. 'Janmanaa jaayate Hinduhu' ('every one is a Hindu by birth')! In truth, every man has but one caste at birth-human. But at least so long as other religionists such as Muslims and Christians keep aside that lofty aim and consider themselves Muslims and Christians by birth and endeavour to swallow the Hindu, we too must cling to the identity of our race. On every occasion and especially during census, register yourselves as Hindus only. Consider all castes as occupations. (1930, Jatyuchchedak nibandha or essays on abolition of caste, Samagra Savarkar vangmaya, Vol. 3, p. 479)

Present-day Caste Divisions are Scripture-based

Scripture-based caste division is a mental illness. It gets cured instantly when the mind refuses to accept it. The seven indigenous shackles whose breaking will liberate this Hindu Nation from the illness and demonic possession that is caste division are as follows: vedokta bandi (prohibition of Vedic recital and worshipping according to Vedas), vyavasaya bandi (prohibition of certain occupations), sparsha bandi (untouchability), sindhu bandi (prohibition of sea faring), shuddhi bandi (prohibiton of re-conversion), roti bandi (prohibition of inter-dining), beti bandi (prohibition of inter-marriages). (1935, Samagra Savarkar vangmaya, Vol. 3, p. 497-499)

I felt like rebelling against the caste system: Just as I felt I should rebel against the foreign rule over Hindusthan, I also felt that I should rebel against the caste system and untouchability in Hindusthan. (1920, Letters from the Andamans, Samagra Savarkar vangmaya, Vol. 5, p. 490)

The social discrimination amongst different castes should end: ...The present-day birth-based caste division and social discrimination amongst different castes should go forthwith for this social revolution to succeed. This is imperative for the rise, rejuvenation and prosperity of the Hindu Nation. If the root of this poisonous tree dies, the poisonous creeper of special privileges that thrives on it will automatically die. (1936, Samagra Savarkar vangmaya, Vol. 3, p. 641)

Every one possessed by the craze of caste: This craze of caste is not limited to the Brahmin alone; it pervades the non-Brahmin Chandala, indeed the whole of Hindusthan is imbued with it! The societal body has become wasted with this disease of caste arrogance, caste hatred and caste conflict. (1930, Jatyuchchedak nibandha or essays on abolition of caste, Samagra Savarkar vangmaya, Vol. 3, p. 440)

Caste division is not the conspiracy of a handful of Brahmins...it is not the joint conspiracy of the Brahmins and

Kshatriyas. (1930, Jatyuchchedak nibandha or essays on abolition of caste, Samagra Savarkar vangmaya, Vol. 3, p. 450-451)

Every one preserved caste division, reform is a collective responsibility: Indeed, the blame for the atrocities perpetrated by the higher castes on lower castes due to scripture-based caste division lies with all castes, from the Brahmin to the Bhangi (Balmiki), not with Brahmins and Kshatriyas alone! This scripture-based caste division enabled the Bhangi to assert his superiority over the Domb, hence every one in his own way preserved and is still preserving it. The blame for unnecessarily allowing it to thrive rests on every one...so the best way is to accept that every one is to be blamed and that the responsibility of reform is collective! Every one destroyed the edifice (* of society) together. Now in the fitness of things, let all of us Hindus together rebuild it on the firm foundation of all-embracing Hindutva. (1935, Ksha kirane or X-rays, Samagra Savarkar vangmaya, Vol. 3, p. 178)

There should be no link between caste and human discrimination/ special privileges: ...The aspect of caste division that we have to mainly abolish because it is nationally undesirable is not merely its basis in birth but its link to discrimination and special privileges...If one were to remove its basis in birth and the resulting discrimination and attendant special privileges without regard to merit, then even if the other causes of caste division were to somehow remain for several years, they would not cause much harm. In that case, if each caste were to continue to maintain its specific occupations, names, caste-based organizations, its non-discriminatory and harmless rituals, familial duties and practices as well as gotra traditions, these per se would not cause any significant harm to the Hindu Nation. (1935, Hindutvache panchapran or The Spirit of Hindutva, Samagra Savarkar vangmaya, Vol. 3, p. 55-67)

Wrong to label an entire caste as 'wicked' or 'harmless': ...In Brahmins and Bhangis (*Balmikis) alike, just as you would find caste egoist, discriminatory and wicked people, in the same measure you would also find reformers who stand for equality and abolition of caste. If a champion of abolition of caste division were to hold that only Brahmins and Kshatriyas are wicked while others are altruistic, harmless gentlemen who stand for equality, such a person would inadvertently prove the validity of caste division and contribute to caste hatred through his slogan of abolition of caste. For to say that the entire caste of the Brahmin or someone else is wicked and that of some others is unexceptionably good is to say that these castes are not man-made or scripture-based but that they are innately different. (Samagra Savarkar vangmaya, Vol. 3, p. 541)

The use of the term 'non-Brahmins' is improper: The use of the term 'non-Brahmins' is improper. It means that on one side you have all non-Brahmins including Englishmen and Americans! (1924, Hindu samaj sanrakshak Savarkar or Savarkar as the defender of Hindu society, p. 69)

Primacy of Priests

Though the word 'priest' instantly conjures the image of the Brahmin, yet the Guravs, Gurus, Jangams, even the Mahar Bhats amongst the Mahars are all priests! Though they are all non-Brahmins, there is nevertheless primacy of the priests (original word used by Savarkar is bhatshaahi). (1935, Hindutvache panchapran or The Spirit of Hindutva, Samagra Savarkar vangmaya, Vol. 3, p. 74)

Priest should be based on merit: ...If you must have a priest, every reformer should choose him not on the basis of caste but on merit. (1935, Hindutvache panchapran or The Spirit of Hindutva, Samagra Savarkar vangmaya, Vol. 3, p. 75)

What should be the nature of religious practices? The priest is redundant on hundreds of occasions. One may read the scripture oneself and worship after expressing sentiments in chaste Marathi. Thanksgiving alms may be given away to institutions doing useful work. (1935, Hindutvache panchapran or The Spirit of Hindutva, Samagra Savarkar vangmaya, Vol. 3, p. 74)

God Himself would be more pleased to see His devotee perform worship on his own without help from others! ((1934, Hindu samaj sanrakshak Savarkar or Savarkar as the defender of Hindu society, p. 304)

Caste Organizations and Hindu Consolidation

Caste organizations are inevitable though undesirable in a period of change...So long as most castes have their organizations, the remaining ones find it difficult and harmful to shun them...As of now, the institution of caste is deep-rooted and alive with an innate sense of high and low appended to each caste. Hence, they have their specific issues of their interest. When caste-specific disabilities, injustices or needs gradually disappear, when all castes reach the same level or in other words when caste discrimination decreases leading to loosening of caste divisions, such caste organizations will automatically become redundant and tread the path to extinction...To organize the Hindu Nation, it is extremely difficult to bring together individuals. It is relatively easier to begin by bringing together different castes.. Bringing people together can be initially done by caste organizations...if you talk of organizations of sub-castes, some sub-castes will be excluded. If you talk of an umbrella organization of castes, you increasingly tend to amalgamate sub-castes. If umbrella organizations of different castes make keen efforts in the right direction then it will not be difficult to tread the path leading to the national temple of Hindu consolidation...

Though caste organizations are obstacles in the path to abolition of caste, yet in the absence of other means, if these organizations are skillfully made use of, these obstacles may be paradoxically used to weaken the foundation of caste division to a great extent; it is imperative that they are put to such use. (1937, Samagra Savarkar vangmaya, Vol. 3, p. 620-624)

The Policy of Caste Abolitionists Towards Caste Organizations

The first essential thing is to start a caste abolitionist group in each town and village that would have no link whatsoever to any caste organization...We should not start any caste organization. We should not claim any caste as our own present day-caste. However, just as it is unexceptionable to say that I was born in such and such family, it is also unexceptionable to say that I was born in such and such caste. To deny it would be laughable...It is foolish and even harmful for caste abolitionists to totally boycott all caste organizations for they need to use the desirable element in caste organizations to abolish caste itself...Amongst existing caste organizations, there are those that have been established with the sole aim of asserting their caste superiority.

Abolitionists who belong to that caste would have to give up their own freedom to reject caste divisions and participate in inter-dining if they wish to participate in such organizations. If that is the case, abolitionists should have no truck with such caste organizations...Our Hindu caste abolitionist brethren should most certainly participate in progressive caste organizations to make them more receptive to abolitionist principles, ensure that they abolish sub-castes, cause elimination of the practices of untouchability, prohibition of inter-dining etc. and encourage them to do useful things such as education and the like. In fact they should go in such organizations in numbers large enough to create their majority and make their brothers in caste receptive to its abolition. ((1935, Samagra Savarkar vangmaya, Vol. 3, p. 624-628)

Conversion and Shuddhi

Note: The term 'shuddhi' literally means 'purification'. It refers to the re-conversion into the Hindu fold of non-Hindus, especially of those Hindus who have been converted to other religions by hook or crook. The word 'shuddhi' has been retained throughout in this section. Prohibition of shuddhi or re-conversion was one of the seven shackles that chained Hindu society in Savarkar's time. Savarkar's assorted views on the other six shackles are given in another section. Given below is an English translation of Savarkar's assorted views on 'conversion and shuddhi'

Grateful remembrance of those Hindus who suffered due to the prohibition of shuddhi and caste ostracism

"Tyajedekam kulasyaarthe, graamsyaarthe kulam tyajet
graamam janapadasyaarthe, dharmaarthe pruthiveem tyajet"

the loss of land which happened in their time. (1963, Sahaa soneri pane or Six Glorious Epochs of Indian History, Samagra Savarkar vangmaya, Vol.4, p. 780, 782)

The Game of Foreign Christian Missionaries

Bharat was not divided on the basis of which community is more patriotic or has produced more scholars! Punjab and Bengal were divided on the basis of demography and it is the same old game of numbers that foreign missionaries are playing to this day. (1953, Kranti ghosh or The bugle of revolution, p. 141)

When is tolerance to other religions (original word used is "paradharmasahishnutaa") a boon and when does it become a bane?* Every Hindu imbibes along with his mother's milk, the teaching that 'tolerance to other religions is a noble sentiment'. But no one ever teaches him the spirit of this teaching. If that 'other religion' also displays the same tolerance to our religion then 'tolerance to other religions' is certainly a noble sentiment. But this principle cannot be applied without regard to circumstances. It cannot be applied to Muslims who consider the merciless destruction of Hindu dharma and the extermination of kafirs (* infidels) to be a pious act or to Christians. Under those circumstances, reaction to such intolerant actions, showing ferocious intolerance to such atrocities, to those 'other religions' is a truly noble sentiment. (1963, Sahaa soneri pane or Six Glorious Epochs of Indian History, Samagra Savarkar vangmaya, Vol.4, p. 721)

Which nations survived the Muslim menace? ...Most of the nations that could not root out the political and religious power of the Muslims were destroyed and became Muslim themselves. But even those non-Muslim nations who succeeded in toppling Muslim political power but kept Muslim religious power intact could not escape from the persistent and terrible Muslim menace. Only three to five nations did not rest after toppling the political power of Muslims but immediately launched a bitter war against their religious power and made their nation free of Muslims. These nations alone not only managed to survive but actually smashed the Muslim menace. (1963, Sahaa soneri pane or Six Glorious Epochs of Indian History, Samagra Savarkar vangmaya, Vol.4, p. 787)

Hindu-Muslim Unity will be Furthered by Shuddhi

I do not despise, let alone hate Muslim or Christian brethren, indeed even the most primitive tribes in the human race. I oppose the wickedness of individuals and groups belonging to them when I see it. It is my hope and conviction that Hindu-Muslim unity can be based on a permanent and beneficial footing only through the practice of shuddhi. (1927, Majhi janmathep or The Story of My Transportation for Life, Samagra Savarkar vangmaya, Vol.1, p. 511)

Shuddhi not by Force

Each person who comes forward for shuddhi should be asked this one question, "Are you becoming a Hindu out of conviction? Is someone trying to force this dharma on you?" (1928, Shraddhanand weekly, 26 January)

When will the dens of corruption shut down? Once the padre and the pir (Muslim missionary) realize that even though they might provide for a Hindu today or even for ten years, he reverts to being a Hindu by simply swallowing a tulsi leaf (*the tulsi or the basil plant is considered sacred by Hindus), they will shut down their dens of corruption posthaste. (1927, Shraddhananda weekly, 25 August)

Discard the notion of 'ritual impurity': Most of the customs that led to our social and national decline had their seeds in the notion of 'ritual impurity'. Shuddhi has become necessary due to this malaise of 'ritual impurity'. (1929, Shraddhanand weekly, 05 April)

Shuddhi is Meritorious

Rather than install a stone idol, the installation of Narayan (*name of Sri Vishnu) in the hearts of men is far more meritorious! And shuddhi is the enlightened spirit of Narayan in the hearts of men; it is verily a temple full of life! (1929, Shraddhanand weekly, 05 April)

It is slanderous to claim that shuddhi breeds hatred: If shuddhi supposedly breeds hatred, then why corruption (*conversion) is not deemed to breed hatred? In fact, it is because the mullahs and missionaries first embark on a campaign of conversion that we are forced to do shuddhi. If shuddhi breeds hatred, then first shut shops of the Muslims and Christians who convert Hindus by fair or foul means and initiate hatred in the first place. Then the campaign of shuddhi shall stop automatically. If you give freedom to the mullah and missionaries to convert under the pretext of propagation of religion, then the Hindus must also have the right to their shuddhi. To claim that the homecoming of those who have strayed into a foreign religion breeds hatred whilst reserving one's own right to convert is like a thief who guards his right to steal and claims that hatred will breed if his victims take back what he has stolen from them! (1929, Hindu samaj sanrakshak Savarkar or Savarkar, the protector of Hindu society, p. 210)

The expense incurred in shuddhi: The expense incurred in shuddhi work should be borne by the district in which the work is carried out. Shuddhi per se does not involve much expense; more expense goes in its preparation and later success. (1927, Hindu samaj sanrakshak Savarkar or Savarkar, the protector of Hindu society, p. 180)

Christian missionaries and Hindu saints: Christian missionaries come from faraway Europe and America, spend millions of rupees and go to far-flung areas of Assam in the sweltering heat and work day and night to entice the Nagas into the Christian fold.

And on the other side, we have the Shankaracharyas, Vallabhacharyas and other saints and ascetics who, far from spreading Hindu dharma amongst Muslims and Christians, reject the pleas of the Nagas and Satpanthis to admit them to the Hindu fold! (1931, Samagra Savarkar vangmaya, Vol.3, p. 780)

When will the issue of shuddhi become redundant? The issue of shuddhi will become redundant when the whole world is filled by angels! So long as the Hindus are being subjected to demonic attacks, it is incumbent on us to vanquish this devil by the

Raamnaam (*invoking the name of Sri Ram is supposed to ward off evil) of shuddhi. (1928, Shraddhanand weekly, 26 January)

The Nagas...Defeat the evil designs of missionaries by weaving the web of Hindu consolidation amongst the Nagas! Remember that if you delay any further, this job will become well nigh impossible. (Samagra Savarkar vangmaya, Vol.3, p. 750)

ASSOCIATES IN SOCIAL REFORMS

Kashinath Laxman Parulekar: Worked both in Savarkar's social reform and Hindutva movements. Worked with Savarkar during his stay in Ratnagiri and since then worked for the Ratnagiri Hindu Sabha. Was president of Ratnagiri Hindu Sabha from 1948. Took part in the working of Patitpavan Mandir. After Bhagojisheth Keer passed away in 1944, a dispute arose regarding the ownership of the Patitpavan Mandir.

The trust of the Mandir was not registered, so the entire property was taken over by the High Court receiver from 1948 to 1964. At the instance of LB Bhopatkar, an application was made to the Public Trust Chaarity Commissioner seeking a status of trust to the institution. The office-bearers were summoned to Kolhapur with the evidence. But they had no money, so they prayed that the Asst Charity Commissioner conduct the proceedings in Ratnagiri.

This prayer was granted and the Asst Charity Commissioner Apte came to Ratnagiri fr the purpose. CK or Bapurao Parulekar represented the officebearers and was assisted by Gajananrao Damle and Vinayakrao Bhave.. The cost of Rs. 5000 towards these was raised by public contribution. Finally the Shree Patitpavan Public Trust came into being in 1954. However the Trust could not be registered as some houses owned by it were yet to pay municipal tax arrears. It was through the efforts of the recovery officer Abasaheb Kane that this formality was completed. As president of Ratnagiri hindu Sabha, KL Parulekar was a member of the trust appointed by the District Court to look after the Patitpavan Mandir. He donated Rs. 2600 while his wife donated Rs. 1000 to the Patitpavan Mandir.

Shrimant Bhagojisheth Keer : Bhagojisheth Keer was a renowned building contractor in Ratnagiri. He was among those who were inspired by Savarkar's campaign for social reform. He had built a Bhageshwar temple in Ratnagiri fort. On Mahashivratri day in 1928, he invited Savarkar to his temple. Keer explained to Savarkar that he had built this temple because he wished to worship Shiva and being from the lowly Bhandari caste, he was not permitted to touch the idol in other temples. He hence had decided to build a temple where he could freely touch the idol. At this, Savarkar instantly said, " Shethji, you could build a temple because you are well-to-do. You can at least enter any temple. But our ex-untouchable brethren are deprived of their gods, temples; in fact they are unable to have a glimpse of the deity. If they have the same desire as you for a glimpse of the deity should not people like you fulfil their desire.

Hence I pray to you to build a temple of Shri Patitpavan where all Hindus can collectively and with equality worship and pray to God. Hearing this, Keer was moved and in a choked voice he said, "What you say will surely happen as per Bhageshwar's wish. After Keer gave his consent, the Ratnagiri Hindu Sabha began scouting for a place. They found a suitable plot of land in the heart of Ratnagiri. The plot belonged to one Bhargav Krishna Shevde. The asking price of the plot of land was Rs. 8000. Keer was not willing to pay more than Rs. 6000 for the place. The Hindu Sabha collected public funds to the tune of Rs. 1000 while the moneylenders who owned the land gave a rebate of Rs 1000 in the form of a donation to the Hindu Sabha at Savarkar's request. The land was bought in Keer's name for Rs. 8000. Shankaracharya Dr. Kurtakoti laid the foundation stone of the temple on Sunday, 10 March 1929. Shrimant Bhagojisheth Keer spent a total of around two to two and half lac rupees towards the construction of the Patipavan Mandir. Keer helped Savarkar's campaign in many ways. Once, the houses of Ramji Laxman Khedekar and Mahadev Babaji Fansopkar (both belonging to the backward Chamar caste) were burned down in a fire. On hearing this news, Savarkar rushed to the spot and made efforts to help the affected families. Responding to

Savarkar's appeal, Keer arranged to provide them roof tiles. Keer also constructed the Hindu crematorium at Dadar, Mumbai. Keer passed away in 1944.

Shankaracharya Dr. Kurtakoti: Born 1879, was a Sanskrit scholar. Obtained doctorate from American University. At the instance of Lokmanya Tilak, took sanyaas and became Shankaracharya of Sankeshwar Peeth in 1917. Developed differences with Chhatrapati Shahu Maharaj of Kolhapur and had to leave Kolhapur; stayed in Nashik Panchavati. Organized shuddhi programmes and several Hindu conferences. At the inauguration ceremony of the Patitpavan Mandir in Ratnagiri, a Mahar (ex-untouchable) leader PN Rajbhoj performed paadyapuja (ritual washing of the feet) of the Shankaracharya Dr. Kurtakoti. This was an unprecedented event in the history of Hindu society. Was president of Akhil Bharat Hindu Mahasabha twice (Prayag, 1924 and Lahore 1936). Died on 29 October 1967.

Vaidya Mahadev Ganpatrao Shinde (a vaidya is a Ayurvedic practitioner) :* Was an Ayurvedic vaidya by training, had inherited this profession from his father who had knowledge of Ayurveda. When Savarkar was interned in Ratnagiri, many people shunned him for fear of inviting the wrath of the British authorities. Ratnagiri was a stronghold of the conservatives. The elite did not look upon very kindly to Savarkar's social reform activities. Vaidya Mahadev Ganpatrao Shinde was one of those who stood behind solidly behind Savarkar in his social reform activities. For this, he became the butt of sarcasm and anger of his relatives and friends. The police hounded him. But Vaidya Shinde stood firm.

The Shinde family hailed originally from Partavne area of Ratnagiri. MG Shinde's father was employed in the police department and rose to be a sub-inspector. He had a great liking for Ayurveda. He would cure many poor people of simple ailments during his travels as a policeman. Ganpatrao Shinde had five sons, of who three were mute. The responsibility of running the family fell on Mahadevrao after his father's death.

Savarkar and Vaidya MG Shinde first met in 1924. In their very first meeting, Savarkar noticed the word 'Dr.' written on

Shinde's nameplate. In keeping with his love for reform of language, Savarkar suggested that Shinde use the word 'vaidya' instead of 'Dr.'. In 1925, Shinde was inducted into the executive of the Ratnagiri Hindu Sabha and made its vice-president.

When Dr. Keshav Baliram Hedgewar who was to later found the Rashtriya Swayamsevak Sangh (RSS) came to Ratnagiri to visit Savarkar, he had stayed at Dr. Shinde's place. On the next day, Dr. Hedgewar had addressed a small gathering at Dr. Shinde's place. As Savarkar was interned, he could not visit Nagpur after the founding of the RSS. It was Dr. Shinde who went to Nagpur. There he was given a guard of honour by the RSS swayamsevaks and Dr. Hedgewar himself introduced Dr. Shinde. When the Ratnagiri Hindu Sabha sent a letter of felicitation to Prince of Nepal, HRH Tribhuvan Bir Vikram on the occasion of his twentieth birthday, the correspondence was done from Shinde's house. Shinde also took upon himself to send 150 rakhis to 150 prominent Hindus throughout the country.

Vaidya Shinde was a member of the Ratnagiri municipality and the District Board. The Muslim members of the municipality wanted to stop the gymnasium started by Savarkar and managed by the municipality. It was Shinde who struck down the proposal of the Muslim members.

Shinde organized the signatures of 500 people on a petition to invite Dr. BR Ambedkar to speak at the Vithoba temple in Ratnagiri but Ambedkar declined citing lack of time. Vaidya Shinde was the secretary when Sant Panchlegaonkar's speech and discussion of temple entry to ex-untouchables was discussed on 11 September 1929. It was due to the efforts of people like Shinde that the ex-untouchables finally got entry to the Vithoba temple on 13 September 1929.

Vaidya Shinde was the moving force in bringing back to the Hindu fold an actor named Ibrahim and renaming him Ishwardas.

Vaidya Shinde was the president of the Somvanshi Mahar Conference held in Ratnagiri on 09 April 1932.

In 1932, Shinde spoke on behalf of reformists in a debate that took place between conservatives and reformists at the Ganeshotsav. On 01 April 1933, Shinde signed a letter of greeting to the Maharaja of Nepal on occasion of the Hindu New Year. The biography of Maharishi Dayanand Saraswati, founder of the Arya Samaj was banned in Ratnagiri Jail. Shinde took steps and got the ban lifted.

Rationalism

Rationalism was an abiding guiding principle in Savarkar's life. Though he did not start any rationalist movement as such, his thoughts and actions were invariably dictated by reason, scientific temper, utilitarianism and human welfare. It is not surprising that Savarkar's thoughts and teachings were shocking to contemporary society. It is precisely these thoughts and teachings that serve as a beacon to society even today. Savarkar's relevance remains intact even decades after he has passed away. Truly, his entire life is a lesson in rationalism.

SOCIAL REFORM

Savarkar was an illustrious social reformer. He firmly believed that political and social reforms are equally important and complementary to each other. During his time, many self-imposed shackles and superstitions had weakened Hindu society. Through his speeches, writings and actions, Savarkar launched a sustained campaign of social reform. Though Savarkar concentrated on social reform when he was forbidden to take part in political activities, it must be remembered that his commitment to social reform was lifelong. He considered his work in the social sphere to be even more important than his spectacular escape from the ship into the ocean. Savarkar preached and practiced social reform not merely because it strengthened Hindu society and nation. Above all, Savarkar's social thought stemmed from his humanism. He championed social reform even amongst followers of other religions. The period from 1924 to 1937 may be broadly termed as the phase of social reform in Savarkar's life.

Seven Shackles

According to Savarkar, the Hindu society was bound by seven shackles (bandi) viz. prohibition of touch (sparshabandi) of certain castes, prohibition of interdining (rotibandi) with certain castes, prohibition of intercaste marriages (betibandi), prohibition of pursuing certain occupations (vyavasayabandi), prohibition of seafaring (sindhubandi), prohibition of rites sanctioned by the Vedas (vedoktabandi), prohibition of reconversion (shuddhibandi) to the Hindu fold. Given below is an English translation of Savarkar's assorted thoughts on six shackles. The seventh shackle viz. prohibition of reconversion (shuddhibandi) has been dealt with separately. Some of these shackles may seem unbelievable, even laughable to the reader today. The remarkable social reform that has taken place in the last 100 years is due to the tireless efforts of social reformers like Savarkar.

Eating and Drinking

What to eat and drink is a medical issue, not a religious one. One may eat and drink as per individual preference and digestive capacity under specific circumstances. (1937, Samagra Savarkar vangmaya, Vol.3, p. 652)

Hinduism does not die by Partaking of Food Cooked by other Religionists

If the Muslim or Christian does not become a Hindu by eating food cooked by a Hindu and remains a Muslim or Christian after digesting that food, then why should your religion be flushed out by partaking of food cooked by a Muslim? How come the digestive power of your religion has become so weak?...Now brothers, eat and digest food cooked by any one in the world and yet remain Hindu! Only then is there hope (for survival). (1927, Maajhi janmathep or My Transportation for Life, Samagra Savarkar vangmaya, Vol.1, p. 495)

...The place of religion is the heart, not the stomach. (1927, Hindutvache panchapran or The Spirit of Hindutva, Samagra Savarkar vangmaya, Vol.3, p. 41)

Interdining does not Destroy Religion and Caste

There is no harm in eating what is medically permissible with any medically fit individual, not in a common plate but as a common meal. It is insane to believe that caste changes forever simply by sitting and eating next to an individual from a different caste. (1931, Jatyuchchedak nibandha or essays on abolition of caste, Samagra Savarkar vangmaya, Vol.3, p. 480)

Be it a Hindu or a Muslim or an Andamanese-eating and drinking with any one destroys neither caste nor religion. (1935, Hindutvache panchapran or The Spirit of Hindutva, Samagra Savarkar vangmaya, Vol.3, p. 83)

Other Shackles Break with Interdining

Just as there was a regulation in the past that at least one Brahmin should dine in a Ganesh Chaturthi meal, there should be a now be a regulation that there should be at least one Chamar-Mahar-Bhangi (* Balmiki) brother to dine in the Ganeshotsav meal

The poisonous fang of scripture-based caste distinction will be uprooted once the prohibition of interdining is violated! The breaking of this prohibition automatically loosens the shackles of prohibition of touch, seafaring, re-conversion, conducting Vedic rites and pursuing certain occupations! (1935, Kirloskar monthly, September)

Interdining is a Litmus Test of Reformism

Many Chamar, Mahar brethren gladly break bread with Brahmins and Marathas but become Brahmins and Kshatriyas themselves and claim caste privilege when Bhangi (*Balmiki) or Maang brethren seek to break bread with them. Their reformism should also be put to test. Hence in every common meal, there should be at least one or two Bhangi or Maatang brothers in addition to Mahars and Chamars. (1935, Maharashtra sharada periodical, November)

How will Caste Distinction Go?

Interdining is the magic sorcerer that will bury the demon of caste distinction! Caste distinction will not die with sterile arguments. Nor is it easy or even desirable to kill it by force...Oh reformer, violate the prohibition of interdining at this very

a day to an untouchable who belongs to a 'lower' caste-the Chamar to the Dhend, the Mahar to the Bhangi (*Balmiki)! (1935, Hindutvache panchapran or The Spirit of Hindutva, Samagra Savarkar vangmaya, Vol.3, p. 81)

RELIGIOUS DISCRIPTURES

Given below is an English translation of Savarkar's assorted views on religion and religious scriptures

The Different Connotations of the Word 'Dharma'

Like the English word 'law', the word 'dharma' has taken on different connotations. Its original wider meaning is 'law'. The dharma of any object upholds its existence and regulates its behaviour. It is in this sense that we refer to the dharma of nature, the dharma of water, the dharma of fire and so on...This wider meaning led to use of the term while describing the laws governing other-worldly objects, irrespective of whether these laws were verifiable or not! The term 'dharma' gradually encompassed the mutual relation between Heaven, hell, reincarnation, god, individual (soul), creation and the like. In fact, the word 'dharma' soon came to be almost exclusively used in its other-worldly connotation.

...The actions of human beings in this world were thought to affect his existence in the hereafter. So 'dharma' came to also mean that which upheld his life in the hereafter. In the past, the rules that governed worldly relations between individuals and nations were also termed 'dharma'. This is clear from terms such as dharma of war (yuddhadharma), dharma of governance (rajdharma), dharma of conduct (vyavahaardharma) and the like. (1934, Vidnyannishtha nibandha or pro-science essays, Samagra Savarkar vangmaya, Vol. 3, p.309-310)

*What is Sanatana dharma (*lit: the eternal code)?* Those laws of nature that have been experimentally vindicated and have stood the test of time verily constitute Sanatana dharma.

We have yet to experimentally gain knowledge of the hereafter. As such, this subject is still in the realm of speculation and it would be inappropriate to either confirm or reject its existence. None of the religious scriptures that offer various explanations of the hereafter are divinely inspired but have been composed or inspired by human beings. Their explanations lack proof and hence they cannot be said to be timeless and eternal.

The worldly conduct, ethics, practices and laws of human beings may be regarded as beneficial or otherwise solely on the touchstone of benefit to humankind. They should be adhered to and amended also on that very touchstone. It is neither possible nor desirable for the code of human conduct in this ever-changing world to be Sanatana (*timeless). As the Mahabharata says, "hence, decide your conduct according to prevailing conditions." (1934, Vidnyannishtha nibandha or pro-science essays, Samagra Savarkar vangmaya, Vol. 3, p.315-316)

I am well aware that we have not fully comprehended this Sanatana dharma, these laws of nature at the present moment and are probably unlikely to ever do so. What we think we have understood could well be rendered false in future by the march of science. Surely, newer ideas will be added to our existing state of knowledge. (1934, Vidnyannishtha nibandha or pro-science essays, Samagra Savarkar vangmaya, Vol. 3, p.311)

When we append the word term 'Sanatana' to 'dharma', we apply it to the principles and philosophies that expound the nature and the mutual relation between God, individual and creation (ishwar, jeev and jagat). For the nature of the First principle (aadishakti), the First Cause of creation and the First Laws are truly Sanatana, eternal and have stood the test of time. The principles expounded by the Bhagwadgita and the Upanishads regarding these may be sanatana. For it is beyond human power to change the nature of the First Cause. They are as they are and will always remain so. (1930, Jatyuchchedak nibandha or essays on abolition of caste, Samagra Savarkar vangmaya, Vol. 3, p.442)

Sanatana Dharma does not Die if Rituals are Changed: Actions are necessarily mortal and time-bound for they are by and for humans. Hence, Sanatana Dharma will not die even if the entire corpus of rituals, what to speak of caste distinctions, is changed.

It is beyond the power of the human race what to speak of a handful of reformers to destroy Sanatana Dharma. It is doubtful even if it within the power of God to do so! (1930, Jatyuchchedak nibandha or essays on abolition of caste, Samagra Savarkar vangmaya, Vol. 3, p.442)

All religious scriptures are man-made: A close scrutiny of the Vedas as well as the Muslim Quran, the Christian Bible and the Jewish Old Testament and the Book of Moses makes it clear that the so-called divinely written or sent religious scriptures are man-made. No doubt, these scriptures have unprecedented historical and literary value.

It is also admissible that these scriptures are a treasure house of words, worthy of respect and deep study...But they are not literally true.

Several stories (in them) are purely imaginary! What does not stand the test of scientific reason ought to be verily discarded even if it appears in the Vedas, Avesta, Quran, Bible, Book of Moses and the like. It is not true that an age of yore is necessarily an age of truth! It is incorrect to think that everything that is ancient is necessarily sacred and worthy of worship. (1936, Samagra Savarkar vangmaya, Vol. 4, p.579)

No religious scripture is valid for all times: I do not consider any religious scripture to be unchangeable and valid for all times. I hold the shrutis, smritis (* shrutis literally that which is heard and understood refers to the Vedas and are considered to be the most authoritative texts in Sanatana dharma; the smritis are the lawbooks and manuals of Hinduism, and they have lesser authority than the shrutis) and such other scriptures in utmost reverence and gratitude not because they are inviolable holy scriptures but because they are of historical value.

I shall apply the test of present day science to all the wisdom and ignorance present in these scriptures.

Only then shall I unreservedly practice and update what is essential for upholding and rejuvenating the nation! (Vidnyannishtha nibandha or pro-science essays, Samagra Savarkar vangmaya, Vol. 3, p.364)

My Idea of Nature

If I were an artist, I would depict nature as follows:

Her tongue freshly smeared with blood from a recently slaughtered deer calf, a tigress walks towards her cubs. Her cubs cling to and suckle her while she cleans her blood-stained jaw with her tongue. This is the world in its reality. The tigress slaughters and kills a deer calf so that she may feed her own cubs and give them life. She is committing violence on one so that she may shower love on another. This picture harmonizes violence and nonviolence. (1940, Samagra Savarkar vangmaya, Vol.4, p.499)

There is no place for absolute nonviolence anywhere in nature. (1940, Hindutvache panchapran or The Spirit of Hindutva, Samagra Savarkar vangmaya, Vol.3, p.62)

Absolute nonviolence is not a reality of nature and certainly not its underlying principle. (1940, Samagra Savarkar vangmaya, Vol.4, p.499)

What is the limit for practising compassion? Compassion for all living beings is a principle to be practised to the extent it leads to material human benefit. Beyond that, a human being is not guilty of violence if he has to commit it for the benefit of humankind! That guilt lies with nature, with creation, if at all it is god who has willed it! (Ksha kirane or X rays, Samagra Savarkar vangmaya, Vol.3, p.249)

The principle of compassion for all living beings has led to our defeat: We have lost our thrones not to demons but to this principle of compassion for all living beings (*Bhutaanni aamchi sinhasane ghetali naahit pan bhootadayene maatra aamhaas paraabhoot kele aahe are Savarkar's exact words)

Bibliography

Anthony, J. Parel : *Gandhi, Freedom, and Self-Rule,* New Delhi, Vistaar, 2002.

Bhadur, Rai Lala Baij Nath : *The Adhyatma Ramayana,* Cosmo, New Delhi, 2005.

Biswas, C.C. : *Bengal's Response to Gandhi,* Kolkata, Minerva Associates, 2004.

Das, Dipty Moyee : *Gandhi's Doctrine of Truth and Non-Violence : A Critical Study,* New Delhi, Dominant Pub., 2008.

Gangal, S.C. and Anurag Gangal : *Contemporary Global Problems : A Gandhian Perspective,* Jammu, Vinod, 1995.

Gaston, Roberge : *Communication Cinema Development: From Morosity to Hope,* Manohar, New Delhi, 1998.

Gitartha, Samgraha : *Abhinavagupta's Commentary on the Bhagavad Gita,* Indica, New Delhi, 2002.

Jain, Madhu : *The Abode of Mahashiva : Cults and Symbology in Jaunsar-Bawar in the Mid Himalayas,* 1995.

John, W. Hood : *The Films of Buddhadeb Dasgupta,* Orient Longman, New Delhi, 2005.

Prasad, Lal Bahadur : *Indian Political System and Law,* New Delhi, Shree, 2005.

Ray, Satyajit : *Our Films : Their Films,* Orient Longman, New Delhi, 2001.

Sanghavi, Nagindas : *The Agony of Arrival : Gandhi : The South Africa Years,* New Delhi, Rupa & Co., 2006.

Singhal, Rahul : *The Eternal Saga of Love : Devdas,* Pentagon Paperbacks, Delhi, 2002.

Trivedi, P.R. : *Concise Encyclopaedia of India,* Indian Pub., Delhi, 1998.

Yeats, W.B. : *Gitanjali : Song Offerings/Rabindranath Tagore,* New Delhi, Mahaveer, 2005.